Archetypes in Japanese Film

Archetypes in Japanese Film

The Sociopolitical and Religious Significance of the Principal Heroes and Heroines

Gregory Barrett

Selinsgrove: Susquehanna University Press
London and Toronto: Associated University Presses

Associated University Presses
440 Forsgate Drive
Cranbury, NJ 08512

Associated University Presses
25 Sicilian Avenue
London WC1A 2QH, England

Associated University Presses
P.O. Box 488, Port Credit
Mississauga, Ontario
Canada L5G 4M2

The paper used in this publication meets the requirements of the American National Standard for Permanence of Paper for Printed Library Materials Z39.48-1984.

Library of Congress Cataloging-in-Publication Data

Barrett, Gregory, 1938–
  Archetypes in Japanese films.

  Bibliography: p.
  Includes index.
  1. Motion pictures—Japan.   2. Characters and characteristics in motion pictures.   3. Archetype (Psychology)   I. Title.
PN1993.5.J3B37   1989   302.2'343'0952   87-43126
ISBN 0-941664-93-7 (alk. paper)

PRINTED IN THE UNITED STATES OF AMERICA

to my mother

Contents

Acknowledgments

ALL stills are courtesy of Kawakita Memorial Film Institute, Tokyo, and I selected them with the help of Ms. Kyoko Sato there. I wish to thank Tadao Sato, Donald Richie, and Keiko McDonald for all their advice and help.

Note on Film Titles and Personal Names

At the first reference to a film in the text, the Japanese title is given in parentheses after the title in English; all subsequent references have only the English title. The Index contains a listing of all films under both their Japanese and their English titles.

Personal names follow the Western order with the surname last, except for legendary or mythical figures. For example, in the case of *Momo Taro*, while *Taro* is a common given name, *Momo*, meaning "peach," is not a family name.

Archetypes in Japanese Film

Introduction

THIS study is the first iconography of Japanese film: an analysis of the symbolization of its principal heroes and heroines. As symbols rather than signs, they are open to many interpretations and their different meanings can be categorized as social, political, and religious. For example, take the character played by Toshiro Mifune in *Seven Samurai* (*Shichinin no Samurai*, 1954), one of the most famous Japanese films shown abroad. On one level he can represent the ambivalent attitude of the feudal farmer toward the samurai. While respecting the samurai as noble men, the peasant also mistrusts them as members of another social class and fears them as his rulers. Yet the Mifune character can also represent elemental man in need of initiation conducted by his mature mentors. This universal aspect of his character transcends any particular Japanese society, and the religious significance of initiation has been amply demonstrated by Mircea Eliade in his study of rites that symbolize the regeneration of the tribe and cosmos, or divine mysteries.[1]

Types of heroes and heroines have been taken up in previous Japanese film studies. Their authors, however, have been predominately director-oriented ever since 1960, when Joseph L. Anderson and Donald Richie dedicated the first authoritative work on Japanese film in English to "that little band of men" who made it a directors' cinema.[2] In 1961 Richie deemphasized history and ignored industry to give Japanese directors the undivided attention they certainly deserved.[3] Joan Mellen (1976) and Audie Bock (1978) followed in Richie's footsteps: the former judging the "little band" according to progressive, feminist standards[4] and the latter adding biographical material.[5] Even Noël Burch (1979), hardly a Richie follower, concentrated on the "few authentic 'masters'" in his structural analysis of Japanese film in general, for they deconstructed western codes best.[6] Keiko McDonald (1983) also treated the best directors in her structural analyses of individual films.[7] Such an orientation inevitably spawned director studies: Richie on Akira Kurosawa (1965)[8] and Yasujiro Ozu (1974),[9] and McDonald on Kenji Mizoguchi (1984).[10] All this was based on the premise that the best directors made the best films, in the sense of artistic merit.

Richie has noted in his preface to Bock's book that the same situation applies for any major cinema, for usually only the films of directors like Ingmar Bergman, François Truffaut, and their counterparts are known

outside their own country.[11] Still, Anderson and Richie in their pioneer-
ing work gave numerous examples of commercial films of no artistic merit
whatsoever, which nonetheless reflected their times and were thus important indicators of historical change. They also devoted some space to
popular genres that mirrored Japanese sentiments. Few, however, took up
these approaches to Japanese film. Alain Silver (1977) isolated one popular genre, the so-called samurai film, and presented some of its typical
heroes in his structural analysis of representative works.[12] David Desser
(1983) gave a more detailed analysis of that genre in terms of content, with
comparisons to the American western.[13] In Japan Tadao Sato had been
concerned with commercial films reflecting popular sentiments ever since
he began writing film criticism in the 1950s, and with the publication of
the first, book-length English translation of some of his essays in 1982,
non-Japanese film critics and students were introduced to his view of film
as social history.[14]

This iconography joins this minor stream of Japanese film criticism—as
opposed to the director-oriented mainstream—for most of the heroes and
heroines treated here do not appear in a pure form in the best directors'
films, which usually feature characterization. Richie presents excellent
evaluations of characterization throughout his book on Kurosawa, but this
is not iconography. A finely delineated Kurosawa character is very individual and complex, and has depth. The subjects of a film iconography are
archetypes (to be defined later), which, viewed negatively, are stereotypes:
general and very simple, flat and one-dimensional. Characters are the
constituents of realistic drama and literary art. Archetypes are the stuff
fantastic entertainments and commercial films are made of. Yet, archetypes are probably the best way to study popular culture, since they are
not only the focus of popular sentiments but also the simple embodiments
of endearing values.

Everyone who has written a book on Japanese film has probably felt that
he or she was also saying something about Japanese culture. Film is as
much an expression of culture as any other art medium like literature,
painting, theater: they all express the thoughts and sentiments (anything
mental or spiritual) held in common by a group of people. Previous
Japanese film studies in English, though, have focused on the traditional
"high culture" that was the preserve of the upper classes before modernization began in 1868. Richie set the tone in 1961 by listing the tea
ceremony, the Noh drama, and haiku poetry as representative of traditional culture.[15] The lower classes did not indulge in these pursuits before
1868. An example of traditional "low culture" is rakugo, a humorous
storytelling art which began in the Tokugawa period (1603–1868) and is
still popular on commercial TV, in contrast to Noh, which can only be
seen on educational TV. But look in the indexes of books on Japanese film
and see if rakugo is listed! Richie also continually asserts that an essential

key to understanding traditional culture is *mono no aware*, a philosophical, aesthetic concept originating among the courtier aristocracy of the Heian period (794–1185), which he defines as a resigned sadness toward life.[16] This "resigned sadness," however, cannot be found in *rakugo*, or, for that matter, *kodan*, another popular, not particularly humorous storytelling form about the exploits of heroes.

The traditional "high culture," *mono no aware* included, is certainly important in the evaluation of Japanese film. Still, our understanding must be insufficient, if we ignore traditional "low culture," as well as modern popular culture (admittedly Americanized to some extent). In all fairness to Richie, it should be noted that he included the responsibilities of the eldest son, arranged marriage and the so-called family system (a Japanese form of patriarchy) among the values of the traditional culture.[17] Since these social values were primary determinants in the behavior of all social classes, probably few contemporary Japanese would consider them "high culture," even though they did originate in the upper classes to a large extent.[18]

Furthermore, Richie arranged Japanese directors in a conservative-to-radical spectrum according to their attitude to their traditional culture,[19] and found several in opposition and some who had different values entirely. Hence, he gave some presentation of cultural values other than the traditional ones, though without detailing them. Richard Tucker did almost the same thing in 1973, only differing from Richie on the placement of certain directors in the spectrum.[20] Joan Mellen, however, was the only one who devoted considerable attention to the antitraditional elements in modern Japanese culture, though unfortunately weakening her thesis by her almost ethnocentric attack on the Japanese family.

For the most part, the philosophical, aesthetic values of the traditional "high culture" have held sway in interpretations of Japanese film written in English. In an analysis of the transcendental style in the films of Ozu, Paul Schrader (1972) reinforced *mono no aware* with Zen, a meditational Buddhist sect that flourished under the patronage of the military aristocracy in the 14th century.[21] Richie followed suit in his own book on Ozu. Noël Burch also delved into Zen, as well as Heian court poetry, in his study of the masters' "systematization of those traits which are most specifically Japanese."[22] Whereas Richie himself gave some socially critical films high ratings in the 1960s, the main trend in Japanese film criticism in English in the 1970s and 1980s was to determine the best films according to traditional aesthetic standards. Perhaps this was inevitable, for if western aesthetic standards had been used, there would have been no need to study *Japanese* film as such, but only a few Japanese directors who measured up.

A notable exception to the trend is Desser's study of Japan's "most western director," Kurosawa, for Desser emphasizes the adaptation of western modes in Japanese film making.[23] The singularity of this stance, however, only indicates the predominance of the trend.

Because of the trend, interpretations of the contents of Japanese film by Westerners have become very similar: everyone seems compelled to bring up Zen or *mono no aware* or something else traditional. Such similarity easily approaches conformity, which is ironic because Westerners are always accusing the average Japanese of being an unimaginative conformist. In the beginning of Japanese film research in English, an interest in traditional "high culture" was understandable. That which attracted the mind were things that were quite different from what one was used to, and it was only natural to share this new-found knowledge. Moreover, traditional "low culture" was little known and modern culture seemed to be only an imitation of the West. But why did succeeding researchers feel they had to repeat what had already been said quite well, particularly by Richie?

One answer to that question is that Japanese film studies simply reflect Japanese studies in general, at least in the United States. A book about *rakugo* probably cannot be found in any Books-on-Japan section anywhere, let alone a study of *manga*, comic books read by almost *all* Japanese, as evidenced by the fact that they can be classified according to the reader's sex and age group. Japanologists have thoroughly examined the aesthetic, philosophical, and sociopolitical values of Japanese culture, but popular sentiments have hardly been given a glance. Popular culture is either ignored or given side-show status by historians, as something to amuse the reader in between serious discussions of important factors in Japanese history.

The academic bais against popular culture is understandable, since expressions of it have to be made plain and simple to remain popular—that is, to be accepted by the majority—and this inevitably leads to a lowering of intellectual standards. Nevertheless, cultural studies which ignore the popular element are at best incomplete. Accordingly, this film iconography of heroes and heroines as the focus of popular sentiments supplements not only Japanese film research in English but also Japanese studies in general. Moreover, the area of research pursued has been outlined by Anderson and Richie in their chapter on the contents of Japanese film, though they were more concerned with popular genres than with popular iconography.[24]

Academicians could still question whether this supplement is necessary, whether popular sentiments are important, and the answer would depend on what actually constitutes the forms and expressions of Japanese popular culture. The "modern" part is largely modeled on American popular culture, for example, the young pop singers who intentionally imitate the mannerisms of their American antecedents. The "old" part often appears to be a corrupt or watered-down version of something that existed elegantly in the traditional culture. Take for example a gangster movie where the hero is ready to sacrifice his life out of loyalty to his dead boss. He seems to be aping the feudal hero in a Kabuki play, which is more plausible because it is easier to imagine that the samurai were noble men. How could a common gangster pretend to be so noble? (Actually Kabuki became high culture in modern Japan and is not the only example of such a transformation.)

Juxtaposed to the above examples, however, there are contradictory samples. The ghosts in Japanese horror films are often women who rightfully bear some man a grudge and whose antecedent can be found in the vengeful spirit in traditional folklore, which is hardly high culture. In literary studies and histories of Japan, Michizane Sugawara (845–903) is frequently given as an example of a vengeful spirit. He was a courtier aristocrat who died in exile because of court intrigues, and who came back as a ghost to wreak havoc in the imperial capital. The vengeful spirit in Japanese film, however, can hardly be considered a watered-down version of him. Whereas he is only emblematic of the grudges fostered in court politics, the film heroine, a mistreated woman, can be interpreted as an expression of the resentment of the lower classes. Furthermore, modern heroes, apparently imitating American action heroes, genuinely express valid feelings of revolt in Japan's younger generation.

Given such contradictions, this study challenges the widespread view in Japanese studies that the common people were always docile and submissive and that young Japanese are only going through an "imitating America" stage. As such, it could become corrective as well as supplementary.

This iconography began with the classification of the heroes and heroines seen in over a thousand Japanese films. The ubiquitous ones were then isolated to determine principal types. Concurring with Anderson and Richie,[25] it was found that the traditional types had mostly originated in Kabuki, the popular theater of the Tokugawa period (1603–1867), and *kodan* and *naniwa-bushi*, oral narratives performed by a story teller, which were most popular in the nineteenth and early twentieth centuries. The principal types were then traced back for prototypes as far as Japan's first lengthy mythology, *Kojiki* (*The Record of Ancient Events*, first presented to the court in A.D. 712). The chronological development thereafter was pursued in literature, theater, and film. Since each type changed with the times, they became a series of metamorphoses with sociopolitical significance, while maintaining certain universal motifs of a religious nature. Modern heroes became either versions of them or their antitheses.

The above methodology shows that the scope of this study is not limited by the ninety years of Japanese film. Since reference is also made to sources in modern literature ("pure" and popular), comic books, and to the latest developments on TV, it is fairly comprehensive as an iconography.

Ian Buruma has also written a fairly comprehensive iconography of popular culture in Japan.[26] Though he did not start with movies and drew his examples from various other media, his main types resemble mine; however, there are some crucial differences between our approaches.

As Buruma stresses continuity in Japanese culture, his types generally do not change in time. There is not much difference between a present-day stripper and a Shinto goddess depicted in *Kojiki* in A.D. 712. Modern heroes are only versions of old ones, and never antithetical. Modern ideas are inconsequential—loan words given in their Japanese spelling, for example *demokurashi* for democracy, to show that the Japanese recognize them but do not take them too seriously. One is led to assume that the present parliamentary system of government and consitution are merely froth on the waves lapping the ancient shores of Japan. As Buruma is fond of saying in one form or other throughout his book: surfaces change, sentiments do not.

Buruma does recognize one major change in Japanese culture: the introduction of Buddhism and Confucianism. He considers them oppressive foreign influences which turned a fun-loving Shinto, permissive attitude toward sex into a Japanese form of Victorianism: respectable hypocrisy in the everyday work-world, and elegant pornography and prostitution in the pleasure quarters. Within this context, he makes a brilliant, psychological analysis of the effects of repression—particularly sexual—and a chronic mother complex, as they appear in the popular culture. However, by overemphasizing the exotic, like many before him, he has depicted Japanese culture as a perennial freak show and has made inadequate suppositions about the sentiments of contemporary Japanese.

This study differs from Buruma's by giving equal weight to cultural continuity *and* to historical change, and by considering religion a major factor in the formation and metamorphoses of heroes and heroines. These reflections of changes in Japanese sentiments are strongly influenced by the dominant religion of a particular period of Japanese history, whether it is Shinto, Buddhism, Confucianism, or Nationalism (which Arnold Toynbee regarded as an inferior religion). Buddhism and Confucianism should not be considered only oppressive tools of the state, for they also contributed to what Robert Bellah has referred to as "the tradition of submerged transcendence"[27] in Japanese culture. The Buddhist tenet of the illusory nature of the phenomenal world could lead to a denigration of any society as mere artiface. Although the transcendental elements in Confucianism are not very persuasive—and Bellah himself has stated that "filial piety is subordinate to loyalty"[28] toward a superior, in the Tokugawa value system—in chapter 7 it will be shown that the Confucian ideal of parental benevolence could foster opposition toward society and the government, at least in the sentiments of the common people. Because of these aspects of Buddhism and Confucianism, sometimes even traditional Japanese heroes and heroines transcended or opposed their society, and their expression of discontent in the popular culture was not simply a matter of letting off steam, as Buruma would have it.

This study is not confined to a social history of Japan as seen through the development of popular heroes and heroines. In their religious significance they are universal as well as transcendental, and so I call them archetypes and make use of the theories of Carl C. Jung.

Jung found that the term archetype appeared in early Christian writings in Latin, where it meant the God-image in man, or God as the archetypal light.[29] Jung also compared archetypes with Lévy-Bruhl's mythological "représentations collectives",[30] which were often gods and goddesses,and related them to mythological motifs.[31] He distinguished two kinds of archetypes, active personalities and typical situations.[32] While motifs would correspond better with the latter, players are still needed to act out dramatic situations.

Japanese film heroes and heroines are obviously active personalities and as symbols are cultural rather than natural. According to Jung, natural symbols are directly derived from the unconscious, whereas cultural ones have gone through many transformations as a result of more or less conscious development before being accepted as collective images by a society.[33] In spite of the transformations, though, archetypes as the players in myths continually represent certain motifs. Jung noted that "myths of a religious nature can be interpreted as a sort of mental therapy for the sufferings and anxieties of mankind in general—hunger, war, disease, old age, death."[34] Accordingly, Japanese heroes and heroines often appear in modern film myths as therapy for the sufferings that remain, despite progress.

For this study archetypes are defined as changing, personified representations of constant motifs. The motifs considered basic to filmic expressions of Japanese culture are: the inevitable human conditions of suffering and death, parts of the life cycle like initiation, the moral problems of guilt and forgiveness, and the ideals of loyalty, sincerity, courage, justice, purity, and self-sacrifice. These motifs do not change, but sentiments about them do, as expressed through their representations. While Japanese sentiments are different enough to warrant study, their archetypes are often simply their versions of universal myths.

This definition of archetypes differs from common usage of the term in film criticism, where transformations are usually not considered and repetition is emphasized. Critics and researchers seem to be referring to typical heroes/heroines and situations that have continually appeared in the medium, presumably from its inception. Archetypes in this study refer to the chief or principal types, which are not necessarily the original ones. After all, the original heroes in *Kojiki* are not the main ones in Japanese film. Both meanings are contained in the Greek root, *archē* ("beginning", "rule"), and since *archos* means "ruler",[35] one gets the impression of an original reign with a line of succession.

The psychological origin of archetypes is not crucial for this study, since the concern is with cultural ones that have undergone some conscious development. To avoid misunderstanding, though, it should be stated that, rather than Jung's theory that archetypes are derived from a suprapersonal collective unconscious,[36] Bellah's view is followed. Bellah believes archetypes are constructed in a personal unconscious as a result of a child's interaction with its sociophysical environment, for example, the relation with the mother produces a mother archetype. He surmises that archetypes resemble each other in different cultures because early socialization is similar everywhere, and does not attribute their universality to a collective unconscious.[37]

Japanese archetypes are part of the tradition each film maker learns. He can project his own personal archetypes on them, adjust them to the times and/or his own predilections, or reject them by creating antithetical heroes who could become at least as popular as the traditional ones.

Japanese film archetypes can be classified, according to their relation to society, as conservative, problematic, and oppositional. These categories reflect the relation of religion to society. Bellah has concluded that every "religion seeks to proclaim a truth which transcends the world, but is enmeshed in the very world it desires to transcend," and that every "religion seeks to remake the world in its own image, but is always to some extent remade in the image of the world."[38] This paradox of religion indicates two aspects, sociopolitical and transcendental.

Joseph Campbell has elucidated the sociopolitical aspect by referring to religion as an adjunct to police authority in that social duty is enforced by secular and divine authority,[39] and by presenting Emile Durkheim's interpretation of mythology as an "allegorical instruction, to shape the individual to his group."[40] Durkheim stated that the reality of religion is society, which is the individual's refuge, shield, and support,[41] and from this one gathers that the protecting gods and saviors in various religions simply symbolize their societies. The sociopolitical aspect can also be inferred from James Frazer's definition of religion as a propitiation of powers superior to man that are believed to control nature and human life,[42] since submission to suprahuman forces symbolized in religion is easily equated with submission to society and a political state. The cost of submission is repression of individual desires, and the reward is a strong sense of social affiliation, inalienable as long as one believes.

Campbell has given self-subordination a mystical meaning, when self-sacrifice becomes self-transformation in the sense of participation in the consubstantiality of all beings.[43] Since this belief transcends any society or state, it expresses the transcendental aspect of religion without positing another world, as orthodox Christianity does. In Japanese culture, as already noted, the transcendental aspect is usually expressed in the Buddhist tenet of the illusory nature of the phenomenal world, even though Zen meditation could lead a few adepts to a mystical sense of "consubstantiality."

The sociopolitical aspect of religion is well exemplified in the conservative archetypes of Japanese film, since, as a rule, they are models of submission and/or group affiliation. They are dealt with in chapters 1, 2, and 3, where it is shown how the Confucian virtue of loyalty to a superior overrode conjugal and familial considerations, and how Buddhist altars and Zen meditation become tools in the interest of the state. These archetypes all came from the conservative, period film genre (*jidai geki*) whose stories are set in the feudal period before 1868, and its extension, the *yakuza* ("gangster") film. However, the sociopolitical aspect of religion was more important in their formation than genre, since the period film did produce leftist, nihilistic, and socially critical films when the climate was right.

The second category of archetypes, treated in chapters 4, 5, 6, 7, and 8, is called problematic because they not only exhibit the conservative function of inducing submission and containing dissatisfaction, but could exist in a state of tension in relation to the powers-that-be, since they also express the transcendental aspect of religion. For example, the triad of archetypes designated as Prodigal Son, Forgiving Parent, and Self-Sacrificing Sister can be analogous to subject-ruler relations in a paternalistic state that requires self-effacement in exchange for forgiveness. This triad, as expressed in Mizoguchi's *Sansho the Bailiff* (*Sansho Dayu*, 1954), however, can also evoke a Medieval Buddhist concept of justice that applies to rulers too, an idealized parent who almost functions as a transcendental God, and a Christ-like Sister-Savior.

The third category of oppositional archetypes is taken up in chapter 9. They are modern, antithetical heroes and heroines who are the focus of youthful, rebellious sentiments against the dominant culture of the older generation. These sentiments were fostered to a large extent by Western ideas of individual freedom and of unjust exploitation of lower classes—ideas that entered Japan during the modernization begun in 1868.

In the concluding chapter there is a summary of the comparisions made between Japanese film archetypes and their Western counterparts. There is also an assessment of the present condition of all three categories on television, Japan's most popular medium since the 1960s, to determine whether a synthesis of traditional and modern archetypes has been made, and to decide how significant the expression of rebellious sentiments can be in commercial media that are supported by majority society and the powers-that-be.

1

The Loyal Retainer and the Tormented Lord

Introduction

UNTIL the 1960s almost half of the Japanese film heroes were feudal characters, because close to half of the feature films came from the period film genre. Ever since the 1910s this genre was furnished with an extensive ensemble of traditional, familiar characters—in contrast to the other main genre of the contemporary film (*gendai geki*), whose dramas were set in the fairly recent modern era beginning in 1868.[1] Since the feudalistic system of government before 1868 was based on the relationship between lord and vassal, it was inevitable that the loyal retainer would become a major hero. In period film he was the *main* hero because a Japanese lord was seldom presented as a dynamic character. Rather, by falling into some predicament he tested the loyalty of his retainer(s), and so I call him the Tormented Lord. This archetypal dyad, formed by the Loyal Retainer and the Tormented Lord, represents the ideals of loyalty and sincerity, and served as a metaphor for the required attitude of the governed in Japan until at least 1945.

Ivan Morris gave examples, from each period of Japanese history, of sincere noblemen and samurai who suffer defeat at the hands of practical politicians and thus became tragic heroes.[2] The fact that some of them were also paragons of loyalty is not at all strange, since sincerity and loyalty are closely related. For a retainer or vassal, sincerity could consist solely of loyalty toward a sovereign. Moreover, both of these virtues have to be put to the test to determine whether they are genuine or not. Suffering is their common motif. Death is the ultimate demonstration of fidelity.

The theme of loyalty-to-the-death was expressed very early in Japanese culture, for example, in the following stanza written in 749 and included in the *Man'yoshu*, Japan's first major anthology of verse:

> If we go to the sea our corpses shall soak in the water.
> If we go to the hills our corpses shall rot in the grass.
> We will die by the side of our sovereign,
> We will never look back.[3]

This stanza was turned into an extremely popular, martial air during World War II, when Emperor Hirohito assumed the role of the Tormented Lord. He was believed to be grieving over the fate of the nation, and only victories by his loyal retainers in the imperial army and navy could relieve his suffering heart. Accordingly, countless soldiers who had sung the modern version of the 749 stanza made the lyrics come true in a suicidal demonstration of the virtues of sincerity and loyalty in the modern era.

To a Westerner, it seems like martyrdom, and Japan's most famous martyrs for the sake of absolute loyalty were the forty-seven retainers from the feudal fief of Ako.[4] In 1703 they avenged the death of their lord or daimyo by killing his enemy, and later commited *seppuku* or harakiri (ritual suicide by disembowelment). As they were poor *ronin*, samurai made masterless by the death of their lord, they appealed to the popular imagination, and their story, *Chushingura*, became a national epic, which was made into a film over eighty times from 1907 until 1962.[5] Oishi, their leader, and Lord Asano, their daimyo, became the best embodiments of the archetypal dyad of the Loyal Retainer and the Tormented Lord and served as models for countless period film heroes. In fact, in order to understand the period film genre's main heroes and its principal motifs of loyalty and sincerity, it is better to trace the development of Oishi and Lord Asano from Kabuki to film and TV than to give numerous examples of their replicas, which usually appear in films singly. Beforehand, though, some historical background is necessary to understand the sociopolitical significance and the importance of the ideal of loyalty in the Japanese cultural value system.

The incident of the forty-seven Akō ronin occurred during the Tokugawa period (1603–1868), a watershed in Japanese history. Previously, loyalty toward a superior had not been an absolute virtue. Tadao Sato claims that during the civil-warring period from 1482 to 1603 samurai warriors prized honor and courage above loyalty, for they often changed masters in their search for one who would appreciate them.[6] Moreover, the warlords or daimyo then did not have absolute power in their own fief, since Buddhist temples with huge congregations resisted their authority.[7] With the final victory of Ieyasu Tokugawa, a powerful daimyo who became shogun in 1603, peace came to Japan. The power of rebellious Buddhist temples had been crushed[8] and Confucianism became the dominant religion.[9]

The Confucian virtue of loyalty toward a superior suited the purposes of the Tokugawa authorities, for they still demanded the loyalty of the fiefs outside their direct rule in their semicentralized government. The loyalty of a retainer toward his daimyo, however, could conceivably conflict with his duty toward the state. This problem was raised by the forty-seven Akō *ronin*, and the way the Tokugawa government handled their incident was an important step toward the formation of the modern state of Japan.

When the incident became a subject for Kabuki and puppet plays, the popularization of the samurai virtue of loyalty began. This was not engineered by the Tokugawa government, for, although they intermittently excercised censorship, they had no department of propaganda as such. Nor was it the result of obsequiousness on the part of playwrights, since samurai seldom deigned to attend their popular entertainments.[10]. Rather, it was mainly the effect of servility engendered by a society ruled by samurai, whose arbitrary power was exemplified in their right to cut down any commoner they thought had insulted them (*kirisute gomen*).[11] For popular playwrights and their audiences, the loyalty of a fictionalized retainer for his lord was the sublimation of their own submissive attitude toward a government that had more control over their lives than any previous one.

Modern versions of the story of the forty-seven Akō *ronin,* or *Chushingura,* were not simply expressions of residual feudalistic sentiments. The changing representations of Oishi, their leader, and Asano, their lord, reflect the process in which feudal loyalty became modern patriotism. Hence, *Chushingura* can be called a myth with a modern political message.

Chushingura

The myth of *Chushingura* begins with the Tokugawa government's judgments on the actions of Lord Naganori Asano and Kuranosuke Oishi, his chief retainer. Later interpretations of their motivation were what Ivan Morris called the projection of archetypes onto actual historical figures.[12] In the spring of 1701, Lord Asano drew his sword and wounded Lord Yoshinaka Kira, his mentor, when the latter evidently did not give him instructions during an important ceremony. Since the incident occurred in the shogun's palace and could thus be considered an act of defiance against the government itself, Lord Asano was ordered to commit *seppuku* that same day. On 30 January 1703, Oishi and forty-five other retainers broke into Lord Kira's residence and beheaded him.

The beheading of Kira presented the authorities with a problem. All recorded vendettas since 1603 had been for the sake of filial piety, usually to avenge a dead father, and had not upset the social order since they were considered "private" affairs.[13] Oishi and his men, however, had not only created a public disturbance but had also raised the insurrectional possibility of a conflict between loyalty toward a feudal lord and the central government. The problem was solved by letting all of them commit *seppuku* rather than executing them. Their loyalty was thereby honored, while their illegal action was properly sanctioned. The primacy of law, a prerequisite for a modern state, was firmly established. Thereafter until

Chushingura (1962), directed by Hiroshi Inagaki. Arrayed for battle, Oishi (Koshiro Matsumoto), the best representative of the Loyal Retainer, prepares to avenge his lord. His feudal loyalty became a sublimation of the submissiveness of modern Japanese toward their government.

1868, there was only one other, rather insignificant case of a servant avenging a master.[14]

The archetypal dyad of the Loyal Retainer and the Tormented Lord first assumed definite shape in 1748 in *Kanadehon Chushingura*, the most famous of the seventy or so Kabuki and puppet plays on the subject written between 1706 and 1891.[15] Kanadehon's Oishi is an agonized witness to his lord's painful death and afterwards takes possession of the *seppuku* sword. This "keepsake" becomes like a fetish controlling his whole being until he plunges it into his lord's enemy. Symbolizing Oishi's unswerving devotion, it anticipates the sword as the fundamental icon of the period film.[16] Since it is also a reminder of an intense, personal relation, the loyalty of Kanadehon's Oishi is significantly different from the institutionalized variety it would later become.

Kanadehon Chushingura changed the attitude of the authorities toward Oishi and his men. As historical personages they had been a threat to the government. In fact the first play about them had been prohibited after only three performances, and in 1706, Chikamatsu Monzaemon, Japan's greatest playwright, could present a play about them only by more carefully concealing their identity in a previous historical period.[17] The authors of *Kanadehon Chushingura* followed Chikamatsu, and Oishi and his men, disguised with pseudonyms, became heroes in a popular play who were perfect models of loyalty toward a superior, a social virtue still desirable in a legalistic state. Moreover, the *seppuku* of Lord Asano, Oishi and the others suggested that, while other samurai virtues like honor and courage are commendable, they could be costly and that loyalty in the form of submission was the best course. Thereafter, the authorities not only supported further dramatizations of *Chushingura*, but also had historical models of loyalty put into school books for commoners. Before the Kanadehon version in 1748, it seems commoners had not been taught much about loyalty but had only been admonished to fear the strong and to respect authority.[18] Henceforth, that fear would be internalized and rationalized as loyalty.

The character of Lord Asano underwent a major change when *Chushingura* became subject matter for nineteenth-century Kodan storytellers. Kanadehon's Asano is actually a minor player. Though he bravely commits suicide for his honor, his torment is short-lived. He is so quick-tempered and imprudent that he slashes at Kira because he cannot bear even a slight insult. He provides a striking contrast to the patient Oishi, who endures many humiliations to avenge him. Kodan's Asano, on the other hand, is a sincere youth who is constantly picked on because he did not give his mentor a bribe. When Kira gives misleading instructions for ceremonies Asano is conducting, he reflects the pecking order of the apprentice system of Japan's traditional craftsmen, the main audience for Kodan.[19] Accordingly, Kodan's Asano suffers various humiliations in addition to a painful death and is truly transformed into the Tormented Lord.

Oishi and the other retainers also change in the Kodan version, where the women involved become insignificant. In *Kanadehon Chushingura* Kira's lust for Asano's wife is the catalyst of the tragedy, and a few love affairs are depicted. Moreover, although Oishi and the others sacrifice their wife or sister for the cause, they are distressed over this necessity. In Kodan, though, they do not give it any thought at all, since the honor and courage of men are almost the sole concern. This difference doubtless reflects the different lifestyles of the audiences. In the Kabuki-viewing merchant family the wife had an active role in the family business, whereas Kodan-listening craftsmen like carpenters usually left their wives at home and went out in all-male work gangs.[20] As a result of this sociological difference, loyalty toward Asano rides roughshod over any conjugal or familial consideration in Kodan, and behind the macho blustering of its retainers an even more submissive attitude can be discerned.

Submissiveness was further emphasized in the beginning of the twentieth century, when the Kodan version of *Chushingura* was adapted for *rōkyoku* or *naniwa bushi* ("storytelling with samisen accompaniment"). *Rōkyoku* artists shed the romantic interludes of Kabuki origin, particularly the story of Kampei Hayano, whose amorous dallying leads him to neglect his duty toward his lord. Wholehearted loyalty was stressed even more than the manly honor and courage appreciated in Kodan, and *rōkyoku* artists thereby ingratiated themselves with military and political leaders during the Russo-Japanese War (1904–05) and its aftermath. The feudal loyalty praised in *Chushingura* was easily associated with the modern variety toward the emperor, and in fact the imperial family became patrons of this performing art, which had previously entertained only the lowest social classes.[21]

Film versions of *Chushingura* combined episodes from Kabuki and Kodan and eventually became spectacular productions with all-star casts. As they were generally box office hits, they disseminated the ideal of loyalty on a mass scale. In the oldest extant print from 1910 to 1912, director Shozo Makino deferred to women viewers by drawing out the parting scene between Oishi and his wife. Still, primary relations were between men. This was exemplified in the classic scene showing a close retainer kneeling in the courtyard below, while Asano walks down the veranda toward the area for his *seppuku*. As Japanese cinema technically advanced in cinematography and editing, their tender parting looks would be expressed through close-up exchanges reserved for lovers in European and American movies.

Chie Nakane has likened *Chushingura* to a male love affair.[22] The same can be said for action genres in other cinemas. For example, in American westerns, Desser has noted that the camaraderie of men is prized above the society of women.[23] But Chushingura and other period films are extreme in this respect. One reason is that Japan lacks a tradition of chivalry toward women. In political terms, though, through the retainer's "love" for his lord his servile position is glorified. This is more important than Joan Mellen's interpretation of sexual politics,[24] for the film retainer was a model for the attitude Japanese males should take toward their superiors, no matter what tyrannical airs they put on in front of their wife.

Besides expressing loyalty in terms of love, Japanese cinema through the 1920s and 1930s made few changes in the Kabuki- and Kodan-inherited contents of Chushingura. Major innovations in the story came from popular literature and modern Kabuki.

In the 1927 novel, The Ronin from Akō (Akō Roshi), Jiro Osaragi turned the loyalty of Oishi and the retainers into indignation at the injustice of their lord's death sentence, and interpreted the beheading of Kira as a protest against a corrupt government, rather than as a private grudge. As Osaragi was extremely interested in French history,[25] he probably wanted to draw an analogy with the French Revolution. The liberal trend of the 1920s in Japan, the aftermath of the so-called Taisho democracy (1912 to 1926), permitted such an expression. Militaristic ideology, however, had by no means vanished then, since Oishi was a hero in primary school textbooks from 1920 to 1945, partly because of the popularity of the patriotic rōkyoku version of his tale.[26] In the textbooks, as in Osaragi's novel, Oishi's times were described as degenerate because the frivolous shogun then favored dogs over human beings, and Oishi became the embodiment of a masculine, martial valor highly favored during a time of militaristic expansionism on the Asian mainland.

Osaragi's liberal theme of upright men in corrupt times appealed not only to conservatives but to rightists as well. On 26 February 1936, some officers from the radical faction of the imperial army attempted a coup d'état because they thought the government was run by capitalists who bribed corrupt politicians. These officers have been likened to the Akō ronin by Tadao Sato,[27] and the resemblance is a fitting one. Whether influenced by Osaragi's novel or by their primary school textbooks, they failed and were executed. The conservative faction of the military, however, used the incident to increase their own power to fascist proportions.

In 1934, a modern Kabuki play about the Akō ronin, Genroku Chushingura was first performed. Genroku is the name of the era when the incident took place, and its inclusion in the title indicates playwright Seika Mayama's emphasis on historical authenticity. The central theme of the play is Oishi's fears that his loyalty toward his dead lord could be construed as disloyalty toward the imperial court, and his torments are resolved when he learns that the emperor pitied Asano for not being able to kill Kira.

Since Mayama solves Oishi's "To be or not to be" dilemma by equating loyalty toward a feudal lord with that toward the emperor, he could be accused of intellectualizing the *rōkyoku* version. However, in Oishi's doubts can be gleaned the rationalization for the transfer of loyalties that led to the modern concept of patriotism. Throughout most of the Tokugawa period (1603–1868) *samurai* were theoretically loyal to their feudal lord and to the shogunate, the central government. Near the end of the Tokugawa period they were divided into factions either supporting the shogunate or advocating restoration of imperial rule. Eventually, in countless novels and films on the Meiji Restoration in 1868, both factions were deemed loyal because they had the best interests of the nation at heart. Since they had not been loyal to a feudal lord, however, in place of the old word for loyalty, *chūgi*, a new term, *chūseishin* was coined for patriotism.[28] Mayama's Oishi was simply one step removed from Japan's modern patriots.

Mayama's *Genroku Chushingura* was made into a two-part film in 1941 and 1942 by Mizoguchi. Mizoguchi had previously made films highly critical of feudalism, and he hoped to escape from the wartime demands for propaganda by concentrating on history.[29] Ironically, though, his superb cinematic techniques exaggerated Mayama's theme of absolute loyalty.

The film begins with Kira insinuating that Asano is incompetent and Asano losing his temper and striking him with his sword. True to history like Mayama, Mizoguchi had scrapped the tormenting scenes, which were Kodan accretions. Consequently, however, Oishi's loyalty becomes unconditional. It does not matter what kind of man Asano was, whether he suffered or not. Affection for the dead lord is erased. Oishi's loyalty is not personal but institutionalized, for it is simply directed toward anyone in a superior position, and Mizoguchi illustrates this cinematically.

Oishi is shown slowly bowing low toward the ancestral altar containing Lord Asano's memorial tablet (*ihai*). Since this drawn-out scene is shot from a high angle, Oishi appears to be a subject bowing in front of the overhead camera as if it were some kind of god. After the vendetta, Oishi is shown, from the same camera angle, bowing reverently before the written proclamation granting him the privilege to commit *seppuku*. His devotion to his lord has been transferred to the shogun and the emperor, or perhaps nothing has changed and the objects of his devotion were just different manifestations of his total submission to absolute authority.

Mizoguchi's Oishi illustrated the required attitude for the entire Japanese nation during World War II. This Oishi was unusual in Japanese film history, though, because his predecessors and successors exhibited a strong sense of personal loyalty. In fact, this sentimental interpretation of his character interfered with postwar attempts to democratize *Chushingura*.

In the script for ToEi's *The Ronin from Akō* (Akō Roshi, 1956), Kaneto Shindo intensified Osaragi's theme of protest against an unjust government by downplaying loyalty to Lord Asano and presenting Oishi as a cool-headed organizer, who resembles modern union or guerrilla leaders. During the filming, however, Shindo was overruled by director Sadatsugu Matsuda and Utaemon Ichikawa, the superstar who played Oishi. In Ichikawa's performance tears perpetually come to Oishi's eyes whenever he is reminded of his dead lord, and he is often shown with a Buddhist rosary in his hands, as if he prayed for his lord's soul every chance he got.

Similarly, in *The Fall of Akō Castle* (Akōjo Danzetsu, 1978), director Kinji Fukasaku had wanted to portray the loyal forty-seven *ronin* as *Wild Bunch*-like desperadoes. Superstar Kin'nosuke Yorozuya (formerly Nakamura) had other, orthodox ideas and got his way,[30] but at least did not blubber as much as Ichikawa.

These two film versions demonstrate that while very few postwar Japanese would subscribe to the feudal virtue of loyalty toward a superior, Oishi's devotion to his dead lord was still appealing. This devotion was best justified to modern audiences through Toho's 1962 version of *Chushingura*, the most popular outside of Japan.

Director Hiroshi Inagaki presents Lord Asano as the incarnation of sincerity, the cardinal virtue of youth. The tormenting scenes are lengthened and clearly connected with Kira's greed, thereby stressing Asano's integrity and making his attack on Kira an inevitable result of his nobility and honor. It is the universal contrast between pure youth and corrupt adulthood. Kira is a materialization of all the vices attendant on aging and the loss of innocence.

Previous directors had also emphasized Asano's innocence. In the 1910–12 version Shozo Makino had had a liberal amount of face powder applied to his star Matsunosuke Onoe so that he appeared like a lamb surrounded by Kira and other dark-complexioned tormentors. In 1941 Mizoguchi showed Kira in the shade and Asano out in the sunlight. In 1962 Inagaki used color composition.

Asano is usually dressed in blue robes, often of a light hue, while Kira wears brown and tarnished gold. Once Asano wears a sash with delicately painted, green bamboo leaves. Blue is perhaps universally associated with youth, but the Japanese enhance this symbolization by confusing blue and green, the same word, *aoi*. Hence, the sky blue of youth is combined with the young leaves and green shoots of spring.

For the *seppuku* scene, Asano is dressed in white robes, which symbolize purity and death. When he reaches for the short, silver sword, the camera cuts to cherry blossoms silently falling, and the screen becomes a white blur. Cherry blossoms are a hackneyed symbol for the fleetingness of life, but when associated with Inagaki's Asano they come to represent a pristine purity that perhaps can be preserved only through death. Accord-

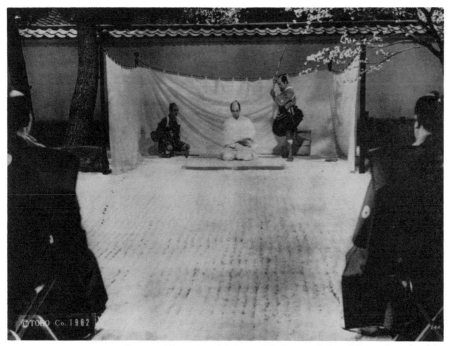

Chushingura (1962), directed by Hiroshi Inagaki. Dressed in white robes for his *seppuku,* Lord Asano (Yuzo Kayama) represents a pristine purity that can be preserved only through death and that is also associated with the young kamikaze pilots during World War II.

ingly, Oishi avenges him more in anger over the death of an innocent than out of loyalty.

Yet, Inagaki's Asano is not simply a universal, pure youth. For many Japanese he probably represented the young kamikaze pilots in World War II. Their death too tends to be regarded as an inevitable consequence of the purity of their youth, rather than as a modern expression of the loyalty-to-the-death ideal, which served so many feudal governments in the past. Consequently, Inagaki, like previous Japanese film makers (and probably just as unintentionally), concealed the self-abnegation inherent in this ideal through the emotional treatment of a theme in which cinema excells.

The sentimental attitude toward *Chushingura* also prevailed in the year-long TV drama serials of it on NHK, the government network, and the 1964 and 1975 productions effectively undercut Osaragi's theme of resistance against a corrupt government. Furthermore, in the 1982 production sentimentality was used to fashion a contemporary message of patriotism through the sympathetic treatment *everyone* receives. Lord Kira is not such a bad guy after all, since he sought bribes for the revival of his house.

Shogun Tsunayoshi, often presented as somewhat effeminate in film versions, now firmly responds to Oishi's test of *his* samurai spirit by granting the correct judgment on the case: honorable suicide. In short, the old feudal loyalty was not such a bad ideal, as everyone's superior was a well-meaning, honorable man, after all.

In 1982 NHK not only suggests that there were no bad superiors, but also that there were no disloyal retainers either. While the loyal forty-seven are awaiting their honorable suicide, they pass the time in pursuing traditional arts like calligraphy and in holding parties. When they get drunk they reminisce about the *other* retainers, who have such a bad reputation these days. Finally, Oishi himself magnanimously concludes that they were not really disloyal, for they must have had their own reasons for not participating in the vendetta.

Watered-down dramas are a trademark of Japanese TV because, as in the United States, by trying to please everyone they become common denominators of all popular sentiments. Still, NHK's *Chushingura* bears a remarkable resemblance to the Japanese family drama in which no one is to blame for arguments resulting from misunderstandings that are ironed out in the final reconciliation scene. In fact, NHK's *Chushingura* is the family drama writ large. When Kira, Tsunayoshi, and the not-so-loyal retainers are "forgiven," the prime-time viewing populace is told that there were no villains in Japanese history, and by extension none in the present government. Since the Japanese have always been members of one big, well-meaning family, feudal loyalty or modern patriotism were only an inevitable result of a tender affiliation and an unshakable sense of unity.

The sentiments expressed in NHK's *Chushingura* in 1982 are a far cry from the sentiments that must have prevailed during the civil-warring period from 1482 to 1603. Still, they may well have been an inevitable consequence of the process whereby a political incident in 1703 became the springboard for a myth that popularized a samurai virtue more conspicuous by its absence theretofore. As the archetypal dyad of the Loyal Retainer and the Tormented Lord changed dress, or were interpreted differently, to suit the times, it still remained amazingly constant to its motif. One cannot help but marvel at how the Japanese from 1703 until 1982 could get so many renditions from the single tune of loyalty.

Loyalty

Loyalty is also a social virtue in the West, and in European history too it was transferred from feudal lords to a modern nation. In Japan, though, loyalty became absolute and submission total. The cultural reason can be shown by a comparison with the story of King Authur and Sir Lancelot. The most recent film version is John Boorman's *Excalibur*, which was based on Malory's *Le Morte d'Arthur*, written in the fifteenth century.

Lancelot appears as a wandering knight in search of a worthy king and, after Arthur defeats him in a jousting match, he is all too happy to serve him. Although Japanese warriors sometimes searched for lords to serve during civil wars, they never fought with them. The almost egalitarian relation between Arthur and Lancelot can be attributed to the Magna Carta tradition, which gave barons rights vis-à-vis their king and thereby made feudal loyalty conditional in the West.

Since Lancelot's loyalty is conditional and voluntary, his adultery with his lord's queen may be regrettable, but not inexcusable, as would be the case in feudal Japan. Lancelot chose to serve Arthur, but then fell in love with Guinevere. True to his own feelings for her he betrayed his king, but still seems sincere.

Oishi would not recognize such choices. Without a Magna Carta tradition, his loyalty is regarded as absolute. Furthermore, since he inherited his role as a family retainer, his relation with his lord is involuntary. Lord Asano could be true to his feelings, but Oishi his retainer can only be true to him.

There *is* a relation between Oishi and Lady Asano, his lord's widow. In most film versions of *Chushingura* Oishi pays her a visit on the night of the attack, but cannot reveal his plans because of the presence of one of Kira's spies. He even lies to her, saying he has found a new master. Disgusted with him, she refuses his parting request to light incense in front of the altar with Lord Asano's memorial tablet.

In contrast to the Lancelot-Guinevere-Arthur triangle in which they all loved each other, in the *Chushingura* triad the sole love object is the spirit of Lord Asano himself. Perhaps his widow felt she had triumphed over Oishi in that she had remained faithful and he had not. However, Oishi wins in the end by avenging the lord whose memory she could only be faithful to. This is graphically shown in the otherwise undistinguished 1958 DaiEi film version when Lady Asano gets down on her knees in the snow and reverently bows in Oishi's direction as he and his men go marching off with Kira's head. Even though Asano's widow is Oishi's Lady, in the triad she is subordinate to him in terms of loyalty toward their lord, which is absolute in either case.

Oishi's loyalty is so single-minded that it is akin to religious devotion, and thus *Chushingura* can also be compared to the story of Christ and his disciples. Lord Asano is like the Lamb of God, a martyr grieving over the troubled hearts of his loved ones. Oishi is even better than Peter in that he never forsook his lord even once. If Asano had left behind some doctrine, surely Oishi would have proselytized it. As it is, he has to be content with avenging him, which has religious significance in Japan. According to folk belief, if someone died experiencing deep resentment like Asano, his spirit is restless and continues to suffer after death until appeased.[31]

Chushingura, though, differs crucially from the Judaeo-Christian tradition. While Oishi, like Abraham, would sacrifice his family to show that his loyalty to his lord was ultimate, Asano is not transcendental like Yahweh. Oishi's devotion to his memory, represented by the Asano family altar, is a symbolization of their relationship when Asano was alive. There is nothing beyond the altar except society at large. Oishi is affiliated with it through his position in the Asano family, and he submits to it by commiting *seppuku* after avenging his lord. Oishi's belief in Asano does not conflict with his social role. In fact, his religion *is* his social role. His loyalty is absolute not only because it is involuntary and unconditional, but also because he has no distracting, transcendental reference points.

There is a Buddhist, transcendental aspect to Japanese culture, but this was suppressed during the Tokugawa era (when the myth of *Chushingura* originated), thereby strengthening the sociopolitical aspect of religion even more. The Tokugawa government forced its subjects to register with a Buddhist temple as a disavowal of Christianity, which was being persecuted. The main effect of this measure, however, was to turn religious faith into a family rather than an individual matter, for the focus of worhsip became the family graves at the temple and the ancestral tablets in the household Buddhist altar. Hence, Japanese Buddhism was changed into a religion of affiliation instead of one of belief.[32]

Oishi's affiliation as a retainer of the Asano household was the source of his religious sense of loyalty toward his dead lord. As nothing transcended his affiliation, loyalty toward it became his religion.[33] Since such an indivisible bond had formed between loyalty and affiliation, as late as 1982 NHK could still use *Chushingura* to foster patriotic sentiments by appealing to a sense of affiliation, even though feudal loyalty toward a superior had long been antiquated.

NHK's devillainization of Kira was not such a radical interpretation after all. Fictional villains in the West could be representations of Satan, but in Japanese culture there is no single archdemon, just as there is no one transcendental God, but a pantheon of Shinto gods and goddesses resembling Mount Olympus in Greek mythology. Japanese villains are simply like Greek antagonists, who oppose protagonists. Like Kira, they pick on their victims, but do not really intend to bring about their downfall.

Variations

Given the insignificance of Kira and the subordinate position of Lady Asano, the relationship between Oishi and Asano is the one that really

counts in *Chushingura*. In period film there are other significant variations
of the Loyal Retainer-Tormented Lord dyad. While they lack the religious
ambience of *Chushingura* because their lord remains alive until the end,
they are often more touching because of their depiction of a warm relationship between living human beings.

In *The Men Who Tread on the Tiger's Tail* (*Tora no O o Fumu
Otokotachi*, 1945), Yoshitsune Minamoto, a famous twelfth-century general, becomes a weak, effeminate lord who is protected by Benkei, a
supermasculine retainer. Directed by Kurosawa, this film was based on the
Kabuki *Kanjincho*, which in turn was taken from *Ataka*, a Noh drama.[34]

The Paltry Ronin Forces His Way Through (*Suronin Makaritoru*, 1947)
is based on the story of Ten'ichibo, a pretender to the shogunate who is
aided by his scheming retainer, Iganosuke. Director Daisuke Ito, however,
differed from prewar film versions by changing Ten'ichibo into a sad,
fatherless boy who was protected and guided by Iganosuke in his role as
surrogate father.

Iemitsu and Hikoza (*Iemitsu to Hikoza*, 1941) concerns the third
Tokugawa shogun, Iemitsu (died 1651), an able but tyrannical admin-
istrator, and his chief minister, Hikozaemon Okubo. Director Masahiro
Makino turns Okubo into a kind uncle who gives Iemitsu piggyback rides
when he is a child, admonishes him during his youth, and rescues him
from a plot against his life, calling upon all the strength left in his aging
body.

Nobunaga Oda (*Oda Nobunaga*, 1940) is about the young Oda (died
1582), who eventually became a cruel warlord, and his chief retainer
Hirade. In Masahiro Makino's film—as well as in the 1959 remake by
Kazuo Mori—Oda is presented as a misunderstood, motherless boy who is
nurtured by Hirade, who eventually commits *seppuku* to end his own
worries and admonish his charge to mend his eccentric ways.

These variations share with *Chushingura* the tendency to portray a male
love affair, and Buruma has already alluded to the sublimated homosexuality in the relationship between Yoshitsune and Benkei.[35] More important in terms of inducing submissive attitudes, though, is the fact that a
retainer, who was usually only affiliated with a family, becomes an active
family member as a surrogate uncle or father, or even substitute mother.
This familization of the lord-retainer relationship is extremely ironic,
since, according to the ideal of loyalty, a retainer should be prepared to
sacrifice the lives of his own family for his lord's; and this was the subject
of several Kabuki plays that popularized the social virtue of polity over
family.[36]

These film directors were not really suggesting that "lower family members" should be sacrificed for "higher ones." Rather, by portraying the
lord-retainer relation in familial terms, they made it more emotionally
acceptable to their audiences and themselves. Through such sentimen-

talization, however, they covered up the actual relation between a powerful daimyo and an economically dependent retainer—and, by extension, an authoritarian state and weak subjects. They also adhered to an old theatrical convention in which cruel warlords and tyrants were transformed into boyishly appealing love objects for a docile populace.

Attempt at Antithesis: The Nihilistic Hero

Most period films sentimentalized or sanctified the lord-retainer relation. Some, however, questioned loyalty through a nihilistic hero, a samurai without any loyalties, whose creation was influenced by western ideas.

The prototype of the nihilistic hero was Ryunosuke Tsukue, the main character in Kaizan Nakazato's voluminous, popular novel, *The Great Bodhisattva Pass (Daibosatsu Toge)*. Nakazato began writing his epic in 1913, and it was still incomplete when he stopped working on it in 1941.[37] In his youth he had been influenced by Russian literature[38] and perhaps drawn to its nihilistic characters. Like Russia, Japan had a long history of authoritarianism, and, in the absence of a tradition of liberal democracy, in both countries revolt could take the form of nihilism. Siegfried Kracauer pointed out a similar situation in Germany during the 1920s when democracy was often equated with anarchy.[39]

The Great Bodhisattva Pass was not made into a film until 1935, since Nakazato was apprehensive of sensational treatments of his masterpiece,[40] and perhaps because the film rights cost too much.[41] Nihilistic heroes modeled on or influenced by Ryunosuke Tsukue began appearing in Japanese film as early as 1923,[42] however, and a prime example in extant print is *Orochi*, directed by Buntaro Futagawa in 1925. *Orochi* concerns a young samurai who is expelled from an academy of Chinese learning (*kangaku*) because he got in scraps with fellow students for which he was wrongly blamed. Thereafter, he continually gets in trouble with the authorities as a result of misunderstandings until he is finally apprehended and taken to prison. The theme of the original script by Susukita Rokuhei is simply that dropouts like the hero are actually the good guys and that many of the powers-that-be are evil hypocrites. It was revolutionary at the time because previous heroes usually came from the establishment and most authorities were considered benevolent rulers.

Since the hero in *Orochi* is often shown resisting arrest by fighting off hordes of constables or policemen, his desperate display of courage is certainly a form of protest. Nevertheless, it is meaningless and doomed to failure because of the immense power of the feudal authorities he is up against.

No one will aid him. He is all alone. In the climatic sequence a town crier is shown climbing up the bell tower to alert the populace to the hero's inevitable capture. Shots of the bell ringing are intercut with the hero fleeing until he has his back to a wall. From a high platform the camera presents a birdseye view of him surrounded by the constables, with the townspeople forming an outer circle of onlookers, many of whom cheer on the constables who poke at him with poles and try to lasso him with ropes. When he cuts himself free, the firemen join the attack with hooks and poles. Even the towncrier begins throwing roof tiles at him from above.

The message is clear. Rebellion in an authoritarian society is a solitary, suicidal endeavour. Even the submissive townspeople, who are too timid to join in the attack, will either betray the rebel or at least shun him. Eventually the nihilistic hero drops his sword and turns himself in. As he is led to jail the cheering townspeople form a procession behind the constables.

In 1928, Maijiro Aoe, an intellectual playwright, criticized nihilistic period films like *Orochi* for their portrayal of individual sorrow and looked forward to those showing a group struggle based on a clear social consciousness.[43] In that same year Masahiro Makino came out with *The Street of Masterless Samurai (Ronin-gai)* and showed camaraderie overcoming submissiveness when a few friends come to the aid of the lone hero. Nevertheless, the fact that proletarian period films showing a group struggle were only popular from 1929 to 1931[44] indicates the futility of protest in modern prewar Japan.

The best form of persuasion was an appeal, and in this respect the agonized face of the *Orochi* hero (often shown in close-ups) was more effective than his martial prowess. Abused and misunderstood, he is shown sitting in the temple grounds, head slightly bowed. When he glances up, he resembles James Dean, who is still popular with Japanese audiences because for them he represents misunderstood youth instead of youthful protest. Tsumasaburo Bando, who played the hero in *Orochi*, was in his day as handsome as Dean, and just as appealing, particularly when turned down by heroines. His hurt looks in *Orochi* seemed to suggest that he would call off the rebellion if only someone up there understood him. His appeals for sympathy move neither the townspeople nor the authorities, however, and just before his capture he is shown with blood streaming over his eyes from two wounds on his forehead, as if the director wanted to suggest his hero was as tragic as Oedipus Rex.

Although the nihilistic hero in *Orochi* is antithetical to the Loyal Retainer, he has a lot in common with the Tormented Lord. In one scene while he is walking down a street in town, some rice gruel is accidently spilt on his head from the balcony of an inn. When he complains, the innkeeper tries to buy him off with money. Furious at this affront to his honor as a samurai, he proceeds to beat the innkeeper until the constables

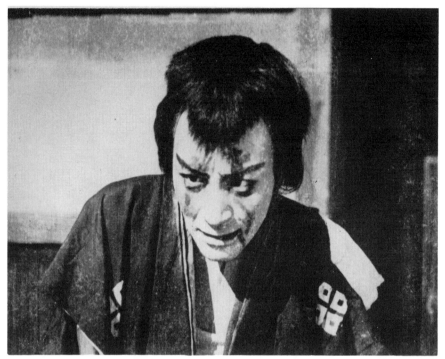

Orochi (1925), directed by Buntaro Futagawa. Since protest in an authoritarian society is futile, this nihilistic swordsman (Tsumasaburo Bando) becomes a tragic figure like Oedipus Rex.

subdue him and take him off to jail. Quick-tempered like Lord Asano, he refuses to suffer affronts, and no less sincere, he also undergoes tragic consequences. He is not a lord, however, and there is no loyal retainer to protect, rescue, or avenge him. Still, he is as representative of Tormented Youth as Lord Asano was.

The nihilistic hero who appears to be the best antithesis of the Loyal Retainer is Sazen Tange, the deformed master swordsman who had lost an arm and one eye in a vendetta. In the original novel, first serialized in a newspaper in 1927, Sazen Tange had been a villain; however, in the 1928 film version, *The Judgements of Magistrate Ooka—New Edition (Shinpan—Ooka Seidan)* director Daisuke Ito transformed him into an originally loyal retainer who is betrayed by the lord he risks his life for.[45] Although only fragments exist of Ito's prewar film and its subsequent series, Ito's script generally remains intact in the postwar remake, *Sazen Tange (Tange Sazen,* 1953), directed by Masahiro Makino.

Makino first presents Sazen Tange as the only retainer faithful enough to volunteer for a dangerous mission on behalf of his lord, a sword collector who wants him to steal a priceless sword set with a long and short blade. Sazen Tange manages to obtain the long sword after defeating its owner in a duel. Thereafter he continually battles the son, who still has the short sword.

The sword set has a magical quality, and when the long sword is separated from its mate it seems to crave blood. As a consequence, Sazen Tange becomes possessed by it and often goes on a rampage, killing innocent victims. Sazen Tange's case of sword possession resembles the fetishlike effect Lord Asano's *seppuku* sword had on his retainer Oishi. However, while Oishi had consequently been imbued with a definite purpose, Tange's failure to successfully complete his mission by obtaining the short sword drives him into fits of madness.

In Makino's sequel, *Sazen Tange II* (*Zoku-Tange Sazen*, 1953) Tange learns that his master betrayed him by denying that he knew him and thereafter he degenerates into self-ridicule and self-abandonment. Not only possessed but betrayed, he becomes a tragic figure because he has lost faith in his sole object of worship, his lord.

In an essay on Daisuke Ito, Tadao Sato states that the two themes of trust and betrayal consistently alternated throughout Ito's long film career. Besides nihilistic heroes like Tange, Ito also portrayed paragons of loyalty, and the fact that there was no middle ground between these two extremes is characteristically Japanese.[46] Accordingly, the insane, one-eyed, and one-armed Tange, both mentally and physically deformed, becomes a grotesque parody of a loyalty-centered Bushido, a betrayed retainer.

In *Sazen Tange II* the role of the insane, betrayed Tange is counterbalanced with that of the cool, sagacious Magistrate Ooka, who represents the authorities and is loyal to the system. The fact that the same actor Denjiro Okochi plays both roles (as he did in prewar versions) is not unusual, for in Japanese cinema such situations were frequent. However, in respect to the archetype of the Loyal Retainer, Okochi's double role is significant, for it suggests that Tange and Ooka are but two aspects of the same personality. One recalls Dr. Jekyll and Mr. Hyde, and Janus, the Roman god who is represented artistically with two opposite faces.

James Hillman, a Jungian psychologist, has proposed the theory that what appear to be two opposing archetypes are actually two aspects of one archetype. He gives as examples Senex, the old man who represents tradition and Puer Aeternus, the eternal youth who always breaks the rules.[47] Hayao Kawai applies Hillman's theory in his own Jungian analysis of Japanese folk tales and views Senex and Puer Aeternus as complementary rather than opposing aspects. In a typically Japanese triad the Senex equivalent helps the youth oppose a possessive mother.[48]

When Magistrate Ooka and Tange are viewed as complementary rather than opposing forces, the denouement of *Sanzen Tange II* assumes greater significance. Edo (modern Tokyo) is in turmoil because of the machina-

Sazen Tange (1953), directed by Masahiro Makino. Betrayed by his daimyo, this one-eyed, one-armed swordsman (Denjiro Okochi)—both mentally and physically deformed—becomes a grotesque parody of a loyalty-centered Bushido.

tions of Tange's lord. One night a deranged Tange appears staggering down a street. The constables try to stop him, but their chief, Magistrate Ooka, orders them to let him pass. Tange proceeds to the Edo residence of his lord and outside the gate cries out to be let in. After he enters a grand melee follows in which he eventually cuts down his lord. The film ends with a crane shot providing a birdseye view of Tange sitting on the ground dejectedly in front of the body of his slain lord, and Magistrate Ooka and his men outside the gate restoring order to the streets of Edo.

Rebellion has been contained. Omnipotent authority has not been breached. Ooka used the betrayed Tange to get his lord, a daimyo who could do as he pleases in his own fief but who would not be permitted to disturb the peace in the shogun's capital, which is protected by Ooka and his men. In terms of archetypal patterns *Sanzen Tange II* is simply a variation of the relationship between Lord Asano, his chief retainer Oishi, and Lord Kira. Ooka, the loyal one, used Tange, the tormented one, to destroy the villain, Tange's lord. For Tange, who was merely an instrument of Ooka's purpose, revenge was not sweet, however, for he slew his lord, not his lord's enemy.

Conclusion

The attempt at antithesis ultimately failed because the nihilistic hero's rebellion was contained and even used to support an authoritarian government. His protest was suicidal, and suicide was the starting point for the myth of *Chushingura*, for Lord Asano and Oishi paid for disturbing the peace with their lives. Still, the formation of the nihilistic hero was significant because it expressed on a popular level a rejection of the sentimentalization of the Loyal Retainer-Tormented Lord dyad. Many artistic period films, like those by Mansaku Itami and Sadao Yamanaka (prewar), and Masaki Kobayashi's *Rebellion* (*Joiuchi*, 1967), have been critical of feudalism, but they mainly appealed to an intellectual audience.

Nihilistic rejection was also expressed in many commercial period films from the 1960s on. Alain Silver labels their main characters "the Alien Hero," and they doubtless take after Sazen Tange in their antitraditionalism and "dramatic de-construction in one way or another of the older, unreflective archetype of the samurai ethos."[49] Daisuke Ito's Tange differs from them, however, in that, when disillusioned about loyalty he did not become cynical but went insane. This indicates the strength of the ideal of sincerity in the period film. Its antithesis, cynicism (for Japanese-style sincerity is always naive), did not become a principal motif until the 1960s when the genre had actually lost its popularity.[50] As a rule, popular period filmmakers could neither attack the marriage between sincerity and loyalty, nor orchestrate rebellion in other than fatalistic tones.

In Japan cynicism is a very modern attitude, and as such, can best be expressed in the postwar, contemporary film genre. This will be demonstrated in the chapter on modern antithetical heroes, through films about contemporary Japanese salarymen, who are not simply modern versions of the loyal retainers in *Chushingura*.

2
The Chaste Warrior

Introduction

WARRIORS, and their modern counterparts such as soldiers, policemen, and gangsters are probably the most popular heroes in any country's cinema. They best represent the universally admired ideal of courage because they put it to the ultimate test in battles where they stake their own lives. To win they must overcome the fear of death. Even the supermanlike heroes for children usually have some Achilles heel, which actually represents this universal fear. Warrior heroes are perhaps no more than the expression of the vicarious triumph over the ultimate universal fear no living human being probably ever totally subdued. In fact, because they do so, they *are* superhuman and even have the right to be inhuman at times.

The warrior heroes in Japanese period film, usually swordsmen, hardly ever show any fear of death. Through their composure and bearing they exhibit a tranquil state of mind which has more to do with their victory than their skill or strength. In contrast, their losing opponents' Achilles heel is often a disturbed or distraught mental state caused by excessive emotion. Accordingly, the Japanese way of overcoming the fear of death is connected with quelling weakening emotions. The most important of these is passionate love for a woman. Mere affection is not a great obstacle.

The Loyal Retainer archetype willingly sacrificed his wife for his lord. In the case of a middle-aged hero like Oishi passion does not seem an important consideration. For young warriors it is different, though. For them to win in battle, the rule in period film is that they must not show strong emotion for a young woman, and in this sense I call them the Chaste Warrior. The best embodiment of this archetype is Musashi Miyamoto.

Just as *Chushingura* is Japan's national epic, Musashi is her national hero. Like Oishi, Musashi is a historical figure, who was probably born in 1584. He claimed in *Gorin no sho* (The Book of Five Rings), which he finished writing just before he died in 1645, that he had fought in over 60 duels and had never lost.[1] He thereby achieved a reputation as Japan's greatest swordsman during an age when dueling and kendo flourished, and became the subject of many books and about thirty movies since 1909.[2] Unlike western heroes who overcome all obstacles to win the heroine, Musashi is usually presented as a celibate who regarded women as weakening influences.

Japan's first warrior heroes in *Kojiki* were by no means celibate. As emperors and gods, they had to have many offspring from which the noblemen of the ruling Yamato clan could claim divine ancestry. Consequently, the records of their exploits often read like the Book of Numbers in the Bible. Thereafter, however, antecedents for Musashi's attitude can be found in medieval chronicles of a literary and military nature.

Women are first presented as weakening influences in *Heike monogatari* (The Tale of the Heike), about the twelfth-century war between the two major clans for political control over Japan. In contrast to the eastern or Minamoto warriors, who regard battle as more important than their families, the western or Taira warriors find it extremely difficult to part from their wives. One chapter in *Heike monogatari* even rivals in poignancy Hector's parting from his wife and infant in Homer's *Iliad*.[3] Although very human, like Hector, the western warriors lose in battle, and the prototype for the Chaste Warrior is the war-loving eastern warrior. Distinctions between east and west fade and wives all but disappear in the *Taiheiki*,[4] about the "grand pacification" campaign in the thirteenth century, which was another civil war. All ideal Japanese warriors then became chaste in their single-minded devotion to battle.

Musashi became the incarnation of this single-minded devotion, and, as a popular hero, performed the sociopolitical function of preparing ordinary Japanese men for battle on behalf of their nation. He complements the peacetime Loyal Retainer, for during war courage is required in addition to submission. Musashi's chaste warrior also complements *Chushingura* in terms of period film iconography. Since, unlike Oishi, he had no master to serve, his brand of courage is divorced from loyalty and even mounted in a peculiar egoism. Accordingly, important motifs in the period film genre that were not derived from *Chushingura* can be demonstrated by tracing the metamorphoses Musashi underwent as he changed from a feudal hero to one with modern implications, which even include postwar pacifism in Japan.

Unlike the Loyal Retainer, who had something of an antithesis, the Chaste Warrior archetype did not produce a counterpart to the nihilistic hero, for Musashi was actually his own antithesis. There are variations of Musashi's chaste warrior, though, and they are presented in the discussion of period film heroes and sex, which comes after the metamorphoses and a cross-cultural comparison between Musashi and non-Japanese equivalents.

Musashi

The myth of Musashi begins with confusing "historical" accounts of his life that allow diverse interpretations of the context of his courage. His most famous duel took place at the Isle of Ganryu in 1612, but the motivation behind it is unclear because of the discrepancies concerning the age of his opponent, Kojiro Sasaki. In *Nitenki* (Chronicle of Two Heavens), compiled in 1755, the authors state that Kojiro was eighteen but contradict themselves by relating that he was a disciple of a famous swordsman, which would have made him an old man in 1612.[5] Eighteenth-century Kabuki playwrights and storytellers preferred Kojiro as an old man whom a young Musashi defeats to avenge the death of his father.[6] Then, a filially motivated vendetta was a popular theme—as it was in prewar period films—and provided a good pretext for displays of courage.

Storytellers went on to invent episodes of harsh training that Musashi first undergoes under a stern father and thereafter on his own. This Kodan version continued to be popular in the early part of the twentieth century long after the Kabuki version was forgotten.[7] The training doubtless reflected the tough apprenticeship Japanese craftsmen went through in their hierarchical guilds, and the Kodan Musashi thus represented an ideal of courage as the endurance of hardships.

The Kodan version was adapted into a short novel by Tachikawa Bunmeido Publishers, whose cheap paperbacks for boys were popular in the 1910s and 1920s.[8] After such childhood training as jumping over hedges that increase in height each year, the Tachikawa Musashi goes on to slay mountain bandits and monsters. He became the model of present-day comic book versions, which also serve the social function of encouraging young boys to train or study hard to become successful adults.

The first Musashi films—about fourteen between 1909 and 1936—were based on the Kodan and Tachikawa versions of his life,[9] and there are no extant prints. He seems to have been presented then either as a supermanlike hero for boys—the principal audience of Japan's first period films—or as a filially motivated avenger. The latter image can be gleaned from Mizoguchi's *Musashi Miyamoto* (*Miyamoto Musashi*, 1944), where he helps a brother and sister avenge their father's death. Such a Kodan-styled Musashi, however, was not nearly so popular in prewar period films as Mataemon Araki, a swordsman who specialized in aiding such vendettas.[10]

Musashi changed from a not overly popular, feudal film hero to a national hero because of the popularity of Eiji Yoshikawa's historical novel about him. Serialized from 1935 until 1939 in *Asahi Shimbun*, Japan's largest newspaper,[11] Yoshikawa's novel was so successful that nowadays the average Japanese is hardly aware of a Kodan Musashi or any other. A detailed discussion of it is warranted here, since it formed the core of all popular Musashi films from the 1940s on, and even of the 1985 TV drama about him.

Yoshikawa's novel was successful for two main reasons. First, he developed the harsh training in Kodan into a Japanese version of the universal initiation myth, which is an important theme in modern literature, according to Mircea Eliade.[12] Second, he changed the context of Musashi's courage from filial piety and endurance of hardship to the conquest of the fear of death. This led to the formation of a new period film hero that had important, political implications, particularly in wartime Japan.

In most initiation ceremonies young men are forced to show courage in the face of death in order to be psychologically weaned from their mother and to gain entrance into the adult male world.[13] Yoshikawa's Musashi, however, displays unbridled courage from the start. As a soldier from a defeated army, he kills provincial border guards on his way back to his village, where he hides out in a nearby forest like a wild animal savagely killing those who stumble upon his lair.

In order to restore peace to the village, Takuan, a Zen monk who acts as a tutelary figure, decides to capture Musashi himself by appealing to his human sentiments. Takuan takes Otsu, a girl who was Musashi's child-hood friend, into the forest with him, and one night while he is cooking potato stew over an open fire, Otsu plays a plaintive tune on her flute. She is an orphan like Musashi and the tune reminds both of them of their dead parents, and, along with hunger, entices Musashi from his hiding place. Takuan then appeals to Musashi's concern for his sister and beats him for all the trouble he has caused. Here, Yoshikawa has Takuan replace Mu-sashi's strict Kodan father to train him to be human rather than simply strong.

Musashi's punishment is by no means over, though, for Takuan binds him and has him suspended from an ancient cryptomeria tree some thirty feet from the ground, during fair and foul weather. The giant tree boldly alludes to primitive phallic worship, and Musashi represents wild phallic energy now bound by the thick hemp ropes often seen at the entrance to a Shinto shrine. He now recalls Susano O, the Shinto god in *Kojiki* who wrought havoc on the Plain of Heaven (*Takama no Hara*) by breaking down the ridges of rice paddies and covering up ditches. Susano O so embarrassed his sister, Amaterasu the Sun Goddess that she hid in a cave.[14] Light returned to the world when she was enticed outside by music, just as order returned to Musashi's village after Otsu's flute brought him out of hiding and he was reminded of the trouble he was causing *his* sister. Musashi and Susano O during the early stages of their development are both simply manifestations of the Untamed Male archetype.[15]

Otsu falls in love with Musashi and sets him free to search for his sister, but Takuan gets a hold of him again. The ordeal has taught Musashi that his strength and courage had been of the inhuman sort. He is tamed, and now Takuan decides to civilize him. He cajoles Musashi into entering the daimyo's castle and manages to lock him up in one of the towers with only volumes of books for his companions. Three years later he emerges from the womblike tower, and Takuan gives him the new name of Musashi— previously he had been called Takezo—to signify his second birth. Now respectfully seated below the daimyo, Musashi exemplifies the cultivated samurai, well-groomed and neatly dressed, and proficient in the use of courteous speech. For the sake of spiritual training, he turns downs the position offered, and later rejects Otsu on a bridge, a meeting place for lovers that also represents a new phase in character development.

With the rejection of Otsu, Yoshikawa's novel diverges sharply from the pattern in initiation myths. While psychological weaning from the mother is necessary, alienation from the female gender would lead to the extinction, rather than the regeneration, of the society. After the bridge scene Musashi continually turns his back on an imploring and pathetic Otsu before going off to some duel. He even seems to derive his courage from the repression of the human sentiments Otsu represents and Takuan had taught him to value. Accordingly, Musashi differs from western mythological heroes, who usually win a woman after a battle, and even from Susano O, who was transformed from a naughty brother to a dragon-slaying hero who mated with many maidens and engendered countless offspring.[16]

Yoshikawa also differed from Kodan and Tachikawa versions by creating Otsu. Since previous Musashis had been passionless celibates, Yoshikawa's Musashi seems more human because he often wrestles with his desire for her. In fact, the passage where he cools off under a waterfall, with his hands tightly folded to show intense concentration, would be recreated ad infinitum in subsequent film and comic book versions.

In this respect, Musashi was the crystalization of the sexual repression Japanese youths experienced in the 1930s, when Yoshikawa wrote his novel. They were aware of western ideas of romantic love and yearned for it; however, with the rise of militarism, Confucian restraints tightened and even seating in theaters was sexually segregated.[17] In Confucian morality sex is not a sin, but amorous escapades are frowned upon because they could lead one to neglect his duty. And duty became of supreme importance in a militaristic Japan where individual desires were castigated. Yoshikawa's Musashi, thereby, became a perfect model for Japanese soldiers then. They repressed their desires and weakening emotions and figuratively became chaste warriors as they left their wife and family behind and marched off to war in China.[18] Ironically, in Chinese literature there is no counterpart to Musashi, since in China Confucianism never combined with militarism in such a self-abnegating manner.

The celibacy of Yoshikawa's Musashi, and the self-abnegation it implies, is related to his quest for spiritual development, which was quite different from the training in the Kodan version, and which had a more subtle political implication than the simple separation from loved ones. Yoshikawa obtained his spiritual interpretation of Musashi from *Gorin no sho*,[19] which had previously only been read by scholars.[20] In this manual of practical advice on warfare Musashi had advocated a state of mind free

Musashi Miyamoto (1954), directed by Hiroshi Inagaki. Musashi (Toshiro Mifune) the Chaste Warrior turns his back on Otsu (Kaoru Yachigusa), a pathetic beauty who represents tender emotions that would weaken him in battle.

from worldly considerations and the inhibiting of rational thought as a precondition for the spontaneous physical reactions necessary for victory. This mental state is similar to the "mindless" consciousness Zen Buddhists try to attain through meditation.[21]

By connecting Musashi with Zen, Yoshikawa placed him above other swordsmen in the early seventeenth century and created a different hero. Although Zen had influenced warriors since at least the fourteenth century, Yoshikawa's Musashi was the first really popular spiritual swordsman.

In prewar period film, along with loyal retainers, Kodan heroes who valued honor above all else had dominated the genre. Some of them, like Musashi himself, were modeled on *ronin* who had fought on the losing side during the Battle of Sekigahara in 1600, which ushered in the Tokugawa shogunate. Since they no longer had masters, loyalty was meaningless for them. Although Yoshikawa's Musashi had a strong sense of honor like his historical contemporaries and Kodan heroes, as he develops spiritually under the influence of Zen he avoids suicidal battles and duels he could easily win, and even submits to some ridicule no other honor-abiding samurai would bear.

In the climactic ending of Yoshikawa's novel, Musashi uses Zen to defeat his ultimate opponent, Kojiro Sasaki, who is transformed into a young man. This is graphically shown in Hiroshi Inagaki's 1940 film version. Other film versions of Yoshikawa's Musashi had been made since 1936, but Inagaki's was the first to attempt to include the whole story and was the first big box office hit.

The only extant print of the trilogy, Part Three, *The Spirit of the Sword is One Way (Kenshin Ichiro)* begins with Musashi telling Otsu he loves the way of the Sword more and leaving her. Then shots of him at a temple meditating and following Gudo, a famous Zen monk, are intercut with her on the road searching for him—once a Buddhist image is superimposed on the countryside scene for continuity. It appears he has forsaken her to attain enlightenment, but once his mind is free of attachments he goes off to the Isle of Ganryu for his match with Kojiro, and we realize Otsu was not so important after all. She is last shown praying for his success, in a beautiful three-quarter profile shot which resembles Christian medallions of the Virgin Mary. But her prayers are unnecessary. Zen has given Musashi the spiritual detachment needed to defeat Kojiro, a technically superior opponent.

In the matching of a "spiritual" Musashi with a "technical" Kojiro one can find a metaphor for the propaganda line during World War II that the spiritual strength of Japan *(Yamato damashi)* would ultimately defeat the technical superiority of the United States and Great Britain. Zen, of course, is on a much deeper spiritual level than such nationalistic sentiments, but the mind free of attachments, which Musashi supposedly attained, could also be used in the war effort.

Freedom from attachments is a selfless state, for when a self is recognized, so are desires, that is, attachments. This selfless state is related to mu (nothingness) or kū (the void). While such philosophical concepts usually presuppose a nothingness from which everything springs, they can also be used to resign young men to war and death. It was to such usage Zen-like selflessness was put in the popular wartime film directed by Kajiro Yamamoto, *The War at Sea from Hawaii to Malaya* (*Hawaii-Marei Oki Kaisen*, 1942).

A young naval cadet returns to his home village on leave and tells a young war hero there that he is troubled over the death of a classmate. The hero tells him that he should not think that way since they themselves are nothing (mu) and the only thing that counts is the Japanese race. Flashbacks follow showing how he realized his own selflessness while lost in meditation before a statue of a famous naval hero in the Russo-Japanese War.

Yoshikawa's Musashi also attained such a Zen-like mental state, and by erasing the fear of death, it enabled him to achieve victory. Musashi became Japan's most popular, fictional hero during World War II. Yoshikawa's novel was serialized into a radio drama that aired on NHK from 1939 into the early 1940s.[22] The first popular edition of *Gorin no sho* came out in 1942,[23] and there was a Musashi film each year before 1945 and the end of the war.[24]

After World War II it seemed most Japanese identified with Kojiro, the loser, and, judging from the fact that one of two Musashi films in 1952 was a comedy,[25] they seemed reluctant to take their World War II hero seriously. Then, between 1954[26] and 1956 Inagaki came out with a new film trilogy based on Yoshikawa's novel, which was shown abroad as *Samurai*. It differed from the original novel and Inagaki's own 1940 film version in that Musashi does not meditate before his duel with Kojiro. David Desser has noted that this Musashi is not much of a "Zen fighter,"[27] and the lack of Zen elements in this version is probably due to the mixed feelings many Japanese felt as a result of Zen's wartime usage.[28]

Instead of Zen, Musashi takes up farming and practically lives together with Otsu as husband and wife. Of course, their "marriage" is not consummated, but since he has by no means completely overcome his passion for her, he appears to be shy and strong, rather than chaste and savage. Before the duel at the Isle of Ganryu, Otsu tells Musashi that she wishes they could simply live together peacefully. Of course, he admonishes her to act like a samurai wife who sees her husband off to battle with a smile on her face. But the impression he gives is just the opposite, and we feel he is forced to play a role. After he kills Kojiro, the tears in his eyes suggest that their match was a tragedy rather than an ultimate test of spiritual development.

Inagaki's postwar Musashi has the common touch. He is an ordinary human being stuck in the archetypal mold of the chaste warrior who rejects love for battle. He has been called "a modern man" by Donald Richie,[29] an observation which suggests a sympathetic character instead of a fanatical samurai. Because of this, part 1 of Inagaki's trilogy won the 1955 American Academy Award as the Best Foreign Picture, for it mainly consisted of the initiation, when even Yoshikawa's Musashi was at his most human.

The metamorphosis Musashi underwent through Inagaki's direction could be attributed to postwar pacifism in Japan. Still, while being a master director of period films, Inagaki did not necessarily share their feudalistic sentiments even in the early 1940s. In the twenties and thirties he was a close friend of Sadao Yamanaka and Mansaku Itami, liberal directors who continually made films satirizing supersamurai and self-sacrifice. In fact, Itami wrote the script for Inagaki's greatest film, *The Life of Matsu the Untamed (Muho Matsu no Issho)*. The version which won the Grand Prix at the 1958 Venice Film Festival was simply a remake of his 1943 film. Its workingman hero differed from Kabuki- and Kodan-derived heroes simply by not being a samurai, and he could be more human than Musashi because he was without a constricting feudal mold. Looking back on Inagaki's long, prolific career as a period film maker, it appears that he too had often been forced to play a role which did not suit his liberal, humanistic sentiments.

Between 1961 and 1965 Tomu Uchida directed a five-part film version of Yoshikawa's Musashi that expresses pacifist sentiments by emphasizing Musashi's monstrous side, which is analogous with war. Uchida's unsentimental Musashi never lives with Otsu and feels no passion for her whatsoever before his duel with Kojiro. Hence, he becomes chaste again, rather than shy. His savagery is emphasized by the sheer number of battles and duels—Uchida's ten-hour version is twice as long as Inagaki's—and the difference in directorial styles.

Inagaki—like his prewar contemporaries, Yamanaka and Itami—favored an indirect presentation of a duel, consisting of a montage showing angry glares, spectators, and inanimate objects, but often not including the fatal sword stroke. Consequently, violence was artistically circumscribed. Uchida, on the other hand, used a direct approach that utilized advanced sound effects and blood-spurting devices, such as those found in Kurosawa's *Yojimbo (Yojimbo*, 1961). Through a liberal use of red liquids, punctuated with thuds, groans, and screams, Uchida seemed to be trying to recapture the horror of the battles he had witnessed as a filmmaker on the China front during World War II.[30] Consequently, the bloodthirsty rages of his Musashi overshadow signs of spiritual development.

Uchida's Musashi is not only savage but cruel. During the Battle at Ichijoji he first kills the thirteen-year-old heir apparent of the Yoshioka family, the standard bearer of their fencing school. If this slaying was shown in previous film versions, it was attributed to the heat of battle or Musashi's chagrin at facing about seventy swordsmen. In Yoshikawa's novel it is stated that it may have been intentional, but Uchida leaves no doubt that it is premeditated. Musashi is shown on a hillside drawing a map of enemy positions. After he draws an X indicating his first intended victim, Uchida's wide-lensed camera zooms in for a close-up of the innocent-looking boy. Hence, Musashi, who formerly slew monsters in Tachikawa books for boys, becomes a monster himself.

Uchida de-emphasizes Zen even more than Inagaki did, by having Takuan and other Zen monks trick Musashi, rather than enlighten him. In Yoshikawa's novel Zen was at least on a par with the Way of the Sword. As Uchida diminishes the former, the latter becomes an obsession with winning the duel in whatever manner necessary. Uchida's Musashi gloats over his fallen foes. He becomes a megalomaniac who needs a keeper instead of a teacher.[31]

Without teachers Musashi is reduced to a form of self-worship that is a distortion of the Zen principle of meditation as *jiriki*, or self-power, for within Uchida's Musashi there is neither a Buddha-Nature nor a Kingdom of God.[32] Moreover, unlike the World War II Musashi who served the sociopolitical function of encouraging citizens to sacrifice personal pleasures for the good of the state, Uchida's "peacetime" Musashi simply represents an antisocial obsession with individual success at all costs. He cannot even be considered as a model for postwar Japanese businessmen who came to be called "economic animals," for they probably viewed success in terms of their family and nation.[33]

The narcissistic side of Uchida's Musashi can best be seen in his relationship with his worthy opponent,[34] Kojiro Sasaki. Desser has pointed out the similarity between the action hero and his antagonist.[35] This was not always the case with Musashi and Kojiro, however, since Kojiro also underwent a number of metamorphoses.

When Yoshikawa changed the David and Goliath setup in Kodan by making Kojiro a young man too, he was left with two similar swordsmen out to achieve fame. Besides giving Musashi a spiritual dimension, for character contrast Yoshikawa presented Kojiro as an arrogant sadist who delights in slicing up people. By the time of their duel, however, Kojiro has acquired some dignity as a fencing-school master. This is shown in Inagaki's 1940 film by the elegant garments he wears in contrast to Musashi's plain garb. Since the militaristic censors then had a penchant for images of pure-hearted farm boys—they made such good soldiers—Musashi became the rustic samurai taking on the corrupt, urban one.

With the slackening of Confucian sexual inhibitions in the immediate postwar period, Genzo Murakami wrote a best-selling novel about Kojiro in which he became a lover boy and tragic hero who dies without fulfilling his ambition to be the best swordsman in Japan. Inagaki made this Kojiro

Musashi Miyamoto—Duel at the Isle of Ganryu (1965), directed by Tomu Uchida. Uchida's Musashi (Kin'nosuke Yorozuya [formerly Nakamura]) is a savage megalomaniac who distorts Zen into self-worship.

the hero of a film trilogy in 1950, and, in his 1954–56 Musashi trilogy, gave Kojiro the aura of a courtier aristocrat who combines urbanity, amorous inclinations, and *aware*, a poignant sense of sadness. Beside being arrayed in gorgeous robes, the handsome Kojiro now wears his silky black hair long and uses white facial powder. While waiting for a crude Musashi who is carving a boat oar into a club, Kojiro admires a branch of cherry blossoms that symbolizes the evanescence of all things. (No wonder Musashi cries after he slays him.) This new, postwar setup not only recalled the twelfth century in Japanese history when courtier aristocrats were overthrown by provincial warriors, but also revealed the homosexual aspect of the worthy-opponent relationship.

Uchida's Kojiro loses his accrued elegance and becomes as arrogant as he was.in Yoshikawa's novel. He continually claims that the Way of the Sword is simply power and skill, and a Musashi stripped of spirituality agrees with him, after he kills him with a carved oar. Their former differences—urbane vs. rustic, technical vs. spiritual—slip off like thin accretions, and we are left with two similar swordsmen who simply want to win. Musashi's chastity and Kojiro's amorous escapades also seem beside the point because in both cases women do not interfere with their ambitions. Both men are basically egoists. Herein lies the narcissistic nature of the worthy-opponent relation: each one sees himself in the other. Rather than a Janus-faced coin, we have one with the same face on both sides.

From Uchida's portrayal of Musashi as a savage, narcissistic megalomaniac, it is obvious the director did not like his subject. Musashi's human side is only shown through some remorse he felt for slaying the thirteen-year-old and for blinding a rather pacifist swordsman.[36] Within ten hours of film footage mainly devoted to carnage, however, Musashi's belated qualms formed a rather small eddy. In Uchida's next film on Musashi, *Battle of Life or Death* (*Shinken Shobu*, 1970) Uchida attempted to make a more forceful, antiwar statement.

Battle of Life or Death is based on a single episode from Yoshikawa's novel in which Musashi takes on Baiken, a warrior who uses a sickle and a small iron ball and chain to defeat swordsmen. Uchida diverges from the original when he has Musashi ruthlessly seize Baiken's infant as a hostage during their duel. Baiken still wants to avenge his brother's death at Musashi's hands, though, and Musashi is forced to draw both of his swords.

Large titles appear on the screen identifying these as the Life-Giving Sword and the Life-Destroying Sword. Yoshikawa had used such terminology to give Musashi's two-sword method some spirituality. Uchida quickly refutes this, however, with the following titles: The Sword is Simply Large Scale Destruction. Then the film ends with a wide-screen close-up of Baiken's crying infant against a background of burning fields.

Uchida died while the film was being edited, and it is not certain if he

Musashi Miyamoto—Duel at the Isle of Ganryu (1965), directed by Tomu Uchida. With a club carved from a boat oar, Musashi (Kin'nosuke Yorozuya) takes on Kojiro (Ken Takakura), a worthy opponent who is a reflection of himself.

had wanted it to end that way. Daisuke Ito, who like Uchida had been making films since the 1920s, wrote the script for *Battle of Life or Death*. In Ito's own 1943 film version of the same episode, *Duel at Hannya Hill* *(Ketto Hannya-han)* the child died and Musashi held it in his arms and chanted a sutra for it.

Although it is uncertain what ending Uchida intended, one can find a saving allegory in this uneven and melodramatic film. The burning fields represent the large scale destruction during the Sino-Japanese War, which Uchida himself had witnessed. Baiken is the Chinese forces who were willing to sacrifice the children the Japanese forces (Musashi) were in effect holding hostage by inviting their death. The crying infant recalls a famous parable known to both Chinese and Japanese. In order to demonstrate that the human heart was good, Mencius, the fourth-century B.C. Chinese philosopher who is invariably linked with Confucius, hypothesized a situation in which a child is about to fall into a well and concluded that even the worst adult would try to save it.[37]

Perhaps Uchida was inferring that only through such humane feelings as parental love could mankind be saved from the total annihilation war always invites. Perhaps his ending was inconclusive because chaste warriors, of course, have no children.

The next Musashi film in 1973 continued Uchida's pacifistic theme on a smaller scale by attempting to domesticate Musashi. After Takuan ties him to the tree he cries like a baby, and the scene where he returns in a boat after killing Kojiro is intercut with a mother singing a lullabye. Director Tai Kato thereby alluded to Musashi's orphan background. NHK continued in a like vein in their serialization of Yoshikawa's novel, which totaled about thirty hours of viewing time from April 1984 until March 1985.

The spiritual development of NHK's Musashi mainly consists of suffering because he *unintentionally* killed that thirteen-year-old. This deepens his humility toward teachers like Takuan and his sympathy for the common folk, and he becomes a nice guy with an amiable smile. NHK also domesticates Kojiro, for on the night before the big duel he embraces his woman for comfort and support, rather than simply for sex.

While NHK's *Chushingura* was the family drama writ large, their Musashi is writ small, for it does not have the purely political purpose of instilling patriotism. Rather, it reminds present-day Japanese males in nuclear families of their social role, which consists of placing work, not war, above conjugal considerations. While Musashi is tenderly caring for the bedridden, ever-failing Otsu, he hears of Kojiro's challenge. Soon he makes his preparations, and at every stage of his journey toward the designated site, he is seen off by old friends. For a man, duty comes before personal affections, and this even goes for mediocre office clerks. If the Japanese male plays his role conscientiously, he will always be enveloped by a warm circle of friends and kin, who understand.

Non-Japanese Equivalents?

Although NHK's Musashi, of all the metamorphoses, showed the most affection for Otsu, he remained true to the Chaste Warrior mold by repressing his feelings when he hears the call of duty, and in this respect continued to provide a model for service to society in general or a nation at war. As stated in the introduction, such swordsmen are the heroes in many period films, and so Musashi is not unusual in a Japanese context. When compared to hardboiled American heroes, however, he seems like a perversion. For example, while Clint Eastwood in the *Dirty Harry* series may appear to be emotionless, he often has sex with women and even falls in love sometimes, and this never seems to have a weakening influence on him. The same can be said for the heroes in American war movies.

Mythological and anthropological equivalents to Musashi's Chaste Warrior do exist. Joseph Campbell has noted that the son of the Hindu deity

Shiva is called Kumara, the "chaste youth" because he is "wedded alone to his army,"[38] and Campbell also treated Cuchulainn, a Celtic hero who drops his guard when embarrassed by naked women.[39] James Frazer stated that many primitive people refrained from women in time of war on the principle of sympathetic magic—that is, the belief that close contact with women would infect them with feminine weakness and cowardice.[40] In modern America such a notion remains in the superstition in boxing circles that sex should be avoided during training, but treatment of this theme tends to be humorous rather than serious, as in Martin Scorsese's *Raging Bull*. Musashi, on the other hand, was only treated humorously in the immediate postwar period when Americanization was quite strong. Generally, his chastity is taken seriously and this makes him crucially different from Western warrior heroes. For a Westerner, the temptations of Saint Anthony are acceptable but those of Musashi are not. His battles could be regarded as demonstrations of courage, but not as stages in spiritual development.

Frazer pointed out that ancient kings were commonly priests and were often warriors.[41] But in the West the temporal and spiritual aspects of the warrior hero separated. Perhaps they did not do so in Japan because of the long tradition of an emperor descended from Shinto gods, which was official ideology until 1945. The relation between Zen and Bushido also has to be considered an important factor, though. Shinto gods and heroes were not only far from chaste but were often helped by women, as were Greek heroes. Take for example, Takeru Yamato, Japan's first earth-bound hero, who received a magic sword from his aunt.[42] While the influences of Zen Buddhism and Confucianism combined to eventually separate Japanese heroes like Musashi from women, they did not separate them from religion. They could no longer be lovers like their Shinto predecessors, but they could still be priestlike.

Women distracted both Christian and Buddhist monks from spirituality, but warriors were not monks in the West. Even in modern Japan, however, Musashi could become not only a national hero but a saintly swordsman. In Zen Buddhism, enlightenment can be attained not only by meditating monks, but also by devotees of the tea ceremony, and also through a dedication to the Sword that included chastity.

Period Film Heroes and Sex

Although Musashi and Kojiro underwent metamorphoses, Otsu never really changed from the way Yoshikawa first conceived her in the late 1930s. After she falls in love with Musashi, she is totally devoted and subservient to him. Men adjust to their times, but women are only supposed to be loyal to their men. Musashi and Kojiro do not fight over Otsu.

She is simply attached to Musashi, but can never be his wife because he is chaste. As the Pathetic Beauty, a type often found in Japanese film, she does not reach the level of an archetype, for in the period film genre where males are in the spotlight, she cannot compete with the Tormented Lord. However, in contemporary film feminine suffering triumphs over weak males, as will be shown in chapter 6.

Despite Otsu's weak showing compared with Western heroines, she was still one of the first females to achieve heroine status in period film, since she was at least an obstacle to Musashi's training. Most young period film heroes do not pay much attention to women at all, since according to Confucian ethics they should be solely concerned with loyalty toward a superior and filial piety. Young nihilistic heroes like Orochi could be tempted and worthy opponents like Kojiro could be flippant, but they were both unorthodox.

Orthodox middle-aged heroes like Oishi could have a wife, but the nihilistic ones like Tange had a mistress to show they were not respectable. Good women and fallen women were drawn to the orthodox hero because of his "virtue," and like Otsu often pursued or trailed him. After Orochi, young nihilistic heroes attracted fallen women because they were handsome. Only villains pursued women, however, often kidnapping good ones and trying to rape them, only to be foiled by heroes. Villains were also free to indulge their lust with fallen women, but such scenes were only suggested.

Such puritanical attitudes toward sex prevailed in the period film even in the postwar period, since very few new heroes were created after Musashi. Consequently, the period films of Akira Kurosawa were truly innovative and demonstrated their artistic level by being true to human nature. The bandit played by Toshiro Mifune in *Rashomon* (1950) is both the Untamed Male and a believable character. His sexual desire for the nobleman's wife is natural rather than perverted, and he is a likeable villain since his actions result from simply human failings. In *Seven Samurai* the chaste youth's desire for the farm girl is not a shameful urge to be exorcized and his shy embarrassment is humorous.

Innovations like those made by Kurosawa, though, were few and far between, and most period films, like American western potboilers, were for little boys and their heroes were appropriately neuter. A good example is the Tengu Kurauma series. Created by popular novelist Jiro Osaragi, Tengu Kurauma is a legendary hero who secretly aids the royalist forces that finally restored imperial rule in 1868. From 1927 through the early 1960s about fifty films were made about him.[43] Dressed in black and riding a white horse like Zorro, besides his sword, he carried one or two six-shooters, which were not incongruous due to the approach of modernization. Unlike Zorro, though, he preferred to rescue little boys in distress rather than damsels.

Tengu Kurauma series (1950s). With a six-shooter and a sword, this avuncular, neuter hero (Kanjuro Arashi) rescued little boys in distress rather than damsels.

Kanjuro Arashi starred in forty of the Tengu films and is most associated with the role.[44] He was a slim actor with a long face and his 1928 Tengu hardly looks different from his 1958 one. While apparently ageless, he does not remain young, since from the start he appeared as the uncle every little boy would like to have.

Although it is impossible to imagine Arashi in a love scene, his Tengu, like Musashi, also has a woman following him, but rather than a pathetic beauty, she is a viper woman (dokufu). Being a pickpocket, she is on the road a lot and is often hired by the villain to either spy on Tengu or kill him. She is never a match for him, though, and generally in the end she is won over to his side and helps him out, even though it means betraying her boss.

Such a femme fatale would never appear to tempt a children's hero in an American film. She is not incongruous in a Japanese film, since there are precedents for a woman following the Chaste Warrior. Moreover, if she is a bad one, he can demonstrate his virtue by converting her to goodness.

As most children's heroes went over to TV, which became the main medium in the 1960s, sex finally entered commercial period films. The best example is Kyoshiro Nemuri, a seventeenth-century, young master swordsman created by Tosaburo Shibata, whose popular novel was made into a film series with twelve entries from 1963 to 1969.[45] Played by the handsome Raizo Ichikawa, Kyoshiro greatly differs from Tengu in that he usually has sex with the women spies he gets the best of. He even takes on respectable women who give themselves to him in exchange for his services as a bodyguard or assassin. His favorite technique is to disrobe women by lightening fast sword strokes which slash through their outer and inner garments, and his only deference to the Chaste Warrior tradition is that he never kisses them.

Although Kyoshiro is a relatively new hero, an antecedent for his womanizing can be found in Kojiro. Moreover, aspects of his personality suggest the old heroes of period film.[46]

His nihilism is signified by his surname, Nemuri, which literally means "sleepy" and refers to his blasé attitude. He never gets emotionally involved and sometimes seems so bored he is about to fall asleep. This is in direct contrast to the orthodox young hero who constantly shows his sincerity by his earnest look and serious demeanor.

The Tormented-Lord aspect of his character is suggested by his personal name, Kyoshiro, literally meaning a "deranged fellow." His father was a Portuguese Christian missionary who was forced to apostatize, and who got revenge on the daimyo who tortured him by raping his daughter. Kyoshiro was the issue of their illicit union, and although he never exhibits abnormal behavior, Japanese viewers naturally assume that underneath he is tormented.

The fact that Kyoshiro is a child of mixed parentage also serves as a

Kyoshiro Nemuri—Flaming Sword (1965), directed by Kenji Misumi. With the appearance of the tattooed lady (Junko Kozakura), sex enters the commercial period film but does not deter the handsome warrior (Raizo Ichikawa) from battle.

pretext for his immorality and allows him sexual behavior denied to "pure" Japanese heroes. He actually reinforces the Chaste Warrior as an ideal by implying that lewdness is due to foreign influences.

Yet, Kyoshiro also resembles Musashi in some respects. In *Bewitching Female Sword* (*Joyo Ken,* 1964), directed by Kazuo Ikehiro, Kyoshiro visits a captured priest. (Christianity was prohibited in seventeenth-century Japan.) He gives him water, not out of pity, he says, but because he wants to learn about the "power" of the Christian faith. Here he is like the Musashi who used Zen meditation not to achieve enlightenment but to become invincible in battle.

In the film's denouement Kyoshiro has a showdown with the bewitching beauty of the title, who is both the villain and his worthy opponent. By posing as Sister Theresa she deceived Christians in hiding in order to further her smuggling business. While he is slashing away at her nun's habit, she uses psychology on him. Since she is the daughter of his nursemaid, she knows his past and informs him that he was conceived as the result of a pagan ceremony in which his father used his naked mother as a sacrifice. For once the blasé Kyoshiro is visibly agitated, and Sister Theresa is down to her semitransparent undergarment. But he regains his cool and cuts her down.

Although Kyoshiro's sang-froid is spiritually far removed from Musashi's Zen-like freedom from attachments, functionally speaking both mental states enable warriors to defeat worthy opponents through action uninhibited by thoughts and feelings. In this respect, slaying the bewitching beauty is not very different from overcoming passion for the pathetic beauty.

Conclusion

Even though sex entered the period film in the sixties, Eros did not shake its foundation, for ultimately it is a genre that manifests Thanatos, or the death wish. Killing is a dominant motif, whether make-believe and bloodless as in films for children, or blood-splattered and chilling as in realistic films for adults. The lack of battle scenes in prewar Itami and Yamanaka films attests to their artistic caliber rather than the nature of the genre itself. Death is an essential element even in Mizoguchi's *Ugetsu* (*Ugetsu monogatari*, 1953) and *Sansho the Bailiff* (*Sansho dayu*, 1954), despite their noncombative heroes. Inagaki tried to humanize Musashi, and Uchida used his monstrous side as an antiwar message. But still the final result of their Musashi films in terms of footage is wholesale slayings.

American westerns have their share of killings, too, which suggest the near genocide of many American Indian tribes attendant on the development of the West. This negative side is shared by all action genres with warrior heroes, no matter what particular culture they express. The period film differs only in its motif of self-annihilation, which comes from Bushido.

The period film genre was from its inception an expression and popularization of Bushido, the feudal Way of the Warrior. Its ideals were simply loyalty, honor, and courage. Loyalty toward a superior resulted in self-abnegation, which was ultimately realized in the group suicide in *Chushingura*. The masterless Musashi denied himself through the repression of his sexual desire, which resulted in chastity.

Tadao Sato has interpreted honor as the cornerstone of Bushido.[47] If honor is superordinate, then loyalty becomes subordinate, and a samurai could conceivably rebel against a master who insulted him. The courage of such rebellious heroes is appealing to Westerners, too, as is the theme of coping with adverse situations, which Sato stated is central to postwar period film.[48] This is the positive side to the genre, and to other action films as well. For example, in American westerns honor is often as important for the cowboy hero as it was for knights of old.

Yet, the examples Sato gives from period film—*The Abe Clan* (*Abe Ichizoku*, 1938) and *Harakiri* (*Seppuku*, 1962)—end with self-annihilation as the price for rebellion.[49] Death prevails in the period film, no matter how Bushido is interpreted, for it celebrates a death cult whose god is Thanatos.

Given such a genre tradition, *Seven Samurai* really stands out. There, after the death of the bandits, comes life symbolized by the farming cycle of planting and harvesting. This is the Japanese version of "the sacrificed divinity from the buried fragments of whose dismembered body the food plants sustaining human life arose."[50] As indicated by the final shot of the graves of the dead samurai, the "sacrificed divinity" is the seven samurai who helped the farmers defeat the bandits. Figuratively, they are chaste warriors, like many other period film heroes. Even if they had sons, they would be dedicated to death also, and their daughters would be subservient to samurai husbands. The only escape from the Bushido code of death is to become a farmer, which the youngest of the seven could not do in the end.[51]

Richie stated that *Seven Samurai* was perhaps the best Japanese film ever made.[52] But Kurosawa's *Ikiru* (*Ikiru*, 1952) came out before *Seven Samurai* and was probably its subliminal inspiration. There, too, in the dying hero's fight against corruption, from death came life, or rather meaningful life in place of the ennui of a petty official. But there were no samurai in *Ikiru*, a contemporary film and thus free from the fatalism of Bushido, whose popularization in period film helped attune a populace more to war than to the natural cycle, and fostered chaste warriors who preferred death to life. By rejecting human emotions they overcame the fear of death. But the price was an emotionless life close to death.

3

Yakuza Heroes

Introduction

FROM 1963 to 1973, *yakuza*, or gangster, films, usually set in the 1920s and 1930s, became Japan's leading action film genre,[1] with period film heroes and stories moving over to the TV circuit. The word, *yakuza* comes from gambling jargon where it signifies a losing number, and the general public came to use it for good-for-nothing people like gamblers and outlaws.[2] Films about feudal *yakuza* had been an important subgenre of period film,[3] but after 1963 they were seldom major heroes in either films or TV dramas.[4]

George De Vos has noted that the *yakuza* code was a parody of the samurai's Bushido, and that their hero ideal was drawn on samurai models.[5] Ian Buruma has aptly summarized the modern *yakuza* film genre as an expression of the death cult and a continuation of the *Chushingura* mentality.[6] In terms of iconography, the genre's heroes simply combine elements of the Loyal Retainer, the Tormented Lord and the Chaste Warrior, and do not undergo significant metamorphoses. In fact, because of the tenacious hold of period film archetypes, modern *yakuza* heroes were models of submission, and were quite unlike American film gangsters, who in the 1930s represented the rising social class of recent immigrant families.

Yet, modern *yakuza* heroes also differed from their samurai antecedents by being closer to the common people, and from the *Chushingura* ethos by making the object of loyalty more the group than a superior. This is probably the main reason they replaced period film heroes in the theater circuit, since the male audience there could more easily relate to a group than a feudal superior. For modern Japanese, the sacrifice of individual desire for the sake of the group—the message inherent in the ritualistic melee modern *yakuza* films climax with—is extremely relevant. This will be discussed after the genre's iconography is presented.

The Tormented Father Figure

The leader of a *yakuza* gang is called *oyabun*, which literally means father figure, and his henchmen are called *kobun*, or "son figures." This

alludes to a quasi-familial relation suggestive of the feudal relation between a family retainer and his lord. In modern *yakuza* films, though, the
dramaturgy of *Chushingura* is turned upside down by making the father
figure the Tormented Lord in place of a young Asano. The Loyal Retainer
could be young or middle-aged.

The Tormented Father Figure is usually a gambling boss or union leader,
who is getting old and often looking forward to retirement. A big rival gang
wants to take over his turf and he suffers their encroachments either to
avoid bloodshed or because of a "peace treaty" he agreed to at the urging of
big-time gangleaders. He is continually restraining his men who are justi-
fiably indignant at the underhanded methods employed by the boss of the
rival gang. This contrast between the good boss and the bad boss not only
recalls Japanese folk tales with their good and bad old men (*yasashii/
ijiwaru jiisan*) but also the noble Asano versus the base Kira.

The feudal antecedent for such a noble father figure is Chohei Banzuiin,
a construction union leader in the seventeenth century who also became a
big-time gambling boss.[7] Under his leadership some construction workers
became a gang who would get into fights with the young *hatamoto* samurai who were retainers of the shogun. Since the latter often gave vent to
their dissatisfaction over their low, peacetime income by harassing the
townspeople, the myth evolved that Chohei's men were defenders of the
common people,[8] and Chohei himself became a hero of Kabuki and Kodan
and one film, Daisuke Ito's *Five Men from Edo* (*O-Edo Gonin Otoko*, 1951).

Models for more popular feudal *yakuza* film heroes, though, were Chuji
Kunisada and Jirocho of Shimizu, nineteenth-century, rural gambling
bosses who extended their territories through successful battles with rival
gangs.[9] In the famous trilogy, *A Diary of Chuji's Travels* (*Chuji Tabi Nikki*,
1927) director Daisuke Ito turned Chuji into a young nihilistic hero who
battles the authorities until he dies tragically.[10] In the postwar period,
however, most Chuji and Jirocho films have happy endings, and like
Chohei Banzuiin, both of them are portrayed as kindly father figures who
battle and defeat a larger gang for the sake of the common people, or for
honor, or to avenge the cruel death of one of their charges.

The Tormented Father Figure in a modern *yakuza* film differed from his
feudal antecedents by suffering much more and by often being killed by
the bad boss early in the story. He thereby became an honorable martyr
whom a young or middle-aged Loyal Retainer eventually avenged. Unlike
Chushingura, though, this Loyal Retainer would go up against a big rival
gang either alone or with one or two helpers. In the bloody melee he thus
assumed superhuman proportions like Musashi.

The Young Hero

At To Ei studios where the most popular modern *yakuza* movies were
made, the young hero role was usually played by the muscular Ken

An Account of the Chivalrous Commoners of Japan (1964), directed by Masahiro Makino. True to the Chaste Warrior tradition, this modern *yakuza* hero (Ken Takakura) keeps his back to the heroine (Junko Fuji).

Takakura, whose performance evoked Musashi and other chaste warriors. When he parted from the heroine before the melee, he was invariably photographed with his back to her, and her pleading face appeared in the frame just above his slouched shoulder. His inclined head showed that he was listening to her and that she had an emotional claim on him, but nothing she said could change his resolve. Even in the few films where he has a wife or lover, scenes where he actually faced her were few and far between, and he would embrace her only if she were dying. In most of his *yakuza* films he either carried a torch for a woman who had married a childhood friend, or he had a platonic crush on his boss's daughter, who thereby became a pathetic beauty like Musashi's Otsu.

In some respects, though, the Takakura hero differed from Musashi. In *Violent District* (*Boryoku-gai*, 1963, directed by Tsuneo Kobayashi) Takakura returns from prison to find that his ritual younger brother, or *ototoki*, has been engaged in illegal activities besides gambling. When he informs the dead boss's daughter, she tells him she had acquiesced because of their financial difficulties. In the ensuing argument *ototoki* even tells Takakura that he has slept with the daughter, his platonic crush.

Takakura eventually recovers from his disillusionment. One day he is walking in a park with the daughter after their visit to her father's grave and she begins to cry. He comforts her, but when he realizes their embrace is going too far, he breaks it and asks her to sing the boss's favorite song, a certain *samurai* air. She consents and the sequence ends with him doing a masculine dance to it.

Besides the psychological relation between repressed sexual desire and escape valves like war dances and violent acts, here the Takakura hero also exemplifies a connection between his loyalty to the memory of his dead lord and his feelings for the daughter. The latter must remain platonic to ensure the purity of the former. In this respect, he diverges from Musashi, for whom chastity was simply a precondition for strength and bravery and had no relation to loyalty. Still, both repressed sexual desire for the sake of masculine activity.

In *Violent District* in 1963 the pull of archetypal configurations was not as yet overwhelming in the nascent genre of the modern *yakuza* film. The *ototoki* was not painted as a villain because he had had sex with the boss's daughter, nor was *his* loyalty thereby diluted. In fact, the chastity of the Takakura hero even seemed humorous then. As the genre developed, however, all the boss's daughters became as virginal as Otsu and the humorous one would be the *ototoki* whose sexual escapades embarrassed the loyal, chaste hero.

The Takakura hero further differs from Musashi in that he exhibits no sword technique whatsoever in his melees, for he simply lays into his enemies with his long sword, hacking or stabbing them to death. He overcomes through brute strength, determination, and a tremendous capacity to withstand near fatal wounds. He has no technique since he did not undergo any training.

Japanese films featuring the training of young combatants enjoyed some popularity before modern *yakuza* movies in the 1950s in the form of *judō* action films *(kōdōkan mono)*.[11] Their forebear was Kurosawa's *Sanshiro Sugata* (*Sugata Sanshiro*, 1943) in which a young *judō* student's most important training consisted of one cold night immersed in a pool as reparation for his arrogant display of fighting skill the day before. The self-realization he experienced has been aptly described by Donald Richie[12] as a baptism and a Zen awakening. An analogy can easily be drawn between the relation of Sanshiro to his *judō* master and that of Musashi to Takuan. Such initiations, however, are never shown in a Ken Takakura film. In one run-of-the-mill movie he first appears as a rough and ready ricksha man, unshaven and uncouth, the workingman's Untamed Male. He leaves his native village and returns four years later as a neatly dressed *yakuza* who has learned self-restraint and the rules of etiquette in the *yakuza* code. However, the viewer is not shown how this character development came about. He is better in a melee than before, but this is probably the result of four years of fighting. In short he has become an experienced street fighter.

The lack of initiation and training in the development of the Takakura character may be attributed to the sentiment that, although he is a hero, he is a disrespectable *yakuza* after all.

The Takakura hero also lacks a worthy opponent, since even the strongest henchmen of the bad boss are not appealing. Instead, he is often aided by a noble friend, the admirable ally.[13] This role was played by Ryo Ikebe in *An Account of the Last Knights of the Showa Era* (from 1925 on) (*Showa Zankyo-den*, 1965–72), one of Takakura's most popular series.[14] In all nine entries the relation between the two men is more important than their loyalty to any boss, and this marks a significant departure from the *Chushingura* ethos, which kept the male love affair in its place.

Ikebe, a popular leading man in the 1950s, had maintained his good looks, like a weathered Robert Mitchum. In the first entry directed by Kiyoshi Saeki in 1965 he played a world-weary, wandering gambler who becomes a guest of Takakura's gang. He lives only for his sister and after she dies he joins the hero in the final melee in order to end his mean-

An Account of the Last Knights of the Showa Era—The Chinese Lion Peony (1966), directed by Kiyoshi Saeki. The young *yakuza* hero (Ken Takakura) has an older, admirable ally (Ryo Ikebe) who aids him in his final melee with a large gang.

ingless life. Impressed with Takakura the first time he meets him, the bonds between them are cemented when he extracts a bullet from Takakura's wound, as they gaze deeply into each other's eyes. Although Ikebe always plays a middle-aged *yakuza* in the series, he never becomes the young hero's older ritual brother. Their relationship is kept on an egalitarian basis and they simply respect each other as individuals. The only big difference between them is the cynicism of middle age and the sincerity of youth.

After the first entry in the series Ikebe was often in the opposing gang; however, he would become incensed at their underhanded dealings and would become Takakura's ally. Triangles often formed because Ikebe's sister or even his wife seemed to love Takakura too, but these complications only seemed to deepen their regard for each other. No matter what, in the grand finale of each entry they go off to the melee together—a denouement which Japanese film critic Masatoshi Ohba has likened to the *michi yuki*, the journey Kabuki lovers take before they commit suicide.[15]

The journey began on a deserted street at night. An overhead shot showed Takakura in the right background of the wide screen and the camera craned down to reveal Ikebe waiting for him in the left foreground. When they met, Takakura would try to dissuade him but to no avail. Then the overhead camera followed them in the spotlight together as they walked diagonally across the frame. They would cross a bridge, which in addition to its romantic connotation also signified passage into another realm. Ikebe showed his death resolve by tossing away his scabbard. He might ask Takakura to help him tie his hand to his sword handle with a large handkerchief, thereby affording them a last chance to gaze into each other's eyes. The melee itself almost seemed anticlimactic. Ikebe usually died in Takakura's arms, being lifted off the ground somewhat in a bloody embrace.

Such a *michi yuki* ironically seems like a natural denouement in an all-male world where chaste warriors turn their back on pathetic beauties. Its sublimated homosexuality, however, is more similar to that in American westerns like *The Wild Bunch* where the desperadoes die together, than that in the Loyal Retainer-Tormented Lord dyad. Close male relations in Japanese film have an Oriental precedent, though, in the five Confucian relations: ruler-subject, parent-child, husband-wife, older brother-younger brother, and between male friends.[16] The fifth relation was the only egalitarian one and almost seems to have been forgotten because hierarchic relations were emphasized in Japan, particularly before 1945.

The Middle-Aged Hero

Heterosexual repression for the sake of male ties was also an important component in the formation of the middle-aged hero. Koji Tsuruta some-

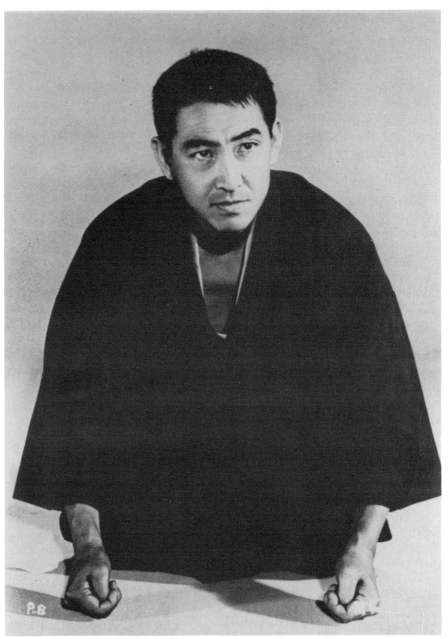

An Account of the Chivalrous Commoners of Japan—Kanto Edition (1965), directed by Masahiro Makino. This middle-aged *yakuza* hero (Koji Tsuruta) represses heterosexual desire for the sake of male ties in his hierarchical gang.

times played Takakura's admirable ally in *An Account of the Chivalrous Commoners of Japan* series (*Nihon Kyokaku-den*, 1964–71),[17] and was also the most popular middle-aged hero in ToEi *yakuza* films. In the early 1950s he had been the most popular leading man in Japanese film,[18] and like Ikebe, had aged well.

The Tsuruta hero was by no means chaste. He would often have a common-law wife, who could not follow samurai strictures and would become hysterical when he marched off to the final melee. If he were not married, he was occasionally shown in a geisha's boudoir having a cigarette or Japanese pipeful of tobacco (*kiseru*) afterwards.

Yet, the Tsuruta hero would often refrain from sex. In *Dissolution Ceremony* (*Kaisan-shiki*, 1967, directed by Kinji Fukasaku) on the night he gets out of prison he refuses the playmate his ritual brother offers him. The following morning he goes off in search of his wife only to find that she would no longer have anything to do with him because she wants to lead a respectable life. Thereafter, like a monk taking a vow of celibacy, he has nothing to do with any woman.

Ironically, the still handsome Tsuruta would sometimes play the role of a cuckold. He would come out of prison to find that his wife had become a prostitute after his boss—a bad one—had raped or seduced her. Under such circumstances he assumed the guise of a betrayed retainer, who might help the young Takakura in the final melee. In *Hishakaku* (directed by Tadashi Sawashima in 1963) he learns that his ritual younger brother has been living with his wife, but he forgives him when he realizes he did not know about their previous relationship, and in the end he even avenges his death.

The most significant triangle the Tsuruta hero gets involved in occurs in the ninth entry of *The Gamblers* series (*Baku-uchi*),[19] *The Card of Life* (*Inochi Fuda*, 1971, directed by Kosaku Yamashita), where he becomes a stoic knight in a triad resembling that between Oishi, Lord Asano, and his widow. When Tsuruta gets out of prison, he finds out that his boss and best friend—they had been ritual brothers—has been murdered. The widow informs him that the boss had found out they had been lovers before she had met the boss. During the funeral the fatal circumstantial triangle is graphically shown by intercutting shots of Tsuruta's strained expression, the widow's sad face, and the memorial photograph of the smiling boss.

During a meeting of big-time gang leaders afterwards, the widow is made head of the gang, but she flees to her hometown, leaving behind a note for Tsuruta. She is next shown on a beach during a snowstorm, evidently contemplating suicide. Tsuruta appears in time, though, and puts a blanket around her. She begs him to leave the gang so that they can lead an ordinary existence as husband and wife. He tells her he can not betray the trust of the dead boss, and that if she can not return as the boss's widow, she may as well die there. He turns his back to her and faces the sea, standing resolutely against the strong wind, with snow clinging to one side of his garments—the epitome of stoicism. She relents and they return to play their roles.

The film ends with an attack on their headquarters by a rival gang—which is treated surrealistically. The wounded Loyal Retainer is holding up the dying widow and both of them are staggering into the reception room toward an altar lined with white porcelain *sake* jugs and plain wooden buckets. These signify the ritual of exchanging *sake* cups, whereby *yakuza* become ritual brothers and vow eternal friendship. On both sides of the long rug leading to the altar, pools of blood form as Tsuruta slashes at the bad henchmen in their way. When he reaches the altar, the background suddenly becomes black and he smashes a *sake* jug with his sword. The last shot is of a red blanket on the snowy beach by the sea.

The stoic knight had been able to break his ritual relation with his boss, but he could not effect a bond with his lady in this life. Their progress toward the altar had been both a wedding procession and a rather grotesque *michi yuki* in a genre which actually frowns on heterosexual love. Any other fulfillment of their love would have undermined the basic ties between men that find ultimate expression in violence in the modern *yakuza* film, and would have also annihilated the archetypes of the Loyal Retainer and the Chaste Warrior.

Parody

The modern *yakuza* film diverged from the period film by eventually parodying its own versions of the Chaste Warrior and the Loyal Retainer. Perhaps this came about because *yakuza* heroes are close to the common people and were from their inception only parodies of samurai.

In the ToEi *Viper Brothers* series (*Mamushi no Kyodai*, 1971–75)[20] Bunta Sugawara plays a small-time gangster. As the antithesis to the Takakura hero, Sugawara is like an untamed Musashi with a strong sexual desire he makes absolutely no attempt to conceal, often cupping his scrotum to show when he is horny. A lot of film footage is devoted to his comical bedroom antics, with his ritual brother and his moll joining in for a foursome. In one film they even try to rape a female prison guard in spite of the cell bars between them.

The comic version of the middle-aged loyal retainer was played by Tomisaburo Wakayama, a heavyset actor. Unlike Tsuruta's stoic knight, Wakayama's hero does not hold back, and his performance is filled with emotional excesses. He cries like a baby at the bedside of the dying boss, dotes on children and pretty maidens, and practically hugs ritual brothers.

Characteristically, he cruelly punishes those who betray him and is vicious in battle.

Wakayama's most popular ToEi series was *Brute* (*Gokudo*, 1968–76),[21] in which he played a lone gangster whose gang had been dissolved. His parting from his chubby, unglamorous wife before the melee was a parody of orthodox procedure. He would slap her when she tried to stop him, but then she would slap him back, repeatedly. Eventually she would burst into tears and begin hugging him and giving him sloppy kisses. Finally she would get the jacket he wore when he was in the old gang, drape it over his shoulders, and see him off.

Ironically, emotional types like Wakayama and Sugawara became the leading roles when *yakuza* films with chaste, stoic heroes were replaced by the semidocumentary series on postwar *yakuza, Battles without Honor and Humanity* (*Jingi Naki Tatakai*, 1973–76).[22] As the title suggests, in this realistic world discord between bosses and henchmen supplanted affinity and concord, and impulsive action was preferred over perseverance and adherence to an outmoded code. Cynicism overthrew parody and dislodged the modern *yakuza* film from its old base in the period film, where sincerity could only be replaced with nihilism.

These new *yakuza* films should be considered part of the contemporary film genre in that they break completely with period film iconography and conventions. The fact that they are set in the postwar period is significant. While present-day Japanese could be nostalgic about the 1920s and 1930s when fabricated *yakuza* heroes were made to roam, the setting of these battles without honor and humanity in the anomic period immediately after the defeat in World War II prevented such a sanguine view.

Ritual

Although the modern *yakuza* film ceased to be popular after 1973, it continued to excite the interest of Japanese and Western critics. In its simple formula many found parables for Japanese culture and society. The concluding ritual of the melee also has universal connotations, though, since it mainly concerns the motif of human sacrifice.

Before the melee the hero usually kneels in front of an ancestral altar with a photograph of his dead, fatherlike boss as its centerpiece, and places a lit incense stick before it as an offering. Sometimes the hero takes with him the sword the good boss bequeathed to him, which is reminiscent of Lord Asano's *seppuku* sword blade. The woman the hero parts from is not only a melodramatic ploy to show his masculine resolve, but also an assistant in the rite, after she stops trying to dissuade him. She may hand him the sword, loosening the string attached to the scabbard and handle first. Her main role, though, is to help the hero dress properly for the ceremony. If it is autumn or winter, she lays out a dark blue kimono, which she may have sown for him herself, thereby reflecting the ancient feminine occupation of weaving. The inner garment is usually white. If it is summer, he wears a light, wrap-around robe or *yukata* with a simple design against a white background.

White is an appropriate color because it symbolizes the purifying aspect of revenge that purges the dead boss, the hero, and the woman of the bitter resentment they feel toward the bad boss. It also symbolizes death and was the color worn for the *seppuku* ceremony. White thereby indicates that the hero as avenger is not only the main actor but also the ceremonial sacrifice. As if conscious of the hero's dual role, the woman decorously folds and lays out his garments as though they were priestly vestments.

Ian Buruma has compared the bloody melee itself to a Spanish bullfight and noted that the death of the hero functions as a purification,[23] which is a universal phenomenon even Christianity is based on.[24] This universal phenomenon has its roots in primitive societies where, as James Frazer pointed out, it effects "new birth and the remission of sins through the shedding of blood."[25] The Christian Mass is thus a bloodless version of this old ritual of sacrifice, previously performed for isolated tribes rather than all mankind.

Such analogies only go so far, however, since the hero does not usually die in the melee. The most popular modern *yakuza* films were series in which the same invincible hero, played by the same actor, appeared throughout. Yet, Buruma's "mistake"[26] is more informative than accurate reporting would be, since the hero always does die symbolically. The admirable ally or someone else may die for him to keep the series going (and this kind of substitution in the ritual of sacrifice probably has pre-historic origins),[27] but this always symbolizes the hero's death for the sake of the gang. The pretext for the hero going to the melee alone was generally that his small gang would be annihilated either by the enemy gang or by big-time gangs through a series of recriminations. During the melee the hero's sacrifice is demonstrated by the wounds and cuts received all over his chest and back, which suggest old paintings of Christian martyrs instead of the stoic endurance of Oishi in *Chushingura*.

Yet, for whose sins does the hero symbolically die? What is being purified beside resentment? He is always presented as pure from the start, and his father figure and ritual brothers are neither sinful nor impure. The henchmen in the bad gang are certainly dishonorable, but the hero's sacrifice will not stop such gangs from continuing to exist. In fact, they are the wave of the future and the hero's own gang is one of only a few still adhering to old principles. Therefore, analogies with purification and "remission of sins" fall short in an analysis of the final ritual in a modern *yakuza* film. The hero simply sacrifices himself so that his still pure, small gang may survive, and this has relevance for modern Japanese film au-

An Account of the Last Knights of the Showa Era—Lone Wolf (1966), directed by
Kiyoshi Saeki. The tattoo of the *yakuza* hero (Ken Takakura) is the gang totem
and symbolizes their solidarity.

diences who probably do not attach much meaning to either Shinto or
Christian symbolism.

Tadao Sato has attributed the popularity of modern *yakuza* movies to
the fact that they "successfully projected the feelings of a small group
shunted aside by social change."[28] One can extrapolate from this to
include even Japanese in large organizations, for they probably most
closely identify with their office section or small work gang.[29] For them
the sacrifice of the *yakuza* hero probably represents the sacrifice of their
own individual desires for the sake of the group (not just male ties), which
the hero's sexual abstinence and repression of conjugal love had been
representing all along, albeit in an extreme fashion. For them, as for the
yakuza hero, group solidarity has become more important than loyalty to a
superior. The fact that the good boss dies early and becomes a nostalgic
symbol, an icon on the ancestral altar, probably indicates the devaluation
of hierarchic loyalty, at least in representational forms like films.

The good *yakuza* gang still resembles the forty-seven loyal retainers,
though, not only in the early death of their leader. In contrast to the bad

gang who are usually presented as a motley crew who dress differently, the good gang all dress alike in traditional garb like kimono, with the crest of their boss prominently displayed as a sign of their strong sense of affiliation. The crest of the Asano family was also often shown in the costuming for *Chushingura,* and in both cases the crest represents a House—that is, the leader's family. This definitely indicated hierarchic loyalty to the family head. In the melee, however, after the hero's white garment has been cut to shreds, a large tattoo of a dragon or Chinese lion is revealed on his back and shoulders. This tattoo, possessed by other gang members too,[30] has no particular relation to the boss's family. Historically, such a tattoo was used to brand criminals,[31] but in the modern *yakuza* film it is the gang totem and symbolizes their solidarity rather than loyalty to a superior.

For the sake of this solidarity, individual desires are repressed, as symbolized in the hero's sacrifice. Hence, the denouement of the ritual in a modern *yakuza* film is very old: simply an expression of one of Durkheim's elementary forms of religion that structure the individual to the group. Still, it is also very relevant to a modern Japanese, who is educated to become a member "of a mythical body to which he sacrifices his life and thought in order to receive his true self."[32] We have here a simple paradigm for socialization, for to become a member of any society individual desires have to be curbed to some degree. The degree expressed in modern *yakuza* movies, and observed in Japanese society, seems extreme to Westerners. So much appears to be sacrificed that it is hard to believe any *self* remains, let alone a true one. Tadao Sato, on the other hand, stresses the warm sense of belonging and friendship obtained as a result of the sacrifice.[33] In either case, the modern *yakuza* hero performs a social function that is at the core of any society, primitive or modern: individual sacrifice for social preservation. As in initiation rites, he dies symbolically for the regeneration of the tribe.

4

Wanderer

Three Aspects

As stated in the Introduction, archetypes are representations of basic motifs in culture, reflecting how human beings think about themselves and existence in general. Basic motifs include human ideals like loyalty and courage, which the Loyal Retainer and the Chaste Warrior stood for, and sentiments about the human condition. Sentiments about the individual and society are symbolized in the motif of wandering that is represented in the archetype of the Wanderer.

Ideals and sentiments about the human condition are not clearly distinguishable. Wandering was part of Musashi's training and Oishi made a journey to Edo, which signified the hardships he had endured before he could demonstrate his loyalty by avenging his lord. In literature tales of courage often include wandering—the search for the Holy Grail—or at least traveling—the Odyssey. In fact, one could say that tales of wandering include courageous exploits. The basic difference between ideals and some sentiments, however, is that loyalty and courage are social virtues (society expects its members to be loyal and its warriors courageous) and that wandering is not necessarily a virtue and could even be regarded as anti-social. While the Wanderer archetype could be conservative, he or she does not always support submission and affiliation, and is thus problematic.

The motif of wandering sybmolizes the human condition as an individual, and the three viewpoints on this problem are expressed in the three aspects of the Wanderer as exile, vagabond, and pilgrim. The Exile expresses the view that, since man is a social animal, life alone is a living death. Loneliness is the worst suffering and to be cast off from friends and kin is the worst fate. In the past, society was simply one's village or tribe and an individual had no human relations outside its cozy confines. And even in the modern age when humanism is preached and international friendship is praised, most people still relate on an intimate level only with their own.

The Vagabond expresses the view that, since man is a free spirit, the individual is severely restricted by other people, particularly his own.

Freedom consists in hitting the road where relations with people you meet do not incur confining obligations, and one can magnanimously help a stranger or appreciate no-strings-attached human kindness.

The Pilgrim expresses the view that, since man is a religious being, the individual cannot be ultimately satisfied by any society in this world. The Pilgrim either prepares for the next life by doing penance for his sins and accumulating indulgences, or endures the rigors of travel to obtain divine favor in this life or in thanksgiving for grace already received. On a higher level the pilgrim searches for religious truth rather than social meaning.

These three aspects are probably universal, but representations of them vary in the arts of all cultures, and Japanese film is no exception. The iconography of the Wanderer consists of pure types and composite forms, whose metamorphoses are simply a change of dress as they appear in period or contemporary film, for they are not confined to any single genre. Conclusions about Japanese culture and society are best drawn when considering the Pilgrim, the most problematic aspect.

Exile

The Exile is a particularly forlorn figure in Japanese culture because there is no strong cultural equivalent to Western humanism, whereby ideally one could feel close to any human being simply because they are a human being. Humanism has its roots in Christianity—all men are brothers in Christ—and in Islam where faith crosses national borders. No one in Japan says that all men are brothers in Buddha, and Buddhism in Japan became firmly connected with ancestor memorialism or worship, which always reminds the believer of particularistic rather than universal ties. Despite Western influence on modern Japanese, altruism is emotionally unacceptable, and when Japanese use "humanism" as a loan word they usually mean the warm affection among people in the same social or familial circle. This is one of the causes of the "groupism" noted by any foreign observer. Where non-Japanese consider the Japanese to be clannish, they themselves regard their behavior as perfectly natural and human.

Being cast off from friends and kin was not always a terrifying idea in Japan. Susano O became the first Japanese exile when he was expelled from the Plain of Heaven for misbehaving, but after playing the all-conquering hero on earth he married and lived happily ever after.[2] The most famous historical example, however, Michizane Sugawara (845–903), lamented his fate in poems that influenced later generations to venerate him as the god of poetry.[3] Like Michizane, aristocratic characters in literature such as Prince Genji in Genji monogatari (The Tale of Genji) and minor figures in Heike monogatari were expelled from the court on account of political intrigue and suffered the fate of the exile. Musashi was in effect an exile from his village. Even in the stable Tokugawa era (1603–1868), with its strict travel restrictions, there were wandering outlaws and gamblers, and they became models for exile heroes in an important subgenre in the period film (*matatabi mono*).[4]

Unlike Chuji Kunisada and Jirocho of Shimizu, the wandering gambler was not a boss or even affiliated with a gang. Often he was forced to leave his native village because of a quarrel with the boss there, and thereafter he would wander from place to place, gambling and joining in fights between rival gangs, often merely in exchange for bed and board. His yearning for home was even implied in his name, for he always introduced himself with the name of his native place and his personal name. For example, for Jirocho of Shimizu the latter is his place of birth, since, like other commoners, *yakuza* were not allowed surnames.

The wandering gambler's love of home is well expressed in *Kantaro of Ina* (*Ina no Kantaro*, 1943, directed by Eisuke Takizawa). When Kantaro returns home, the song of Ina, his native village, comes on the sound track and there is a montage of rushing mountain streams, bamboo groves, and pine forests. The topography is familiar and dear to the hero, and he can relax in the security of being amid those he can trust. In his absence, his old sweetheart has married someone else, but Kantaro accepts it magnanimously and even helps her husband out of a jam. The dream of Camelot, however, is eventually ruined by the bad local boss, who, by playing on the husband's jealousy, gets him to lead Kantaro's old boss and men into a fatal ambush.

The last scene where Kantaro refrains from killing the betrayer is very moving. Kantaro has been standing outside the betrayer's hut, enviously looking in on the warm family scene around the open hearth at suppertime. From the open window he tosses in a mask as a going-away present. The small boy picks it up and shows it to his parents, and they all rush outside. As Kantaro is running down the darkening country road, he hears their voices calling out his name, and looks back only once.

For Kantaro, parting from the human warmth of those he knows and from the beautiful surroundings of his native place is bitter indeed. Like the rushing stream in the last shot, he will be in perpetual motion, restless and homeless.

The creators of Kantaro of Ina were doubtless influenced by Shin Hasegawa (1884–1963), one of Japan's most loved authors, whose popular novels and plays about wandering gamblers created the *matatabi* genre.[5] Film versions of his works are said to be as many as 115;[6] however, most of these were made before 1945 and only three complete extant prints of prewar versions remain.[7] This loss is particularly regrettable, since Hasegawa heroes had their heyday in the 1930s when the vast majority of his fans could not afford to see the expensive Kabuki productions of his works.[8]

Unlike Kantaro of Ina, Hasegawa heroes are hardly ever shown leaving or returning to their native place, which they had been separated from early in their youth. Often their wandering becomes a search for a lost mother or sister, or anyone with whom they have had a close relationship. As such, they are exiled from human bonds rather than a particular place.

In *Mother on my Mind* (*Mabuta no Haha*, directed by Hiroshi Inagaki in 1931 and Tai Kato in 1962) the hero searches for his lost mother.[9] When he finally finds her, she pretends she does not know him because he is a *yakuza* and his presence would ruin her daughter's chance for a respectable wedding. After he leaves her he runs into a gang of thugs who bear him a grudge. Full of despair, he tells them that if they have no parents, he will show them no mercy. Following the theatrical convention that *yakuza* are orphans,[10] none of them claims a parent, and in a bloodthirsty rage he slays all of them. The message is simply that life without familial ties is worthless and the man without parents has license to kill.

The film version of Hasegawa's *Yatappe of Seki* (*Seki no Yatappe*, 1963) begins with Yatappe rescuing a little girl from drowning. He later finds out that his own sister had died in a house of prostitution, and he abandons himself to the life of a hired killer and gambler. Years later he runs into the girl he had rescued, and she now reminds him of his dead sister.

Director Kosaku Yamashita often shoots the scenes between Yatappe and his sister-substitute amid flowers. For example, behind a flowering bush he watches her inside her relatives' house singing a lullaby her mother used to sing. Flowers symbolize his gentle side, which is associated only with her. They form a bright contrast to his ambience of self annihilation, as shown by shots of him alone in a gloomy bar, his face darkened with despair and marred with an ugly scar from a recent fight.

Before he leaves her he says something that makes her realize he is the man who saved her life, but when she runs after him he hides under a bridge in a dry river bed. After she is gone, he goes off to the final melee. The film ends with an extremely long, wide-screen shot of him from the back walking down a country road in broad daylight until he becomes a tiny figure fighting with other tiny figures. Far in the horizon to the left and right of the ribbonlike road are red, flowering bushes.

Yatappe's exit here calls to mind the flower passage, or *hanamichi*, in Kabuki, an elevated runway from the back of the theater through the audience to the front stage. Kabuki actors use it to make colorful and flamboyant entrances and exits. Yatappe's exit, however, is without drama because of the alienating effect of the long shot. For Yatappe there is no glory to be gained in the oncoming battle, no worthy opponent to cross swords with.

Yatappe is just the opposite of Musashi, who parted from Otsu so that he could be strong in battle and achieve glorious victory over warriors like Kojiro. Yatappe parts from his sister-substitute only because he is ashamed of being a *yakuza*, and he goes off to battle only because he has nothing to lose now that he has severed all human ties. Director Yamashita had filmed his previous battles in the rain at dusk to show clumsy thugs slipping in the mud and screaming at each other, and sometimes even panicking and running away from unworthy foes.

Tadao Sato has compared Yatappe and Hasegawa's other wandering gamblers with modern soldiers in that they both kill people they bear no grudge out of obligation to their boss or their nation.[11] In this respect Hasegawa'a stories of *yakuza* are similar to antiwar statements. The senseless nature of their battles is aggravated by the lack of glory, or demonstration of skill after rigorous training, and by the fact that their courage is based on despair rather than on overcoming fear of death. The source of their despair, however, is the loss of those particularistic ties, for example, love of native place and country, which ironically often lead men into wars where they feel justified in killing strangers.

In *Tokijiro Kutsukake—A Solitary Knight (Kutsukake Tokijiro—Yukyo Ippiki*, 1966) the hero kills a fellow *yakuza* to fulfill an obligation to a local boss who put him up for a few days. They both respect each other, though, because of their mutual adherence to the *yakuza* code, and the dying man asks Tokijiro to take his wife and small boy to his relative's place. During their journey they fall in love and live together until she leaves him out of guilty feelings toward her dead husband. They are reunited thereafter but she soon dies from illness.

While they had been living as man and wife, Tokijiro did his utmost to go straight. In one scene where he took a beating from some thugs rather than fight, he revealed how a warrior is weakened by human bonds. However, unlike Musashi who consequently rejected affection, Tokijiro only fights when he is deprived of affection, or in the end to get money for her medicine, which is of no avail.[12]

Director Tai Kato poignantly showed the loneliness of the man exiled from human bonds in the scene following her departure. Snow is falling in the night sky. Then Tokijiro is shown in the lower right corner of the wide screen, his face spotlighted in the darkness. "That was over a year ago," he says gravely. Light fills the room to show him telling his story to a barmaid.

For Tokijiro existence is now a perpetual winter night. Exiles like him are like the restless dead spirits whom the Japanese call *muenbotoke*, unrelated spirits. They are people who died without descendants or unbeknown to their kin, and consequently have no one to perform memorial services in front of their grave, if they have one, or before their ancestral tablet in the family Buddhist altar. The thought of them arouses not only sympathy but fear because they could cause the living trouble if not appeased or pacified somehow.

One example of the pacification of *muenbotoke* can be found on the Isle of Miyake, where criminals were exiled in feudal times. The inhabitants there have set up anonymous grave markers to the seamen who died in

Tokijiro Kutsukake—A Solitary Knight (1966), directed by Tai Kato. The feudal exile hero, a wandering gambler (Kin'nosuke Yorozuya), is shown during a happy interlude with his common-law wife (Junko Ikeuchi) and her son before their inevitable separation.

shipwrecks off their coast. Clusters of these upright, narrow wooden tablets under pine trees swept by tide winds evoke melancholy even in modern tourists.

Since Tai Kato's *Tokijiro Kutsukake—A Solitary Knight* in 1966 there has not been a major film based on a Hasegawa story.[13] However, the Hasegawa exile not only influenced the modern *yakuza* film through 1973, but also the Ken Takakura hero in contemporary action dramas in the late 1970s and the early 1980s. In fact, *Station* (*Eki*, 1981) won Takakura a Japanese Academy Award for his portrayal of a modern, living *muen-botoke*. He thereby demonstrated the appeal the Exile has for even present-day audiences, since Ken Takakura is indisputably the top male film star in Japan.

Director Yasuo Furuhata filmed *Station* on location in Hokkaido, Japan's northernmost island, and most of the sequences were shot during the winter, as if to provide a suitable background for the main character who, like Tokijiro, exists in a perpetual winter night. Takakura plays a lonely police detective who is a master marksman. Through his occupation he is fated to meet lawbreakers, and because of his skill he often brings sorrow to their relatives and friends by killing them. In this respect, he is like Hasegawa heroes who kill *yakuza* like themselves and form karmic ties with their kin or wife. Furuhata adds psychological depth to his hero's predicament by having him recall through flashbacks circumstances in his own life that parallel those of his victims; and the resultant identification causes him to suffer, too.

While on a case, the hero has a love affair with a woman who runs a small bar and restaurant, and he is on the verge of forming conjugal ties. It turns out, however, that her former lover is the man he is after and when they meet by accident he is forced to shoot him to death before her eyes. As in the case of Tokijiro and the wife of the man he killed, guilt separates the police detective from the woman he loves, though in *Station* the guilt is more his than hers.

The film ends in a train station at night, where the hero tears up the letter of resignation he had written when he dreamed of starting a new life.

Station (1981), directed by Yasuo Furuhata. This film begins and ends in a train station to show that the modern exile, here a police detective (Ken Takakura), must also part from loved ones.

He doesn't board his train, however, because he sees the sister of another one of his victims getting on it first. The train leaves and an overhead shot shows him alone at the station in the snow. Like a *muenbotoke* he is doomed to an existence of loneliness. The human bonds he forms are inevitably severed because it is his fate to kill people in the name of the law.

Vagabond

Although the Hasegawa exile is the main wandering gambler in period film, the happy-go-lucky Yataro, created by the novelist Kan Shimozawa, provided some cheerful contrast in the subgenre and spawned several descendants.[14] Yataro's story was first made into a film as early as 1932, but there does not seem to be any extant print of it or other prewar versions. The most popular postwar version is *The Traveling Hat of Yataro* (*Yatarogasa*, 1952, which director Masahiro Makino remade in 1960). In the beginning of the film a smiling Yataro comes to a fork in the road and tosses his umbrella-shaped, reed-woven hat into the air in a Japanese equivalent of "heads I take this road, tails that." Later, when he loses all his outer garments gambling, he keeps a smile on his face and hits the road again in his underwear.

The reason for Yataro's cheerful attitude probably is that he is a dropout from the samurai class who chose to wander because he preferred the carefree life of a gambler,[15] unlike a Hasegawa hero who does so out of despair over the loss of human bonds. All is not sweetness and light in his travels, though. Due to the conventions of the *yakuza* film the boss who befriended Yataro is murdered and must be avenged, and Yataro's love for the daughter must remain eternally platonic. Still, while Yataro is on the road, the sky is blue and the sun always seems to be shining. When he has clothes to wear, they are invariably neat and clean, and he often strikes a gallant pose. Even in a melee he does not work up a sweat and no matter how far he travels he never gets dirty.

The appeal of this make-believe character doubtless lies in his vagabond image. Tadao Sato has noted that travel is popular among Japanese because their circumscribed social circle does not provide them with the opportunity to meet and enjoy different people.[16] Although the Japanese love their own, familiarity breeds if not contempt at least boredom. Many wish they could hit the road alone like Yataro, but realize they are dependent on the security provided by travel in groups. Consequently, vagabonds like Yataro give vicarious pleasure to modern office workers and others who only travel with fellow workers or go to places where they have some social connections.

The most popular wandering gambler hero was Zatoichi, a blind mas-

The Traveling Hat of Yataro (1960), directed by Masahiro Makino. Yataro (Kin'nosuke Yorozuya), a wandering gambler, comes to a fork in the road, but either path will lead to adventure for this happy-go-lucky, feudal vagabond.

seur rather than a gambler, but also a hired sword like Hasegawa's heroes. Although Kan Shimozawa mentioned Zatoichi in his essays on feudal outlaws, as a film hero he is mainly the creation of scriptwriter Minoru Inuzuka, of Shintaro Katsu, the actor who always played him, and of the DaiEi studio directors who worked on the series from 1962 to 1973 and turned out twenty-five entries.[17] As a wanderer, Zatoichi is a cross between the exile and the vagabond.[18]

In the first entry, *The Story of Zatoichi (Zatoichi Monogatari,* 1962) director Kenji Misumi presents the hero as a gloomy figure who is forced to kill a consumptive master swordsman, the only person who treated him as a human being. Most scenes take place at night and there is one memorable low-angle close-up of Zatoichi's blind face with the moon shining above him. For the blind it is always night, and the hero is on a dark journey that leads to death.

In the second entry, *The Story of Zatoichi—Part 2 (Zoku-Zatoichi Monogatari,* 1962) the gloom continues, for the hero has to kill his own brother, a one-armed master swordsman on the other side. However, director Kazuo Mori adds sex when Zatoichi spends the night with a prostitute whose scent reminds him of his dead wife, who had run off with his brother. There is also humor in the blend. One night he gives a gay daimyo a massage, and afterwards is hunted by the retainers who are afraid he will let out their secret shame.

In the third entry (and the first one in color), *The New Story of Zatoichi (Shin Zatoichi Monogatari,* 1963) director Tokuzo Tanaka added more humor—often predicated on the hero turning the tables on those who

The Story of Zatoichi (1962), directed by Kenji Misumi. Zatoichi (Shintaro Katsu), a blind master swordsman, was first presented as a gloomy figure on a dark journey; but as his film series developed, touches of earthy humor were added to his image.

ridicule his handicap—and produced the first box office hit in the series. Thereafter, Zatoichi's travels were so humorous that he seemed to take on the guise of a vagabond. The blind exile never really vanished, however, thereby producing a hybrid hero, who could put on a dazzling display of swordsmanship.

Like the impulsive males played by Bunta Sugawara and Tomisaburo Wakayama in modern *yakuza* movies, Shintaro Katsu's Zatoichi projects earthy humor. Although he never lays a hand on pathetic beauties, usually there are plenty of bawdy women to entertain him.

The precedent for Zatoichi's roadside sex and humor can be found in the novel, *Hizakurige (Shank's Mare)* by Jippensha Ikku (1765–1831), which deals with the comic adventures of Yaji and Kita, two pure vagabonds with no tragic airs whatsoever. Yaji and Kita have been heroes in over forty films.[19] Since most of these were made under puritanical censorship before 1945, however, their ribald mix-ups with prostitutes and their scatological humor were never given full treatment until Yasuki Chiba's *Travel Chronicles of Yaji and Kita (Yaji-Kita Dochuki,* 1958).

Judging from the old Japanese proverb that shame is cast aside when one travels, it seems sex has been associated with travel since feudal times. The reason can be gleaned from *Hizakurige,* where Ikku writes about being tied by convention and cleaning one's life from care by travel.[20] Apparently nosy neighbors acted as a greater restraint on sexual behavior than Confucian morality, and thereby augmented the appeal of the vagabond.

The most popular contemporary vagabond hero is Tora-san, the main character in the *It's Tough To Be a Man (Otoko wa Tsurai yo)* series, in which Yoji Yamada has directed over thirty hit films since 1969.[21] Tora-san is a *tekiya,* an itinerant merchant who falls into the *yakuza* category because he may use confidence-man techniques to sell shoddy merchandise.[22] Often during his travels he gets the urge to go straight—sometimes after looking in on a warm family scene from outside the window like a Hasegawa exile—and in every entry he returns to his hometown only to hit the road again after suffering a broken heart from falling in love with some beauty.[23]

In *Yearning for Home (Bokyo-hen,* 1970) Tora-san probably made his most serious attempt to settle down and lead a respectable life. One day he looks upon his brother-in-law's grimy overalls and with sudden inspiration decides to work at his small printing company. The following morning he goes to work with a comically serious expression on his face. Through conversations in the next scene, however, we find out that he had gotten into squabbles with his coworkers and the clientele and had gone off in a huff. His sister goes on her bicycle to look for him. While she is on the river bank scanning the distance, he is lying in the hull of a row boat down below, taking an afternoon nap in his spotless workclothes.

Using an overhead shot, director Yamada takes a slow pan from bow to stern of this blissful, sleeping figure. A motor boat goes by and the waves rock his boat free from its mooring rope and set him adrift in the river. A final long shot takes in his boat alone in the river until a rowing team glides energetically by. He will always be adrift, a perennial exile from the workaday world.

After suffering from a broken heart, Tora-san parts from his sister, who seems to represent Yatappe's sister-substitute and Musashi's Otsu. Even though Tora-san's parting is sadder then those of a Hasegawa exile or the Chaste Warrior, unlike them his road ahead does not lead to the dark night of battle. Actually, *Yearning for Home* ends with him running into his ritual younger brother at a port, and the last shot shows them gleefully throwing pebbles into the water as ships go out to sea.

A broken heart is not the only reason for Tora-san leaving home after a short stay. In the beginning of *Yearning for Home* he dreams that his uncle is dying and when he returns he mistakes his afternoon nap for a deathbed scene. This comedy of errors results in a family argument, which eventually leads Tora-san to hit the road again, and such is often the cause in the series. He had returned during the Buddhist holiday of *Obon*, when most Japanese return to their native area, symbolically to greet departed family spirits, who are believed to return then also. However, the fact that he immediately got into a squabble made the title, *Yearning for Home* ironical and demonstrated that actually Tora-san is better off on the road.

In *Torajiro's Poems of Pure Love (Torajiro Junjo Shishu,* 1976) director Yamada celebrates the joys of chance encounters during travel. Tora-san is presented walking down a road alone on a sunny day amid high clusters of *susuki,* a common variety of pampas found throughout the Japanese countryside. He comes into a town where there is a festival, which gives him a chance to ply his trade as a *tekiya.* In the midst of all the excitement he runs into a troupe of itinerant entertainers and they have a rousing party together that night. The following morning he gets stuck with the bill and, since he cannot pay it, he winds up in jail. However, he makes friends with all the policemen there and they treat him royally until his sister comes to bail him out.

The ease with which Tora-san makes friends with complete strangers must make him an object of envy, and there is probably no one like him in group-oriented Japan. Judging from film and TV documentaries, real-life *tekiya* appear to a sad lot who feel modern times have passed them by. Tora-san is a complete fabrication, a pure vagabond who finds more joy on the road than at home.

In contemporary film a prototype for Tora-san can be found in the Kihachi character created by Yasujiro Ozu, who worked at the same Shochiku studios that Yoji Yamada does. Like Tora-san, Kihachi is a comical character from the lower classes who is quick-tempered and affectionate. These traits are considered characteristic of people from

男はつらいよ望郷篇[映倫]

It's Tough to Be a Man—Yearning for Home (1970), directed by Yoji Yamada. Tora-san (Kiyoshi Atsumi), a traveling salesman, is better off on the road. Whenever he tries to settle down, he gets into a family argument or suffers a broken heart from a one-sided love.

shitamachi, the workingman's area of old Tokyo. They are believed to be sentimental in contrast to the reserved middle class, who take stoic samurai behavior as their model.

Since Tora-san is a salesman and Kihachi is a laborer, they differ in occupation, and Tora-san's humor is more verbal, though this could also be attributed to the fact that Kihachi was mainly a silent film character. The main difference between the two, however, lies in the varying attitudes of their creators toward travel.

In Ozu's *The Story of Floating Weeds* (*Ukigusa Monogatari,* 1934, remade as *Ukigusa* in 1959) the Kihachi character is the leading actor and head of a traveling theatrical troupe. In contrast to Yamada's joking, itinerant entertainers, this troupe is a pathetic lot who constantly engage in petty arguments. Ozu's silent film begins and ends in the night and the only bright respite is Kihachi's brief reunion with his son. The last shots are particularly poignant. There is a frontal shot of Kihachi and his mistress having a box lunch together on the night train, and suddenly a look of grief appears on his face. Then a shot of a small boy sleeping alone in a booth is followed by one of the locomotive rushing down the track.

Kihachi had apparently remembered his own boy who was now fatherless, which means that Kihachi himself is childless and the road down the tracks is dark indeed. For Ozu, the joy Tora-san experiences on the road with strangers is foreign. Ozu sees only fleeting happiness among friends and kin before the inevitable sadness of separation.

Kihachi further differs from Tora-san because he is a parent, and perhaps a better figure for comparison is Chaplin's Tramp, since, like Tora-san, he projects the image of the eternal bachelor. Their style of comedy is also similar. Anderson and Richie have noted that Chaplin was particularly admired in Japan becuase his humor allowed one to both laugh and weep.[24] Although the joys of travel dominate in the Tora-san series, pathos is by no means absent, for not only does he get jilted every time but also he can never do anything to make his sister proud of him.

Yet, once again differences are more crucial. Nöel Carroll, a film theorist, has presented a structural analysis of Chaplin's directorial style.[25] In *The Gold Rush* (1925) the Tramp's loneliness is interlocked with alienation. Through foreground background juxtapositioning, the Tramp's unique dress and walk, and the casting of taller, heavier actors, the Tramp is constantly being set alone against groups of people who seem unaware of his existence. The overall effect of this "imagery of alienation" is pathos.

In contrast to the Tramp's alienation, Tora-san is often shot *in* small groups whether at family gatherings or in a cheap room at a roadside inn with new-found friends. All the characters are seated on a tatami-matted floor around a low table, eating or drinking, and the camera usually focuses on whoever is talking or reacting meaningfully at the time. Since the famous comedian who plays Tora-san, Kiyoshi Atsumi, is the star, he gets more close-ups, usually of his broad grin or his ludicrous and inept attempt to smile "though his heart is breaking." While Tora-san is pathetic, he certainly is not alienated, and Chaplin's Tramp is more like Hasegawa's exile than he is a vagabond.

Nöel Carroll finds significance beyond pathos in The Tramp's eternal bachelorhood, for as marriage symbolizes integration into society, an unrequited suit would suggest "irreconcilable otherness," and the same could be said for Tora-san. "Otherness" in Chaplin's comedy results in the theme of confrontation, continually repeated between the rich and the poor, policeman and tramp, man and machine. Tadao Sato has noted that compromise between both sides is impossible.[26] In a Tora-san comedy, on the other hand, confrontation does not last long because the invariable arguments are always followed by reconciliation, and usually kept in a familial context that accents sameness rather than otherness. Moreover, confrontation is kept at a minimum because Tora-san easily adapts anywhere, but nowhere completely.

Confrontation in film suggests social criticism and some critics read an impeachment of modern, bureaucratized Japan in the free spirit of Tora-san.[27] He himself, however, has a low opinion of his character because he is a *yakuza*. In this respect, he conforms to one kind of traditional Japanese humor in which the comedian made fun of himself, not society. Tora-san makes a fool of himself through his actions, but draws not only laughter but sympathy, probably because at heart we are all fools.

Pilgrim

Pilgrims have appeared briefly in Japanese films, but have never been central. At the end of Kenji Mizoguchi's masterpiece, *The Life of Oharu* (*Saikaku Ichidai Onna*, 1952) the heroine becomes a mendicant nun who travels the countryside begging like a pilgrim in order to do penance for her sins. However, since she had been more sinned *against*, she also becomes an incarnation of a forgiving Buddha.[28] At the end of Teinosuke Kinugasa's Cannes prizewinner, *Gate of Hell* (*Jigoku Mon*, 1953), the hero goes on a pilgrimage as a mendicant monk in atonement for inadvertently killing the woman he loved and for causing her husband to suffer. In Yoshitaro Nomura's mystery thriller, *Sand Vessel* (*Sunna no Utsuwa*, 1974, released in the United States as *Castle of Sand*) through flashbacks the hero remembers the pilgrimage he went on with his leprous father to obtain divine favor in this life.

The Japanese image of the pilgrim is best projected in films about the *goze*, who are blind women minstrels. Although not exactly pilgrims, they go wandering around the countryside to eke out a meager existence enter-

Banished Orin (1977), directed by Masahiro Shinoda. The Japanese image of the pilgrim is best projected by this blind woman minstrel (Shima Iwashita), who wanders around the countryside entertaining people with her shamisen playing.

taining people with their shamisen-playing. If their guests don't put them up, they have to spend the night in a temple or shrine.

The best film about the *goze* is Masahiro Shinoda's *Banished Orin* (*Hanare Goze Orin*, 1977, also known in the United States as *Melody in Grey*), which takes place during the early part of the twentieth century. The heroine, Orin was abandoned by her parents at six, when she was found by a traveling salesman who put her in the care of a *goze* troupe. The headmistress of the troupe ordered the girls in her charge to concentrate on their music lessons and also admonished them to keep in mind Amida (Amitabha), the Buddha of Infinite Compassion. She told them they were his servants and would never see hell. Besides a pun on their blindness, an allusion was made here to the belief that those who die chanting Amida's holy name would be reborn in the Western Paradise or Pure Land, no matter how many sins they committed. The girls in her troupe led a nunlike existence, for they were expected to be chaste. Contrary to such religious associations, *goze* girls had a shady reputation as entertainers, who in traditional Japan were expected to regard their guests as demigods whose requests were difficult to refuse. Men in the villages they toured considered them easy marks who had no village connections and would have to leave the following day. Since their shamisen-playing was often accompanied by drinking, it was easy to blame anything that happened on the wine. Given such circumstances, it is not surprising that Orin soon lost her virginity, and when the headmistress found out, she was banished from the troupe and had to ply her trade alone.

Thereafter she hooks up with an army deserter who insists on keeping their relation platonic because of sexual inhibitions resulting from his relation with his lascivious mother. Once when they were bathing together in a pond, he says that she looks like a Buddha, which is a natural association since most Buddhist images have closed eyes in meditation. She claims there is a better pose and squats down in the water so that only her head is showing and smiles. Her smile, however, is not tranquil like a Buddha's but mischievous like that of a blind girl who knows the ropes.

In this scene it seemed that not only Orin's sweetheart but also director Shinoda (and even Ben Minakami, the author of the original story) had wanted to imagine her and other *goze* women to be pure, passionless Buddhas. However, like any other woman Orin has natural desires and she parts from her sweetheart after he kills the man who satisfied them.

Later Orin is briefly reunited with him and they both enjoy sexual fulfillment until he is captured. Thereafter, her life takes a tragic turn. When she returns to the house of the headmistress, she finds it empty because she had died and Orin is shown pathetically feeling her way along the walls of the deserted house, calling out for the woman who had been like a mother to her. She winds up on the road again only to die alone in a field. Huge black crows eat her flesh and, flapping their wings, fill the sky at dusk. A human skull is shown facing the setting sun, in the direction of Amida's Western Paradise.

Although Orin was not exactly a pilgrim, her life was a pilgrimage in the old sense of "the course of life on earth."[29] This Webster's definition of *pilgrimage* implies the old Christian belief that happiness can only be attained in heaven, which concurs with the first tenet of Buddhism, that Life is Suffering.

The Solitary Travels of Chikuzan (Chikuzan Hitori Tabi, 1977) is about a blind male minstrel, the famous shamisen-player Chikuzan Takahashi (born 1910). In director Kaneto Shindo's presentation, Chikuzan does not suffer on the road like Orin, but usually runs into interesting travel companions, and his experiences are replete with ribald humor. He is more a vagabond than a pilgrim. He does suffer somewhat when his first wife leaves him after being forced to accommodate a paying guest. However, his mother gets another wife for him and they both seek him out and end his sad solitary travels.

The title of the film was ironical because Chikuzan was seldom on the road alone and, even when he was, such scenes were crosscut with his mother and second wife looking for him. This not only reflects the over-whelming Japanese preference for group over solitary travel, but also indicates why the solitary pilgrim in search of religious meaning is vir-tually absent from Japanese film, and not too important in Japanese culture in general. The first solitary pilgrim in the Buddhist tradition was the historical Buddha himelf, who forsook the pleasures of being a prince to find the true meaning of life. In Japanese Buddhist terminology this is called, *shukke,* literally "leaving home," and when Japanese become Bud-dhist monks they renounce the world and society by symbolically sever-ing family ties. This could be accompanied by a solitary pilgrimage, but perhaps a more typical case is that of Ippen, a famous thirteenth-century religious teacher who added a dance to the chant of Amida's holy name.[30] When Ippen took his Buddhist vows, he "left home" with friends and female attendants and turned his pilgrimage into a field trip. Furthermore, in films about the lives of other thirteenth-century Buddhist teachers like Shinran and Nichiren, they are presented as men who endure hardships with the help of their mother or other women and of their disciples, and not as solitary pilgrims in search of the true meaning of life.

Modern Japanese pilgrims can be discerned in the image of dissatisfied youths who leave their society in search of something else. One example is the sixteen-year-old heroine of *The Weight of Travel (Tabi no Omosa,* 1972). However, although the cinematography is superb, director Koichi Saito's message is hardly profound: life is simply a journey with good and bad experiences.

In *Red Lantern (Akachochin,* 1974) director Toshiya Fujita expresses dissatisfaction with society through the plight of a young couple who cannot find a suitable apartment in present-day Tokyo. They are forced to leave their first place because the building is to be torn down, and thereafter they wander from old to new abodes as a result of misunderstandings with unsympathetic landladies. Just when it seems they have found an apartment with congenial surroundings, they find out that the previous tenants, a family of four, had committed suicide there. The young wife goes insane and is committed to a mental hospital and the young husband goes off in search of a new apartment with their infant.

The search of Fujita's urban wanderers for a suitable apartment can be considered a futile attempt to escape from a restrictive society. The last shot of the young wife shows the shadows of gulls flying across her mentally deranged face. Her flight ends not in freedom but in insanity. The last shot of the young husband shows him sitting in the front seat of a moving van stalled in a congested, exhaust-fumed city street. He is trapped, for all avenues of escape are stopped up.

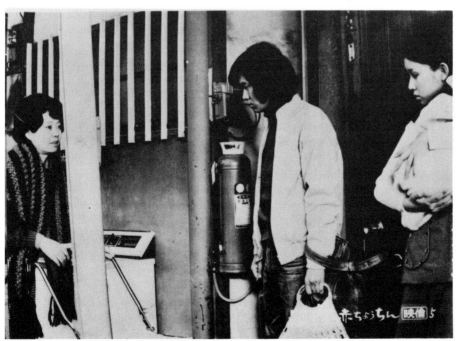

Red Lantern (1974), directed by Toshiya Fujita. Unable to find a suitable apartment on account of an unsympathetic landlady (Kirin Kiki, formerly Chiho Yuki) or neighbors, this young couple (Kenji Takaoka and Kumiko Akiyoshi) become modern pilgrims seeking a fixed abode in this fleeting world.

If the young couple is viewed as pilgrims, it seems the only meaning they find is that there is no fixed abode in this fleeting world. This Buddhist view harmonizes with the modern nihilism of Fujita. Youthful dissatisfaction with society is real, but there is no meaning outside of society.

Fujita's view oddly agrees with that of the respectable members of the Japanese society he probably detests. They are satisfied with the meaning society assigns to their role in relations with people who become as familiar as kin. Existence outside these social circles is not only meaningless but a little terrifying, for such a person could become like a Hasegawa exile, which is still the predominant aspect of the Wanderer archetype in Japanese culture. There are some notable exceptions. Japan's greatest poet, Basho (1644–94) followed the example of Saigyo, a twelfth-century Buddhist monk who renounced society and became a pilgrim who found meaning in life by writing poetry about nature.[31] But there are no Japanese films about such men, one reason being that man-in-nature is not such good filmic material as man versus nature.

Perhaps the best Asian film about the pilgrim comes from South Korea, which is Japan's cultural sister. *Mandala* (1981) concerns two Korean Buddhist monks' search for the true meaning of life. Director Lim Kwan Tag often takes a long shot of them on the road together discussing the agony of their search and the emptiness of satisfied desires. Each seems convinced his pursuit will lead nowhere, but still they wander on. Although they are two tiny figures blending into an Oriental landscape, they maintain their individuality because each searches for truth in his own way. They are also archetypal in that searches like theirs have probably existed since the beginning of religion, which coincides with the beginning of humankind. One of them freezes to death, but the other, after forgiving his mother for having abandoned him as a child, continues down the road alone, shown in a bleak but uncompromising long shot, again.

5

Vengeful Spirit

Introduction

IN Japanese folk religion a vengeful spirit (onryo) is a human being who dies bearing a grudge and appears as a ghost to settle the score. For example, if Lord Asano had not had Oishi and other loyal retainers to avenge him, in the popular imagination he could have appeared as a ghost tormenting Lord Kira. A vengeful spirit is like muenbotoke, or those who die without living relatives, in that both are restless. Still, whereas muenbotoke could be somewhat pacified if someone at least remembers them by erecting a grave marker and/or by making food offerings, vengeful spirits cannot be satisfied until they avenge themselves.

As folk religion is an oral tradition, which might never be recorded, it is difficult to trace the historical development of the idea of the vengeful spirit. On the basis of archeological remains of burial practices, Shoko Watanabe surmises that even in pre-Buddhist times (roughly before the fifth century A.D.) the Japanese believed dead spirits could harm the living and that those who died tragically would take it out on not only those responsible but also innocent bystanders.[1] Tadao Sato states that, although such indiscriminate trouble-making never completely vanished from the popular imagination, eventually the idea developed that such a spirit would only torment the guilty and leave the innocent alone.[2]

The most famous historical example of a vengeful spirit is Michizane Sugawara. After his death in exile, it was believed that his spirit took revenge against the family of Tokihira Fujiwara (871–909), his chief rival at the imperial court, as well as causing indiscriminate damage in the imperial capital through earthquakes and fires.[3] The most numerous occurrences of vengeful spirits are the ghosts of dead soldiers, which are reported in the aftermath of any war in Japanese history.[4] Like Michizane Sugawara, they may have a specific target or may simply express general resentment against war.

In contrast, most vengeful spirits in Japanese film are wronged women, who have traditional precedents in literature and theater. The oldest example is Izanami, the Kojiki goddess who dies after giving birth to many islands and deities. Like Orpheus, her husband Izanagi goes to the land of the dead to bring her back, but she is so ashamed when he sees her in a state of pollution that along with other, ugly female spirits, she pursues him until he escapes to the land of the living.[5]

Shame is also an important characteristic of the female ghosts in medieval Noh plays. In *Kurozuka* one wearing a terrifying *hannya* mask suddenly appears near a mound of corpses. She is full of resentment, but Buddhist monks eventually pacify her, aided by her own shame at having become such a monster.

Ian Buruma puts such examples in his "Demon Woman" category, which he interprets as the reverse side of the "maternal goddess," a dichotomy resulting from a traditionally severe mother complex.[6] On the other hand, Akiko Baba, poetess and critic, states that such Noh ghosts, and their prototypes in Heian literature (794–1185) represent the just grievances of women of antiquity.[7] Like Buruma, though, it seems men of antiquity did not necessarily see it that way.

In *Genji monogatari (The Tale of Genji)* Prince Genji *does* feel sorry when his girl friend is killed by the *living* spirit of his jealous wife. Still, fear of disgrace, that is, shame, outweighs his guilty feelings and he has the incident covered up.[8] In another passage a wife's jealousy at being replaced by a younger girl is attributed to spirit possession.[9]

These cases suggest that Japanese males of old were reluctant to recognize guilt feelings toward their wife or paramour, and even went to the extreme of attributing a woman's jealousy to supernatural causes. As a consequence, however, her jealousy became all the more terrifying in their imagination, leading them to hallucinate female vengeful spirits and/or create them in literature and drama.

With the creation, or hallucination, of a female vengeful spirit with a definite purpose—namely, to take revenge against the man who wronged her—an archetype was formed that represented the motif of justice through revenge. The resentment the archetype of the Vengeful Spirit expressed is the traditional Japanese equivalent to rebellious sentiments, for the grudge borne one man could be extended to include a male-dominated society that oppresses women. The best example of this archetype is Oiwa, the heroine of *Yotsuya kaidan*, Japan's most famous ghost story. After tracing the metamorphoses she undergoes as the Kabuiki play is adapted into modern films, the moral implications of justice through revenge can be discussed.

The Vengeful Spirit archetype is problematic, however, for she has to be considered as one side of a coin with a protective spirit, too. Watanabe has also noted that the Japanese believed in protective spirits, even in pre-Buddhist days.[10] This dichotomy corresponds to Buruma's dualism of the Demon Woman and the Eternal Mother. The latter could forgive male offenses and thus by extension cover up social injustices. This problematic aspect will be taken up in an analysis of Mizoguchi's *Ugetsu* that makes use of C. G. Jung's concept of the anima. Modern versions of the Vengeful Spirit are also treated and an examination is made of the current iconography of the Japanese spirit world in film and on TV.

Yotsuya Ghost Story

Tokaido Yotsuya Kaidan, a Kabuki play by Nanboku Tsuruya, was first performed in 1821.[11] Nanboku based his play on an actual contemporary incident of a lower-class samurai wife who went insane and disappeared after discovering that her husband had got another woman pregnant.[12] In Nanboku's play the husband has someone poison his wife so that he could marry into a rich family, and the dead wife becomes a ghost who haunts him.

The wife, Oiwa, was even more terrifying than her Noh predecessors, for she could not be pacified. The influence of Buddhism had weakened considerably during the secular Tokugawa period, and Nanboku's times were so degenerate he would not even consider having Buddhist monks appear before her rubbing their rosary beads, as was the case in Noh plays. Moreover, unlike Noh ghosts who bore vague grudges, Oiwa has a specific purpose—namely, to get her husband Iemon. In the play her wrath is not indiscriminate, despite the superstition that performers in it must visit her shrine to avoid being cursed.[13] The object of her wrath, Iemon, does not feel any guilt for his actions, but still is presented as a despicable character responsible for the heroine's plight.

Nanboku's play was first performed as a Kabuki double bill with Kanadehon *Chushingura*, and set in the same period, its male characters are either retainers of Lord Asano or Kira.[14] Seeing significance in this relation, Ryosuke Urio, a modern theater director, billed his 1984 presentation of *Tokaido Yotsuya Kaidan* as the other side of the *Chushingura* coin. The designation is an apt one, for Nanboku's Oiwa illustrates the resentment which forms when a loyal wife is betrayed. Her "rebellion" does not end in self annihilation, because she is already dead, and revenge against her husband and master does not support the system, as was the case with the story of Sazen Tange. Perhaps she could have been created only during Nanboku's degenerate times when the social fabric based on loyalty toward superiors was coming apart.[15]

When Kabuki became respectable after the Meiji Restoration in 1868,[16] its presentation of *Tokaido Yotsuya Kaidan* no longer developed the social criticism implied in the original play, and a contemporary avant-garde production is much closer to Nanboku's intentions. The cleaned-up Kabuki presentation was probably the base for prewar film versions, but there are no extant prints for verification. The first notable postwar film version was Keisuke Kinoshita's *The Yotsuya Ghost Story* (*Yotsuya Kaidan*, 1949).

Kinoshita presented the appearances of the dead Oiwa as simply the hallucinations of Iemon's guilt-wracked mind. When he commits suicide—a divergence from Nanboku's inconclusive ending where he remained alive—it is obvious he died from pangs of conscience rather than supernatural causes.

Kinoshita's version was more a pyschological drama than a horror story. In 1959 with *The Yotsuya Ghost Story on the Tokaido (Tokaido Yotsuya Kaidan)* Nobuo Nakagawa (1905–83), Japan's best director of horror films, brought back the old theme of resentment, while keeping the modern interpretation of guilt. Nakagawa's Kabuki-like presentation was unrealistic compared with Kinoshita's version and with Toho's 1965 production directed by Shiro Toyoda. Still, Nakagawa added a religious dimension that made the Vengeful Spirit a sacred figure.

In Nakagawa's version Iemon becomes a somewhat sympathetic character, since he kills Oiwa's father in a fit of indignation at being refused her hand in marriage on account of his lower-samurai-class origins. (This resentment of the lower classes was also implicit in Nanboku's play.) Furthermore, Naosuke, a co-culprit in the original, becomes Iemon's Iago by persuading him to pose as the avenger of Oiwa's father in order to marry her, and later by convincing him that poisoning her is the only way he can marry a rich merchant's daughter. Iemon's reluctance reveals affection for Oiwa that turns to guilt after he kills her.

More than Iemon's guilt, however, director Nakagawa concentrates on Oiwa's resentment. His portrayal of her becomes a summation of period film heroines, for he shows her pathetic beauty and loyal samurai-wife aspects before her transformation into the Vengeful Spirit with a tenacity of purpose.

Like Musashi's Otsu, Oiwa had been frail and prone to illness. It was easy for Iemon to explain away the bitter taste of the poison by saying it was new medicine. When it took effect, she looked in a mirror and found one side of her once beautiful face disfigured by an ugly swelling. Then she suddenly assumed demonic strength and lunged at the masseur who had been attending her and who had insinuated her husband would leave her for another. Dishonored by her husband's betrayal, with samurai resolve she seized a razor and put an end to her own life, and that of her infant.

With Oiwa's facial disfigurement, Nakagawa's presentation takes on religious connotations. Oiwa now evokes the ghastly *preta* depicted in horizontal, scroll-like paintings *(emakimono)* drawn in the twelfth century when plague and famine were rampant in Japan. (Kurosawa's *Rashomon* was set in that period.) The *preta* were spirits condemned to starvation in the afterlife because of their sins, and their ugly faces and distended bellies were marks of their punishment. Disfigurement in the monsters of Western horror films could also be considered symbolic of their sins in a

The Yotsuya Ghost Story on the Tokaido (1959), directed by Nobuo Nakagawa. Disfigured by the poison her husband gave her, this samurai wife (Katsuko Wakasugi) kills her infant and herself and becomes a Vengeful Spirit.

Christian context, as well as the mark of their inhuman or supernatural nature. But Oiwa was sinless, and though supernatural as Vengeful Spirit, her disfigurement is simply an emblem of Iemon's betrayal and the grudge she bears him for it.

Oiwa's comb, on the other hand, signifies her previous fidelity toward Iemon, for in Japan it was customary in the event of separation for a woman to break a comb and give half of it to the man she loves. After Iemon's poison took effect, Oiwa had started to comb her long hair, symbol of feminine beauty, only to find it clinging to the comb, leaving behind red welts on her scalp and making her even uglier. The comb is later found by Iemon's accomplice, Naosuke, who shows it to his wife, Osode. Osode says it belonged to Oiwa, her dead sister, and suddenly Oiwa appears before her. She is her old beautiful self, since she bears Osode no grudge. To Naosuke, however, she appears as a wrathful figure, who eventually gets a deranged Iemon to kill him.

The comb symbolizes Oiwa's beauty and her loss of it. It also indicates the dual aspect of Japanese spirits who appear to be vengeful only to those who wronged them.

Dualistic symbolism also occurs in Nakagawa's use of snakes, in place of the rats indicating degeneracy in Nanboku's play. In the beginning of the film when Iemon killed a snake that frightened Oiwa, she told him it was a bad omen because snakes were messengers of the gods. Thereafter, their appearance was intended not only to give the audience a queasy feeling, which may be a universal effect, but also to signify the approach of Oiwa's heaven-ordained and just revenge.

Nakagawa's treatment of the revenge, which begins in "The Temple of the Snakes," adeptly conveys religious symbolism through theatrical and cinematic techniques. Iemon had taken refuge there and an overhead shot shows him praying in the center of a large, serpentlike Buddhist rosary on the floor around him. When the living avengers, Osode and her old betrothed enter, Iemon flees to the sanctuary where there is an altar with a huge image of the Buddha. But suddenly it is rolled back into the darkness where balls of fire swirl and dance. Then a disfigured Oiwa appears in midair with the dead infant in her arms, towering menacingly over a crouched Iemon. The child cries and a tent of mosquito netting comes floating down from the darkness to entrap Iemon. This recalls the summer night when Oiwa, inside such a tent dutifully drank the poison he had given her. He cries out for forgiveness, but he is appealing to the wrong deity, for the Vengeful Spirit has replaced the Buddha of Infinite Compassion.

The scene shifts to a swamp where a fleeing Iemon is finally cut down by Osode and her betrothed. Since they are aided by not only Oiwa but also the Vengeful Spirit of the masseur, whom Iemon had killed for being an incriminating witness, it appears that Iemon's demise is the result of a group endeavour. However, director Nakagawa leaves no doubt in the viewer's mind that Oiwa is the central agent.

After Iemon's final cry for forgiveness there is a split-second montage of his agonized face, a snake, and her disfigured face. In the silence after his death she is shown standing calmly in front of a gravestone with the infant in her arms. Her facial disfigurement has vanished because her vengeance has been spent. The film ends with a dissolve to show her standing suspended in the misty night sky, followed by another dissolve of her as a small figure with the child in her arms, ascended even higher with the moon on her right.

Masatoshi Ohba has compared this final image of Oiwa with the famous painting of The Sad Mother Kannon (Hibo Kannon-zu), completed by Motonobu Kano (1476–1559) just before his death.[17] Doubtless, Western readers will recall paintings of Mary's Assumption into Heaven. It is not necessary, however, to read a Western or Christian influence into the work of either Motonobu or Nakagawa, since representations of the Great Mother Goddess appear in many religions, as noted by C. G. Jung,[18] and Mary and the Buddhist Kannon are but two examples. At any rate, once

Oiwa the Vengeful Spirit achieved her purpose, she could, like Mary, attain eternal rest, which is called *jobutsu* or nirvana in Buddhism.

Revenge and Justice

When Oiwa ascends into heaven, the viewer also feels repose, a sense of relief. The psychological purpose of any drama is catharsis: spiritual release from tension or uneasiness. We are all dismayed over the contradiction between the ideal of justice and the actual state of any society where the weak like Oiwa are used and discarded. In any revenge story there is a calm after the storm. An ideal has been affirmed. Balance has been restored to a world tilted by injustice.

Yet, in the midst of the calm there is often a bad aftertaste. We are glad the hero did it and the villain got punished, but the violence and death somehow make life seem futile. For this reason philosophers and religious leaders have often rejected revenge as a means to justice.

Christ's doctrine of the other cheek has its Oriental equivalents. The historical Buddha saw revenge as a vicious cycle with death begetting more death, and Mencius concurred. Filial piety is the cornerstone of Confucianism and one of its injunctions is that one cannot live under the same sky as the man who killed one's father or brother. Mencius interpreted this as a strong deterrent to any killing because any human being has relatives or friends, who would be bound to kill one's own kin.[19]

Despite the warnings of great teachers that revenge could ultimately lead to the annihilation of the human race, just vengeance still remains a viable ideal realized in countless stories, dramas and films. Although the Japanese know Mencius, in their history and dramas the "same sky" idea led to wholesale slayings of all the relatives of one's enemy rather than a deterrent to killing as such.

Tadao Sato has surmised that there are more vengeful spirits in Japan than in the West because the concept of the Last Judgment has not been so persuasive in Japanese thinking.[20] Still, the Buddhist doctrine of reincarnation, through which the sins of this life are paid for in the next, has been popular in Japan and can be considered a cultural equivalent.

Actually, both ideas are rationalizations that attempt to solve the inequalities and unfairness in society, but that never completely succeed in dispelling the resentment piled up after years of oppression. Hence, the popularity of revenge stories in Japan and the West, and probably elsewhere. Even the long suffering Japanese, who are said to be capable of bearing the unbearable, could not wait for the next life, let alone a too distant Last Judgment. They changed the primitive, troublesome spirit into a vengeful one with a just purpose, which afforded at least psychological relief.

On a less philosophical level, Japanese viewers might not experience any bad aftertaste from a revenge drama, since they seem to completely identify with the avenging side and do not take into consideration the position of the object of revenge. This kind of identification also takes place in the West, where dramatists and filmmakers aid and abet it by painting the culprit as evil and cruel as possible, thereby filling their audiences with absolute loathing for him. In Japan, however, this is not necessary. In Nakagawa's film version Iemon is more a victim of circumstances than a villain.

But Iemon is insignificant. Japanese viewers probably focus exclusively on Oiwa's tenacity of purpose. Called *shunen*, it is not only a chief characteristic of the Vengeful Spirit but also an attribute of women, as Japanese men see them. Just as they would risk their life to be faithful to the man they love, they would also not rest until they got even with the man who betrayed them. Hence, nothing can stop Vengeful Spirits like Oiwa. The ending is inevitable, and the audience is satisfied when her purpose is fulfilled. Thwarted purpose is unjust.

Anima and Folk Belief

Since most vengeful spirits in Japanese theater and film are female like Oiwa, and since most of their creators are male, it is useful to interpret them through C. G. Jung's concept of the anima. The anima is the personification of all feminine psychological tendencies in a man's psyche, "the woman within" who conveys vital messages from the unconscious. She appears in dreams and is projected in myths and theatrical conventions, for example, the Greek Sirens, the German Lorelei and the French *femme fatale*. Viewed negatively, the anima leads men to their doom, but she could be a positive spiritual guide, too.[21] Although Oiwa destroys Iemon, as a representation of male guilt she corrects the imbalance caused by male excesses or injustices.

The positive and negative aspects of the anima coincide with the benevolent and malevolent sides of the mother archetype. (Jung believed the anima was a separate archetype, "which in a man's psychology invariably appears, at first, mingled with the mother image.")[22] In Hindu mythology, for example, Kali is both the loving and terrible mother.[23] A Japanese counterpart to the terrible mother can be discerned in legends about *yama uba*, old women demons in the mountains who devour unwary, solitary travelers.[24] On this level, after Oiwa "devours Iemon" she becomes like Kannon, the Goddess of Mercy in the heavens protecting her own child and all who revere her.

The benevolent and malevolent aspects of the mother archetype, and the anima, correspond to the dichotomy of departed spirits in Japanese folk belief. Ancestral spirits protect descendants who remember them with food offerings, and malevolent spirits cause trouble. A good manifestation of this dichotomy can be found in Mizoguchi's *Ugetsu*, a film version of Japanese ghost stories that won international acclaim.

During a time of civil warfare a sixteenth century potter becomes separated from his wife and little boy and dallies with a beautiful, aristocratic lady who turns out to be a ghost who wants to take him with her back to the land of the dead. He barely escapes and returns home to find his wife waiting for him. She fixes him a warm meal and mends his garments, but when he awakes the next day he finds out that she was a ghost, too.

The ghost of the aristocratic lady was definitely a malevolent spirit, and her maid had told the potter why. Her spirit is restless because she died inopportunely before she could become a bride and experience fulfillment as a woman. Since she never gave birth, she is a *muenbotoke* who has no descendants to pacify her with memorial services. Moreover, she is also a vengeful spirit who bears the living world a grudge because she missed out on a major phase of the life cycle. She is actually more terrifying than Oiwa because her vengeance has no specific target, and one imagines her eternally trying to entrap an unsuspecting male.

On the other hand, the potter's wife has become an ancestral spirit. The last sequence of Mizoguchi's film begins with the potter kneeling before her grave mound and asking her why she died. On the soundtrack we hear her answer: I did not die, for I am still beside you, even though we are in different worlds. The sequence ends with their little son placing a food offering on her burial mound, which recalls previous scenes of the three of them enjoying a warm meal together around an open hearth while she was alive. This cinematic counterbalancing indicates the continuity between the living and the dead in one family as it is symbolized in ancestor worship through food offerings.

The potter's wife has become a benevolent spirit watching over her husband, their boy, and their house. Although she had an untimely death, she still completed the major phases of her life cycle: marriage and childbirth. Therefore, she is not restless and is simply pacified because they remember her.

Although the contrast between the spirits of the wife and of the aristocratic lady is extreme, their frequent juxtaposition in sequences where one's departure is smoothly followed by the other's appearance suggests that they are simply two alternating aspects of the male's anima, whether that of the potter or of Mizoguchi himself.[25] Their original natures did not make one benevolent and the other malevolent. It was the result of the circumstances of their deaths, with the life cycle of one prematurely interrupted. They exemplify the two aspects of Oiwa: malevolent when

Ugetsu (1953), directed by Kenji Mizoguchi. The ghost of this aristocratic lady (Machiko Kyo) is malevolent because she died before she could become a bride, and therefore she eternally tries to entrap an unsuspecting male.

Ugetsu (1953), directed by Kenji Mizoguchi. After the potter's wife (Kinuyo Tanaka) dies, she becomes a benevolent spirit who watches over her husband and son in the land of the living.

bearing a grudge, benevolent when pacified. Oiwa's benevolence is limited, though, for, unlike Mary, she protects only her own descendants, not all mankind or all Christian believers.

Keiko McDonald has noted the forgiving nature of Mizoguchi's heroines like the potter's wife.[26] This can be problematic, however, in terms of the primary function of the anima: to correct the psychological imbalance caused by male excesses. The ease with which the potter is forgiven will hardly induce self-reflection, or a recognition of his own negligence. The protective forgiving side of Japanese spirits can thwart the Vengeful Spirit's purpose of justice through revenge. This was particularly evident in the 1959 Dai Ei film in which director Kenji Misumi has Oiwa forgive Iemon in the end. The ending of the 1965 film version was even worse, for a sweet and gentle Oiwa came for Iemon after he had suffered enough, presumably to guide him to Amida's Western Paradise, where they *both* could attain eternal rest. Such Oiwas lost the power to terrify and simply covered up male sins with unwarranted "motherly" tenderness.

Forgiveness is by no means out of the question. The potter was not such a bad fellow. In fact, he was so nondescript that it seemed as though two powerful female deities were battling over his rather small soul. But Iemon did not deserve to be forgiven by the woman he had killed when she was of no further use. Such forgiveness is only an idealization of the servility of the weak and oppressed.

Living Female Avengers

The main drawback of both Oiwa and *Hannya* ghosts in Noh theater is that their supernatural nature makes their just grievances and vengeance seem like aberrations. Live avengers, particulary female ones, would be better, since men created the societies and are responsible for the injustices therein. However, in traditional Japanese theater and period film, living female avengers were not only poor imitations of their male counterparts but also supported society by only taking part in socially approved vendettas like that of avenging the death of a parent. Living female avengers who were *socially* terrifying only began appearing in Japanese film in the late sixties, and there are only a few examples.

Tales of the Shogun's Harem (Ooku Monogatari, 1967) consists of three episodes about the lives of the female attendants who nightly entertained the head of the Tokugawa government, which ruled Japan from 1603 to 1868. Although director Sadao Nakajima exploited his titilating subject matter to the fullest, his commercial film still gave an accurate, concise picture of the status of women in feudal times. The first episode concerned the competition between the women to conceive a child for their master, since their status would rise if they could provide a successor. Even older women no longer in the running competed by espousing the cause of their younger wards. The plight of all these women was expressed when an old woman dropped a bucket down a deep well, and a wide-screen close-up of its mouth symbolized the womb, the source of woman's pain and status. In the second episode a young attendant committed suicide by jumping in the well because her lover had forced her to abort rather than bring about fatal recriminations from the authorities for their secret affair.

The third episode is about a merchant's daughter who is taken into service as a maid, but whose beauty attracts the shogun so much that he raises her rank to that of a "playmate." Her betrothed suggests eloping after he gets over his initial disgust over her loss of virginity, but he is cruelly killed by the shogun's retainers. The headmistress of the harem tells the distraught girl that at least *she* will be forgiven if she "consents" again. In the boudoir she draws the shogun's own sword, but only succeeds in cutting down the headmistress. The film ends with a shot of the castle in flames behind her. Her hair is disheveled and the sword is still in her hand. She has become a living Vengeful Spirit representing the grudge the commoners bear their exploiters.

Since the merchant's daughter failed to kill the degenerate shogun himself and only got a higher-status member of her own sex, her vengeance was not consumated but simply suggested in the flames. A more terrifying, live female avenger who kills evil, powerful men can be found in *The Red Peony Gambler* (*Hibotan Bakuto*, eight entries from 1968 to 1972),[27] a modern *yakuza* film series set in the 1890s. The heroine, O-Ryu is a wandering lady gambler who is adept not only with the dice cup but with the pistol and dagger as well.

O-Ryu had been a pure maiden whose wedding engagement and chance for a happy ordinary life was ruined by the violent death of her father, which exposed her *yakuza* origins. She vows to avenge him and embarks on her endless journey. Her fate is symbolized by the close-ups of pure white peonies turning into blood-red ones. She resembles the Vengeful Spirit of the aristocratic lady in *Ugetsu* who bears a grudge because a normal phase of her life cycle, marriage, was denied her.

In early entries strong males help her and she experiences tragic love affairs. These "conventions" from the pathetic-beauty syndrome make her seem weak in comparison to her male counterparts, the Chaste Warrior and the Stoic Retainer. The terror she will become, however, is foreshadowed in a scene from the first entry, directed by Kosaku Yamashita. When she pulls a gun on a gambling boss, a close-up makes it seem as if she is pointing it at the audience, which for *yakuza* films is almost exclusively male. As *The Red Peony Gambler* series progressed (and Junko Fuji who played O-Ryu became the most popular Japanese film actress), O-Ryu began killing the evil boss herself, and in the sixth entry, *Enter O-Ryu* (*O-Ryu Sanjo*, 1970) her male helper became an accessorylike, admirable

Tales of the Shogun's Harem (1967), directed by Sadao Nakajima. The head-mistress (Isuzu Yamada) of the harem prevents this distraught girl (Yoshiko Sakuma) from killing the shogun in order to avenge the cruel death of her betrothed.

ally. The director of *Enter O-Ryu*, Tai Kato, was contracted to To-Ei studios to turn out commercial assignments rapidly during the modern *yakuza* film fad; nonetheless, he was capapble of presenting compelling images such as the following of O-Ryu at the height of the melee.

Taking out a long, needlelike hairpin, she flings it into the gun-wielding hand of one of the henchmen. Then she ducks to avoid the sword of another and stabs him in the belly. When she comes up for a full-face, wide-screen, close-up, her disheveled hair occupies half the screen and her clenched, blood-stained dagger is parallel to her face glistening with perspiration. When she sticks it in the evil boss there is a gleam of pure malice in her eyes.

O-Ryu's disheveled hair and malicious gleam during such a melee is striking because usually she is prim and proper. In her elaborate hairdo only a strand or two may be out of place, and like her male counterparts she is trying to hide her emotions. A stickler for formalities, this self-controlled woman has suddenly run amok. In her transformation she recalls Oiwa, who lost some of her hair, and the distraught woman in a Kabuki play (played by an *onnagata* or female impersonator) who removes hairpins from her elaborate wig until her hair reaches the floor.

In the seventh entry of the series, *I Want Your Life* (*O-Inochi Itadakimasu*, 1971), also directed by Tai Kato, O-Ryu reached the fullest extent of demonical transformation. In the midst of the melee, however, she suddenly heard the voices of approaching children, and cringing at their innocence and terrified at the demon she had become, she quickly left the field of battle.

This scene is reminiscent of a passage in *Koshoku ichidai onna* (*The Life of an Amorous Woman*) by Saikaku Ihara, a seventeenth-century prose master. (Mizoguchi based his *Life of Oharu* on the novel.) The old courtesan has a nightmare in which she is haunted by the voices of all the children she never had and thus symbolically aborted. Like her, O-Ryu is obsessed by the ordinary life she missed out on.

As if to pacify O-Ryu, another director, Buichi Saito, turned her into a guardian angel in *Honor and Humanity Come Through* (*Jingi Toshimasu*, 1972), the last entry in the series. Now O-Ryu is continually nursing her wounded *yakuza* brothers, and she even shows some weakness herself by becoming sick and lying down in bed with a few strands of hair drooping over her perspiring forehead. In the melee she even regrets stabbing a turncoat and gives him a look of compassion that inspires him to protect her before he dies.

At the end of *Honor and Humanity Come Through* O-Ryu did not ascend into heaven like Oiwa; however, the actress Junko Fuji retired from the screen, married a Kabuki actor, and became an exemplary wife and mother. This had been foreshadowed in the final film. Looking back on the whole series, her image seems like the two aspects of the anima of

The Red Peony Gambler—Flower Cards Match (Hibotan Bakuto—Hanafuda Shobu, 1969), directed by Tai Kato. Armed with a lethal hairpin and dagger, this lady gambler (Junko Fuji) kills evil gambling bosses who represent male-dominated society.

different directors, alternating between benevolent and malevolent phases, like the good wife and aristocratic lady in *Ugetsu*.

A better representative of just female grievances can be found in the *Scorpion* (*Sasori*, six entries, 1972-77),[28] a contemporary film series about female prison cell mates. After the heroine gets the man who did her wrong, she transcends *Frankie and Johnny* by avenging the victims of rape and late-stage abortions by cruel male doctors. The *Scorpion* series not only includes violent scenes reminiscent of O-Ryu at her finest but also elements similar to *Tales of the Shogun's Harem* that go beyond the lesbian activities of cooped-up women.

The first entry, *Women Prison Cell Mates, Number 701* (*Joshu 701-go*, 1972), begins with the title song about grudges and resentment (*urami bushi*) and a close-up of the heroine's expressive eye. (She is often shown with her hair or her hat brim covering one eye). This is followed by a shot of naked female prisoners walking across a ramp leading to the bathing room. A male prison guard is down below watching them, and a close-up of his lewd eye is followed by a cut back to the heroine's eye of malice.

One eye symbolizes the vagina,[29] which often bleeds. Later the heroine's escape is held up because her cell sister is menstruating, and she recalls her own loss of virginity, crudely expressed by blood on a white sheet. This is followed by a shot of the Japanese national flag with its red circle against a white background. The prison is only an organ of the state governed by men who exploit women. But in the end the heroine will get one of them, her ex-boyfriend and police spy, and make him bleed.

Despite the fact that director Shunya Ito is using this commercial film at least partly to criticize established society, because of his "vaginal symbolism" he could be open to the charge of male chauvinism. Women seem to be defined solely according to their physical characteristics—that is, they are open and vulnerable like the vagina itself. Their sex itself makes them weak—not social suppression—like the deceived heroine herself before she hardened and became a living Vengeful Spirit. In *Tales of the Shogun's Harem* the feudalistic definition of women according to their womb was criticized; but at least the womb has a reproductive function. The vagina as such is only a receptacle for the penis.

Yet, the male villains also come to be defined by their sex. In the first entry the prison warden is wounded in one eye and thereafter resembles a cyclops. In the third entry, *Room of Beasts* (*Kemono no Heya*, 1973) the police detective loses one arm while chasing the heroine. Consequently, these men seem like caricatures of the penis, one-eyed or one-armed. Since the film series was based on a popular comic-book series, such caricaturization does not seem unnatural. Perhaps presenting women, who are on the good side, as vaginas is not chauvinistic after all. It even seems that primitive fertility symbols are being used by a modern film

Scorpion—Cell Number 41 (Sasori—Dai 41 Zakkyobo, 1972), directed by Shunya Ito. This female avenger (Meiko Kaji) starts a revolt in a prison, an organ of the state governed by men who exploit women.

director to further the women's liberation movement, which was quite active at the time of filming.

The fact that the heroine is also presented as a one-eyed figure, however, suggests another interpretation. Akiko Baba has noted the frequency of one-eyed demons in Japanese folk lore and surmised that their prototype was the alleged sacrificial victims in prehistoric times.[30] During festivals of village gods supposedly one leg was broken and/or one eye pierced to prevent such victims' escape. This one-eyed prototypal victim influenced Baba to re-interpret Japanese demons in folklore and myth as sublimations of the resentment of victimized non-Yamato minorities and outcastes.[31] Such groups were even labeled "demons" *(oni)* by majority society.[32] As such, the male cyclopian villains in the *Scorpion* series could be regarded as the terrifying troublemakers demons are usually interpreted to be. On the other hand, the one-eyed heroine is a kindred spirit to Sazen Tange, the one-eyed, one-armed retainer who bore his lord a grudge, and the Noh *Hannya* prototype of the female Vengeful Spirit, which was created by Zeami and others who may have had outcaste origins.[33]

Conclusion

As the Japanese women's liberation movement became less demonstrative, living female avengers like the *Scorpion* heroine ceased to appear in films. Old vengeful spirits like Oiwa did not vanish, however, and even made their way to the TV circuit.

During the eighties a popular TV show called *Anata no shiranai sekai* (*The World You Do Not Know*) has been presenting dramatizations of actual spiritualistic experiences. Iwao Nikura, the show's expert who has published eleven volumes on the subject, has divided contemporary Japanese ghosts into two types: troublemaking demons and purposeful spirits who wish to communicate something to the living. The latter are often wronged women who appear to express their resentment. Unlike Oiwa, though, they can be pacified short of the male culprit's death if he recognizes his old fault—which is then demonstrated by visits to her grave or by making food offerings to her memorial tablet. These TV modifications of the Vengeful Spirit are different from the watered-down film versions of Oiwa in that for them repentance is a precondition for forgiveness. Iemon had suffered but had never really repented. When he was forgiven, his own form of male tyranny simply went unrecognized.

The TV modifications are not nearly so terrifying as Nakagawa's Oiwa, for their resentment is dissipated rather easily, which indicates it is rather simple to contain rebellion in Japan. Still, their pacification price—the recognition of their just grievances—at least curbs male tyranny to some degree, and even reflects the recognition of minority groups in present-day Japan, though the powers-that-be hardly feel guilty about their unequal existence.[34]

The other kind of contemporary Japanese ghosts has been labeled the Exorcist type by Nikura, and he considers them difficult to pacify. This label may simply reflect the popularity of American horror films in Japan since the phenomenal success of *The Exorcist* in 1973. In fact, in the eighties the American variety seems more popular than the old Japanese kind. The label may indeed be superficial. Prototypes for contemporary, troublemaking ghosts may well be the native, one-eyed demon, as well as the demons that entered Japan via Buddhism with its concept of hell. This conglomeration, with its Indian and Chinese origins, included monsters, animallike fairies (foxes were the most popular) who deceived people by assuming human shape, and demons who possessed people or terrified them with apparitions. Monsters were destroyed by sword-wielding heroes, but the others were usually defeated by human ingenuity or kindness, which followed the Buddhist tradition whereby demons were pacified and turned into allies.

Nikura's label may be appropriate, after all. Indian, Chinese, and native Japanese demons could usually be pacified. Christian demons, on the other hand, had to be exorcised. Although the Buddhist rosary could be an exorcising equivalent to the cross, it was only effective in medieval Noh plays. From the seventeenth century on, Japanese spirits generally had to be pacified either by offerings or by revenge. Spirits who could not be thereby pacified had to come from the West.

A good example of the Christian kind of demon changing Japanese iconography can be found in *Hell of Maidens* (*Shojo Jigoku*, 1977), a softcore porno film which Masaru Konuma, a relatively unknown director, raises above the mundane level of the Nikkatsu "roman" subgenre. The story concerns an introverted high school girl who is tormented by classmates and teachers alike, and whom her unsympathetic, lower-class parents consider abnormal. She is befriended by a girl from a rich family and they have a lesbian relationship. The poor girl is later seduced by the principal, who forces her to abort when she becomes pregnant. She tries to get even by sending a letter to a newspaper exposing him, and then setting the school on fire and dying in the flames. Since no one believes the letter, the rich girl continues to avenge her and together with her ghost torments not only the principal but all her former persecutors.

The poor girl's ghost is simply a traditional Vengeful Spirit. The rich girl is a living female avenger, like the *Scorpion* heroine, until she finds out that the principal is her real father. Then she confronts her stepfather with the truth and tempts him, saying the bad seed will be perpetuated, that is, she is just like her mother who made a cuckold out of him.

While "bad blood" is a conventional excuse for lasciviousness in Japanese porno films, her wicked smile suggests she is akin to a Western-style *femme fatale,* and that the sadistic pleasure she gets from tormenting her victims far outweighs the satisfaction of carrying out a grudge. In the climax of the film she transcends the *femme fatale* role and shows herself to be an evil demon.

Dressed in black like a priest, the principal is climbing a volcano, perhaps in atonement for his sins. Suddenly the rich girl appears before him with the poor girl, who is also smiling wickedly. Dressed in white robes like angels, they embrace lasciviously. Then they set themselves on fire, and like witches at the stake are burnt up before his eyes. He goes mad and starts beating his head against a rock, and the film ends with a big white balloon ascending the smoky sky.

The girls had fondled this balloon sensually in the beginning of the film, and it seems to suggest the desires that will always tempt and torment human beings whose efforts toward goodness might simply be hypocrisy.

This theme is new and valid in contemporary middle-class Japanese society. The intrusion of the evil demon from the West, however, weakens the power of the old Vengeful Spirit to evoke a sense of justice. Just grievances are replaced by a vague sense of evil that makes everything seem futile. It also simply recalls the indiscriminate troublemaking of the primitive spirits from which a purposeful Vengeful Spirit evolved. In the cultural hybrid of a livng female avenger and an evil demon, Western influence, which often has a progressive effect in Japan, ironically leads to retrogression and paradoxically induces a yearning for old Vengeful Spirits like Oiwa.

6

All-Suffering Female and Weak Passive Male

Introduction

As stated in chapter two, the pathetic beauty has a subordinate position in period film, for the Chaste Warrior must reject her to be strong in battle and the Tormented Lord is the chief sufferer in the male-oriented genre. In contemporary film, however, she can occupy the spotlight as a suffering female, partricularly in the so-called "feminine films" *(josei eiga)* on tragic mothers and lovers,[1] and the man who loves her is usually weak and cannot possibly match her suffering.

Weak male lovers are not peculiarly Japanese. In popular Chinese literature during the Ming Dynasty from 1368 to 1644 romantic love is often treated as a sickness that particularly afflicts men and makes them weak and pathetic.[2] This view doubtless reflects the Confucian priority for parent-child relations, which could conceivably be threatened by romantic love. While Japan shares a Confucian tradition with China, male lovers in Japanese film through the fifties seemed even weaker than their Chinese counterparts, say in Hong Kong films. This can be attributed to the lack of a Chaste Warrior archetype in Chinese culture. In fact, in China during the the twelfth century the Confucian scholar replaced the warrior as the male ideal.[3] Although warrior heroes did not disappear, they never became chaste like Musashi, probably because Zen and the Chinese equivalent of Bushido were not so persuasive. Thus, a modern kung fu hero like Bruce Lee was not above a love scene. In Japanese culture, on the other hand, the warrior remained the popular male ideal, and lover boys were made even weaker to support the Chaste Warrior contention that women actually were a weakening influence.

Yet the difference is one of degree. Furthermore, weak lovers cannot be attributed solely to Confucianism, for they can be found in the West, too. Stephen Neale observed in his analysis of Hollywood melodramas and musicals the feminization of the men therein and quoted Roland Barthes to the effect that a man is not feminized because he is homosexual but because he is in love. Neale further noted that the agonies of suffering and waiting are experienced predominantly but not exclusively by women, and gives as an example of male agony Rock Hudson in *The Magnificent Obsession*.[4]

Waiting is an expression of passivity; however, Western male lovers, albeit weak, are by no means so passive as their Japanese counterparts. This can be demonstrated by a brief comparison of the male leads in Hideo Ohba's *What Is Your Name?* (*Kimi no Na wa*, 1953-54), an immensely popular Japanese film trilogy, and Mervyn LeRoy's *Waterloo Bridge* (1940). The Hollywood film served as a model for the Japanese one,[5] and both concern young lovers who meet by chance during a World War II air raid and are thereafter kept apart by tragic circumstances.

The Japanese male lead, played by Keiji Sada, is not only powerless to make his love happy but also rather immobile. During three hours of film footage in a digest version he only went to see her three times out of his own volition, and twice then she was on the brink of death because of an attempted suicide and near fatal illness. The dominant image of him waiting for her on a bridge, a meeting place for Japanese lovers, testifies to his passivity. In the Hollywood film however, the male lead, played by Robert Taylor, is only shown once alone on Waterloo Bridge, the scene of the heroine's suicide and their first meeting, and then he was not waiting but simply recalling their life together. A typical, take-charge American hero, Taylor not only pursued his sweetheart but also searched for her; their separations were really the result of circumstances rather than lack of volition on the part of the male.

The difference between the American and Japanese love heroes can be attributed to a tradition of knightly chivalry instead of the Confucianism, as well as Buddhism, which encourages passivity. Japanese lovers were probably more passive than Chinese ones because Buddhism had greater influence in Japan.[6] Hence a Japanese archetype formed, herein designated as the Weak Passive Male.

Given the Chaste Warrior and the Weak Passive Male as mates, it is no wonder that Japanese heroines suffered, particularly more than her Western counterparts. The *Waterloo Bridge* heroine, played by Vivien Leigh, suffered, of course, but she could be vivacious at times. In stark contrast, in *What Is Your Name?* the heroine, played by Keiko Kishi, smiled only once, when she first met the hero, and thereafter invariably wore the same sad facial expression. Hence she represents the Japanese archetype herein designated as the All-Suffering Female.

Keiko Kishi's wooden performance cannot be attributed to a lack of acting ability, for she is almost as accomplished as Vivien Leigh was. Directorial treatment, however, is definitely a factor because Hideo Ohba's melodramatic style makes Mervyn LeRoy's film seem like documentary realism. But genre determined treatment. Even today Japanese often call love stories, melodramas (borrowing the English word and pronouncing it, *merodorama*),[7] as if by their content alone they are melodramatic. Then the treatment itself becomes melodramatic in the English sense of "extravagant theatricality."[8] The most famous Japanese films about young lovers were such "love melodramas" as *What Is Your Name?* They were not so numerous as family dramas, the other principal genre of contemporary film, nor did they reach, or even approach, the artistic level of the family drama masterpieces by Ozu, Mikio Naruse, and others. But they were the biggest box office hits.[9]

Culture determined genre. Japanese considered romantic love in melodramatic terms, since it was so unattainable in everyday life due to the influences of Bushido and Confucianism. The reverse side of a highly valued parent-child relation was a strong yearning for romantic love. Realistic family dramas coexisted with fantastic love melodramas. The latter's archetypes had a social function, for their motifs of suffering and passivity stressed the value of obedience. When suffering is considered a virtue, people accept their social order as a natural rather than an arbitrary phenomenon, and when passivity is the proper mode of behavior, people obey their superiors and submit to the state. Still, the archetypes of the All-Suffering Female and the Weak Passive Male are problematic, for stories about tragic lovers can be considered a protest against the society that would not permit their love.

These archetypes can be transcendental as well as oppositional, for they can also represent a universal desire for an ethereal purity that cannot exist in this mundane world. In the West also *true* love is practically unattainable. One recalls a character in Ingmar Bergman's *Smiles of the Summer Night* saying that in the history of mankind there were only a few true lovers like Romeo and Juliet, and one also remembers that they were kept apart by their families.

Although tragic lovers are universal, the Japanese archetypes of the All-Suffering Female and the Weak Passive Male differ considerably from counterparts in the West and East on account of their development. This can be discerned from the following survey of Japanese love stories from antiquity to modern times.

Metamorphoses

The first Japanese love story is also the *Kojiki* creation myth, a cultural equivalent to the story of Adam and Eve. From the Heavenly Floating Bridge, which is used for travel between heaven and earth, the god Izanagi and the goddess Izanami lower a jeweled spear into the chaos. An island is created and they descend and erect a pillar there. After walking around it they have conjugal intercourse and eventually give birth to more islands and deities—one of whom, the fire god, causes the death of Izanami.[10] As related in chapter five, Izanagi visited her in the land of the dead, but was driven away.

The first Japanese love story is frankly sexual, for not only the pillar but even the jeweled spear can be considered phallic. Like Adam and Eve's, the story of Izanagi and Izanami ends in tragedy, but there is no loss of innocence associated with the knowledge of good and evil. The natural tragedy of death separates Izanagi from his wife, and he grieves over this rather than any fall from paradise.

The earliest love poems appearing in *Man'yoshu*, are also completely natural, for they either celebrate the joy of being with the loved one or bemoan the sadness of separation. In these poems the convention of calling the male's loved one younger sister(*imo*) may stem from the fact that Izanagi and Izanami were brother and sister.

Izanami, who dies giving birth, is obviously the prototype for all the suffering females to come, and not just for mothers. Izanagi is not passive, but certainly weak in the face of death and pollution. When an ashamed and enraged Izanami sends the warriors of the land of the dead after him, he flees waving his sword behind him.[11] Later he is saved by peaches, which are considered vagina symbols in Japan—for example, a folk hero, *Momo Taro* or Peach-Boy, was born from one of them. Since the dead, polluted Izanami is the prototype for the female Vengeful Spirit, the vagina-peaches could represent the benevolent aspect of female spirits. Unlike Perseus and other Western heroes who slay female demons, Izanagi is really no match for them at all, and is by turns threatened and saved by female spirits, like the potter in *Ugetsu*.

In the age following the completion of *Kojiki* and *Man'yoshu*, the Heian period from 794 to 1185, the best prose and verse were written by aristocratic women, who were often ladies-in-waiting at the imperial court in Kyoto, and the subject of their works was frequently love. *The Tale of Genji*, written by Lady Murasaki early in the eleventh century, is considered the world's first novel and concerns the numerous love affairs of Prince Hikaru Genji. Lady Murasaki depicts a world of elegant free sex, replete with clandestine meetings in the women's chambers of the court and at mountainside temples, followed by an exchange of poems the day after since the promiscuity of the courtier aristocracy was always governed by good taste. The joy of being with the loved one, however, was superceded by a melancholy awareness of the fleetingness of the affair itself, for the Buddhist concept of the impermanence of all things (*mujō-kan*) had entered Japanese culture. The Heavenly Floating Bridge in *Kojiki* becomes the Floating Bridge of Dreams (the title of the last chapter of *The Tale of Genji*)—which is a metaphor for the insubstantial beauty of life.

Suffering was not considered ennobling during the Heian period and it was best to escape from it if you could.[12] Still, writers like Lady Murasaki and their heroines pined over their neglect and doubtless were saddened not only by the evanescence of life (mono no aware) but also the inconstancy of male affections. Lovers like Prince Genji were not passive since they usually initiated the affair, but they were far from "masculine" by latter-day standards. Ivan Morris describes them as white-powder-faced tipplers and perfumed womanizers, poets who abhorred violence and left the rough stuff to uncouth, provincial warriors whom they despised.[13]

The literature of the medieval period from 1186 to 1600 contains very few love stories. The principal genre in the thirteenth and fourteenth centuries was tales of the recent wars,[14] and the warrior became the new masculine ideal and hero.

Women continued to suffer in the Noh theater, which developed from shrine and temple sponsorship to patronage by the military Ashikaga shogunate in the fourteenth century.[15] In many Noh plays an itinerant monk comes across female ghosts who return to earth to relive an old tragic love affair.[16] She may undergo the torments of hell because men died on account of her, and this is considered her sin, or she may be denied rebirth at a higher level of existence because she cannot renounce worldly, romantic attachments. At first glance this set-up seems like a variation of the Buddha himself resisting the temptations of Maya, the demoness of illusion. That is to say, the itinerant monk does not succumb to the charms of female ghosts, and worldly attachments must be severed to obtain enlightenment. However, such female ghosts are sympathetic precisely because of their attachments, and their very human appeal is one reason for the excellence of many Noh plays.

In the seventeenth century Saikaku Ihara wrote about the homosexual affairs among samurai in The Great Mirror of Manly Love and about heterosexual affairs in the merchant class in The Life of an Amorous Man and other works. Saikaku's contemporary, Monzaemon Chikamatsu, wrote plays for the puppet theater, which were later adopted by Kabuki, about the tragic love between a geisha and some clerk that leads to their double suicide. The contrast between Saikaku's cynical treatments and Chikamatsu's pathos reveals the official, Confucian morality then, which permitted flippant sex but regarded romantic love as a threat to the social order.

The ruling samurai then maintained social order through a rigid class system in which behavior was regulated by status and appropriate role playing consisted of obedience.[17] When a young man in a Chikamatsu play fell in love with a geisha, he either forsook his duties as a merchant, or disobeyed his parents or master. While it seems the ruling class itself was only concerned with inter-status marriages that would lower samurai prestige, Chikamatsu, a samurai himself, seemed to overgeneralize and conclude that romantic love would inevitably lead a man to abandon his social role. In his plays both love and freedom from society are possible, but only at the cost of death. Social order is affirmed because true lovers are doomed. The audience gets vicarious pleasure and is also admonished that such behavior leads to death.[18]

Yet, albeit briefly, Chikamatsu's lovers do transcend their society. This is graphically demonstrated in one of his greatest plays, *The Love Suicides at Amijima.* When the woman, Koharu, doubts the death-resolve of her lover, Jihei, he cuts of the top-knot of his hair, which signified his familial and social ties.[19] Reassured, she cuts the bow of her courtesan hairdo. Facing each other with their hair hanging down, they are shorn of social status and have simply become pure man and pure woman, like Adam and Eve.[20]

Their transcendental aspect is also signified by the *michi yuki*, or journey the lovers take before their death. In Noh *michi yuki* referred to the journey an itinerant monk went on before the ghosts from the other world appeared to him.[21] In Kabuki *michi yuki* simply means leaving this world.

The transcendental nature of Chikamatsu's lovers is further testified by their belief that they will be reborn together on the same lotus in the Amida-Buddha's Pure Land. It may be doubted whether Chikamatsu himself believed in this, since secularization is a dominant characteristic of his times in comparison to the preceding religious, medieval period.[22] However, his use of this poetic allusion emphasizes the purity of his lovers.

Stories of pure lovers in the West seem to be an attempt to recapture the innocence of Adam and Eve in paradise. But, as stated previously, there is no Fall in Japanese mythology. Chikamatsu arrived at the representation of the universal desire for ethereal purity from a different direction. Unlike Western, teen-age lovers like Romeo and Juliet, Chikamatsu's older lovers do not start out pure. Koharu is an impure prostitute and Jihei is a mundane clerk. They become pure after they fall in love and are ready to die for it.

The theme of Chikamatsu's "love suicide" *(shinjū)* plays becomes pure lovers versus an impure world. While such suicides took place in previous ages, as well as Chikamatsu's own, he was probably the first writer to make them an important subject of literature. Perhaps he arrived at this point of view as a result of his own social position as a samurai writing plays for merchants, that is, because of his own ambiguous status. Still, it would be a mistake to see any considerable social protest in Chikamatsu's "love suicide" plays. Tadao Sato points out that usually Chikamatsu's lovers are weak pathetic creatures who are driven to suicide as a result of tragic circumstances.[23] In the film *A Story From Chikamatsu (Chikamatsu Monogatari,* 1954) Mizoguchi, with the aid of his superb scriptwriter Yoshitaka Yoda, turned the lovers, especially the heroine, into forceful characters who refuse to commit suicide and go to their execution for adultery with a smile on their face. Still, since transcendentalism could

Double Suicide (Shinju Ten no Amijima, 1969), directed by Masahiro Shinoda. In Monzaemon Chikamatsu's best play, and in this modern film version of it, the lovers (Shima Iwashita and Kichiemon Nakamura) become pure after they are ready to die for love. Love suicides are the ultimate Japanese love story.

embody rebellion, however latent, Mizoguchi simply made explicit the protest that was implied in Chikamatsu's originals.

Love suicides became the ultimate Japanese love story and can still be found not only in contemporary film presentations of Chikamatsu's plays but also in films and dramas with modern settings. Both lovers suffered on account of their plight, but the heroine could be considered more noble than her forebears in that she committed suicide out of love. In contrast to the female ghosts in Noh who suffered in the afterlife because of attachment to a former love, Chikamatsu's heroine suffered for love in this life and suicide ended her suffering whether or not she was reborn on a lotus with her lover.

The heroine's lover was usually weak, foolish, and imprudent, but handsome. In Kabuki he was played by the *nimaime,* the actor given second billing after the *tateyaku,* the main lead who played strong *samurai* who did not fall in love. In this dichotomy of leading men one can see reflections of the courtier aristocrat who, as a womanizer, abhorred violence and the warrior aristocrat who disdained romance. The second billing of the former attests to the fact that he was historically overthrown by the latter. In Kabuki the peaceable lover was further weakened by being placed in the lower rungs of the merchant class. Lack of funds often precipitated his tragedy, unlike Prince Genji who was troubled only by the fleetingness of all things. Still, according to Tadao Sato, the Karuki *ni-maime* often outdid the *tateyaku* in popularity,[24] and his appeal probably indicates resentment against the Confucian rectitude that governed the times.

The first "modern" Japanese love stories were written around the turn of the century by novelists who were influenced by Western ideas of romance. Their most popular works were adapted into plays for the new theater, *Shimpa*, which began around 1890 and was the most popular drama from 1900 to the mid-1920s. The first film love stories in the early 1910s were simply filmed presentations of *Shimpa* plays.[25] Although the characters in these contemporary plays were usually dressed in the latest Western fashions, they did not differ greatly from their Kabuki counterparts because their love still ended tragically. Still, their heroes, often college students, were even weaker than their feudal predecessors. Because of their passivity, they seldom had enough gumption to commit suicide with the heroine. In contrast to feudal merchants in a stratified society, they had futures to consider in a modernizing Japan.

The hero of the most famous *Shimpa* play, *The Genealogy of Women (Onna keizu)* is a typical example. He loves a geisha, but says nothing. Her geisha mentor, like an older sister, senses the feelings of the young pair and arranges for them to live together. His teacher and benefactor finds out, however, and orders him to break with the woman, not only on account of her low status but because he wants him to marry his own daughter. The hero dutifully obeys and the heroine suffers and dutifully dies in the end.

In the original novel the *Shimpa* play is based on, the author, Kyoka Izumi, attacked the denial of free love in the traditional Japanese custom of marriages arranged by parents or superiors.[26] However, this Western idea was not acceptable to the Shimpa adaptors, for they, like their audiences and most Japanese at the time, gave top priority to the parent/superior-child/inferior relationship. Romance was considered a rebellion against parents or fictive parents, like one's teacher. It could be tasted, but had to end sadly. The young man should obey and passively let love slip through his fingers. The above situation is called a conflict between *giri* and *ninjo* (obligation and feelings) by the Japanese. The young man loves the girl but is obligated to his teacher, and that is more important. It seems very cold to Westerners; however, the fact that the young man also loves his teacher—he has been like a kind father to him—warms things up emotionally for Japanese audiences. The old teacher may be obstinate but he is never

Genealogy of Women—The White Plums of Yujima (Onna no Keizu—Yujima no Shiraume, **1955), directed by Teinosuke Kinugasa. In this film adaptation of the most famous Shimpa play, the hero (Koji Tsuruta) parts from the heroine (Fujiko Yamamoto) on account of his benefactor. Suicide is out of the question because he has a future to consider in modernizing Japan.**

considered a villain since he has his student's best interests at heart. In terms of dramaturgy, however, he is an obstructing third party that precipitates the tragedy which nevertheless affirms old values.

In *Taki no Shiraito,* another popular Shimpa adaptation from a novel by Kyoka Izumi, modern society precipitates the lovers' tragedy. Taki no Shiraito is the stage name for a female entertainer who practically seduces her college student lover. Thereafter, she acts like his older sister and makes sacrifices so that she can send him the money necessary for his college education. Unfortunately, she later kills for money and ironically the judge at her trial is her lover himself. He has to pass the death sentence on her and out of remorse later commits suicide.

The hero's passivity was perhaps best captured in Mizoguchi's 1933 film version of the story. In one scene he is dozing on a bridge, and suddenly she appears majestically before him. The Floating Bridge of Dreams in *The*

Tale of Genji here becomes the passive male dreaming of romance on a bridge.

The hero's status as a student, like that of many Shimpa heroes, is analogous to the situation in Chinese Ming Dynasty stories where young students came to the capital to study for examinations and had love affairs with female entertainers like Taki no Shiraito. The student-hero has more modern relevance, however, since the Meiji period (1868–1912) college students were the future leaders who would guide Japan through modernization after they acquired knowledge of Western arts and sciences. Tadao Sato has pointed out that, as they rose in status, they inevitably forsook their families and sisterlike sweethearts.[27] This tragic side to modernization as glimpsed in *Taki no Shiraito* not only ennobles the suffering of the heroine but also questions a social system where men abandon women to become successful, and is similar to the social protest in the 1958 British film *Room At The Top*. However, since Taki no Shiraito did not resent this situation, her sacrifice seemed necessary for modernization.

In *The Genealogy of Women* the hero evidently went on to become a success after the suffering heroine died. In *Taki no Shiraito*, however, he committed suicide. While social protest may be implied in such a denouement, his behavior is better explained as an act of atonement for the sin he had committed against the heroine. Tolstoyan remorse had already entered Japanese culture, and *Katusha*, based on *Resurrection*, was in the Shimpa repertoire and had been made into a Japanese film as early as 1914.[28] This individual sense of remorse gave greater depth to the suffering of the Weak Passive Male.

Japanese filmmakers strove to shake off their Kabuki and Shimpa tradition of tragedy by adding a Hollywood-like happy ending and music to their love stories. In the 1930s a new film genre evolved called "melodrama," which for the Japanese then seemed to literally mean "melody" plus "drama." Previously there had been mostly silent "ballad films" (*kouta eiga*) in which a song was played on the sound track while the heroine posed sadly.[29] Even some Shimpa films had a few melodies.[30] The new genre was as melodramatic in treatment as its predecessors, but included more songs besides the title one, had more complicated plots, and eventually became all-sound. The best example is Hiromasa Nomura's *The Compassionate Buddha Tree (Aizen Katsura)*, which broke the box office record in 1938.[31]

The heroine works as a nurse, a modern occupation then that gave respectable girls a chance to meet eligible mates. In this respect she differed from sheltered girls who could only have marriages arranged for them and from geisha and the like who were in an inferior status. However, the man she falls in love with is above her station, since he is a doctor and the son of the owner of the hospital. He opposes his parents and

The Compassionate Buddha Tree (1938), directed by Hiromasa Nomura. Due to the influence of Hollywood movies, these Japanese lovers (Kinuyo Tanaka and Ken Uehara) are finally united in the biggest box office draw in prewar Japan.

suggests they elope, though; but she is not able to meet him at the train station in time because of the illness of her child. (She is a widow.) Thereafter they are kept apart by quirks of fate and misunderstandings until they are united in the grand finale when she sings the title song in her debut as a popular singer.

The heroine in *The Compassionate Buddha Tree* was not very different from her predecessors in the ballad films, for when alone she often posed sadly for the camera while a song played on the sound track, and when together with the hero she modestly bowed her head and averted her glance. Her suffering was not as ennobling as that of Taki no Shiraito because it had no purpose and it was just as fortuitous as her happiness in the end. The hero's weakness and passivity was demonstrated by crosscutting shots showing him also pining away at a different place. Nevertheless, he had broken with tradition by opposing his parents, which a Shimpa hero would not do, and by suggesting elopement rather than a Kabuki-like double suicide.

The initial forcefulness of the hero could be attributed to the Sino-

Japanese War, which had begun in 1937. Like the Japanese soldiers forging ahead on the Chinese mainland, even the *nimaime* should not let anything get in his way. A more pertinent cause, however, was that the barrier between him and his love, their difference in social status, was not so strong as in the past. Modern militarism had an equalitarian side in that poor farm boys inducted into the service suddenly became soldiers of the emperor and potential war heroes. Despite the brutal pecking order within the services themselves, Japanese society in general became more democratic, as is evident by the abolition in 1938 of compulsory filing of social status—nobleman or commoner—on application forms and in hotel registers.[32] Thus, when the hero in *The Compassionate Buddha Tree* decided to elope with a woman of lower status, his action could be regarded as in tune with the times.

Still, since the hero had opposed his parents, he had to suffer for it. Most of the viewers had married in accordance with their parents' wishes and would not permit such a rebellion to go unpunished. But the film ends happily in compromise. They are standing in front of the Compassionate Buddha tree where previously they had vowed their love for each other. She says she will work hard to raise her status so as to please his parents, and he says it is not necessary because they have already approved of her. Despite the traditional motif of the Buddha tree, it is a typically American happy ending that tries to satisfy everyone, liberals and conservatives.

Shiro Kido, who was the head of Shochiku Studios that had produced *The Compassionate Buddha Tree* and other love melodramas, has written that at the time he made wholesome entertaining films that gave the people some relief from their wartime cares.[33] As such, *The Compassionate Buddha Tree* could be considered pure escapism complete with the atmosphere of a Hollywood musical. However, Japanese love stories were only allowed a happy ending on the condition that some other woman would continue to suffer in place of the heroine—that is, the woman who loses the man. While the hero of *The Compassionate Buddha Tree* was pining away for the heroine, the somewhat aggressive sister of his best friend made a play for him. When she found out he loved someone else, though, she not only gave him up but agreed to help him get together with her rival. After she "succeeded" as an admirable ally, she left on an ocean liner for the United States and was granted a close-up of her tear-stained face. Since the heroine was no longer suffering, someone had to carry on the tradition. Furthermore, by showing that aggressive women do not get the man, passive behavior is validated even more.

Stepping aside or yielding one's love to someone else is a conspicuous feature of Japanese love stories even today. While the drama of two women fighting over one man also exists in Japan, it is considered more noble to yield. A good example is *Warm Current* (*Danryu*, 1939). The heroine from a well-to-do family turns down the marriage proposal of the man she loves because she knows that her old high school classmate loves him, too. She meets him again after finding out he is going to marry the other girl, and while walking along the seashore together she hides her tears by splashing water on her face. She suffered nobly because she was unwilling to base her happiness on the misfortune of a friend. Her friend was of a much lower status, and director Kozaburo Yoshimura was considered very modern at the time, since he reversed the old pattern of the poor making sacrifices for the rich.

Such self-sacrifice was increasingly demanded as Japan went down the road toward the Pacific War. After *Warm Current* in 1939 love melodramas gradually ceased to be made, as Japanese citizens were required unselfishly to give up romantic love, as well as any other private desires, for the sake of the nation.

After the Japanese defeat in 1945 the American Occupation forces actively encouraged romantic films based on women's liberation.[34] As a result, in *A Ball at the Anjo House* (*Anjo-ke no Buto-kai*, 1947) the maid in a declining, upper-class family pursues the ne'er-do-well son, and his sister goes after their former chauffeur. Both women get their man. In the final scene director Yoshimura reversed the denouement of his *Warm Current* by having the aristocratic daughter run after her man down the beach, leaving her high heels and pearl necklace in the sand behind her.

While this democratic espousal of free love over status consideration liberated heroines from suffering, it had little effect on the passive male. In 1950 in *Escape at Dawn* (*Akatsuki no Dasso*), an antiwar film directed by Senkichi Taniguchi, the heroine pursued her Japanese soldier boyfriend across the Gobi desert during the Sino-Japanese War. Both Taniguchi and Yoshimura were probably influenced by Josef von Sternberg's *Morocco*, which had been popular in Japan ever since it was first released there in 1931.[35] The vision of Marlene Dietrich following Gary Cooper across the Sahara desert was pure wish-fulfillment for the Passive Male, whom not even the Occupation forces could exclude from Japanese love stories.

After the Occupation, Japanese directors often reverted to traditional ways. In 1953 the All-Suffering Female rejoined the Weak Passive Male in *What Is Your Name?* to set a new box office record[36] in a love melodrama which seemed like a remake of *The Compassionate Buddha Tree*. Once again young lovers are kept apart by quirks of fate and obstructing third parties, like the heroine's husband who will not give her a divorce, and their happy ending is largely engineered by a woman who stepped aside for her. There are also plenty of melodies—eight songs in all—but the music score is marred by a lot of organ music, in Japan considered high-class. It is difficult to say which heroine suffers more, since the exacting mother-in-law in *What Is Your Name?* is balanced by the ailing child that worried her prewar predecessor.

There are visual differences between the two films. The bust shots of the suffering prewar heroine are frequently replaced with full-face close-ups in the postwar film. The heroine in *What Is Your Name?* is often shown wearing hoods or head-covering shawls. It appears the director wanted to create a madonna effect (Japanese use the word "madonna" for heroines) by making her look like a saint with a halo or hood in a medieval Italian painting. (Maybe the organ music was meant to evoke a mood of Christian suffering, too.) These minor differences could be attributed to postwar Western influences on technique and content, as can the pretext for the lovers' first meeting during an air raid. In previous Japanese love stories the boy did not meet the girl completely by chance. In *The Compassionate Buddha Tree* they worked in the same place, which was considered a modern advance over old meeting places like *geisha* houses. The fact that the lovers in *What Is Your Name?* talk to each other on a bridge after the air raid even adds a modern ripple to the old bridge motif. Here two socially unrelated people meet—they do not even know each other's name—and leave behind on the opposite shores their social and familial affiliations. Their chance encounter has a transcending effect which makes them like Adam and Eve, pure from the start, and not like Chikamastsu's lovers who only became pure after they decided to die.

Yet the major difference between *What Is Your Name?* and *The Compassionate Buddha Tree* and other predecessors is that the heroine actually expected the hero to change their circumstances. She was often photographed looking up at him sadly with an unspoken appeal in her eyes. The heroine in *The Compassionate Buddha Tree* never thought the hero could change the status considerations that kept them apart, but her counterpart was not so resigned, probably because of all the changes that had occurred in postwar democratic Japan. However, true to the archetype, the Weak, Passive Male in *What Is Your Name?* ignored her appeal by looking away or telling her to accept her role as another man's wife or to wait patiently for the divorce no matter how long it took.

The change in the heroine's attitude affected the hero. He suffered not only because they were apart, like his prewar predecessor, but also from regret at not having helped her. Thus their happy ending is not fortuitous like the one in *The Compassionate Buddha Tree*, but a catharsis for both of them. Appropriately, it takes place in a hospital and it is their greatest love scene.

The heroine has just recovered from a near fatal illness and the hero is standing over her hospital bed. He gets on his knees and begs her to forgive him for all the suffering he caused her. She gazes upon him and smiles benevolently. The joy in his tear-filled eyes comes not only as a result of being united with her at last, but also because she has forgiven him for his lack of volition, his sins of omission, and his spiritual impotency. And when the All-Suffering Female forgives the Weak Passive Male, she ends the suffering for both of them.

After Part 3 of *What Is Your Name?* in 1954, love melodramas gradually

What Is Your Name? (1953), directed by Hideo Ohba. Near the concrete bridge where they first met, this passive male (Keiji Sada) tells the heroine (Keiko Kishi) to accept her fate, and she continues to suffer in the most popular film of the early 1950s.

declined in popularity in Japanese film. One reason for the decline was the rise of young, active stars like Yujiro Ishihara in the late fifties. They replaced the Passive Male as the lead in contemporary dramas because they were more appealing to young males, who eventually became the principal film-viewing audience in the sixties.[37] Romance was eventually added to Yujiro Ishihara's action films when he matured in the middle sixties, and for about five years he was like a Hollywood star who was equally adept in a fight and a love scene. However, after Ishihara became a TV producer, such romance left Japanese film until Ken Takakura's Chaste Warrior began tasting conjugal bliss in such films as *The Yellow Hand-kerchieves of Happiness* (*Kofuku no Kiiroi Hankachi*, 1977).

Another reason for the decline of love melodrama in film was that the genre simply moved over into TV, where the principal viewer is the housewife, who had been its main supporter from the very beginning.[38] As a result of the shift, however, the genre became more domestic, losing its convoluted plots, locations all over Japan, and Hollywood Musical atmosphere, since a soap opera serial only has one theme song. Consequently, although the All Suffering Female and Weak Passive Male are alive and well in present-day TV dramas, they have lost the ethereal quality they had in *What Is Your Name?*

Japanese viewers who are still interested in that ethereal quality can find it in Hollywood love stories, which are also shown on TV nowadays. They have always been popular, but particularly so since *Roman Holiday* was a big hit in 1954.[39] Many Japanese probably think that, while true love is unlikely for a diligent, hard-working people like themselves, it is very possible for the happy-go-lucky Americans, provided that they suffer a little for it.

Conclusions

Despite Western influence in the form of Tolstoy and Hollywood films, the archetypes of the All-Suffering Female and the Weak Passive Male remained, to a large extent, true to the forms they took in Kabuki "love suicide" plays. From then on Confucian priority for parent-child relations weakened male lovers and made their loved ones suffer. Suffering and passivity supported social stability by stressing obedience; however, the archetypes were not socially engineered by some ministry of propaganda. They appealed to popular sentiments, not necessarily submissive, and not only afforded psychological release from social oppression in the form of theatrical catharsis, but also presented modes of behavior for effective coping in an authoritarian society. This is their sociopsychological significance that will be examined here before taking up their transcendental side, which was heavily influenced by Buddhism.

Suffering in Japan became the virtue of endurance, which is largely a socially instilled value because it maintains the status quo. The poor put up with their lot rather than try to change things. In the Christian tradition the poor received a heavenly reward for their earthly sufferings. In Japan, however, it is believed that you will get what you want in this life if you suffer and wait—that is, endure—long enough. By suffering one not only appeals for sympathy but can also induce guilt. A perfect example is the heroine of *What Is Your Name?* By lying on a hospital bed passively suffering she induced guilt feelings in her husband, who did her wrong, and in her sweetheart, who did not do her right, and in the end she got her divorce and the man she wanted. The Weak Passive Male was no match for her since his suffering was only an appeal for sympathy, as was the case with the nihilistic hero in *Orochi.*

The heroine's behavior was modeled on that of the Japanese mother who, as George A. De Vos concluded, induces guilt feelings in her children by her "quiet suffering" and thereby gets them to do what she wants.[40] This psychology was cinematically expressed in the perennial "mother films" (haha mono), which were at the height of their popularity in the 1950s.[41]

Ian Buruma has stated that "in a sense Japanese love stories are all variations of the haha mono."[42] While his observation is valid, there is a basic difference between the genres. The mother's suffering was based on poverty and in the films of the 1950s she taunted her ungrateful children with her shabby clothes, which reminded them that they had not made her life any better.[43] In contrast to this mundane ploy, the suffering of the love melodrama heroine in a pure white hospital room was ethereal and based on unrequited love. Still, both genres were sentimental expressions of Japanese facts of life. The All-Suffering Female, mother or sweetheart, was not simply putting up with her lot but psychologically working on sons and lovers to better her circumstances and maybe change her fate.

Moral masochism also exists in the West, but it is not so ubiquitous as it is in Japan, where passivity is so highly regarded that it is expected even from males. Suffering and passivity are like two sides of the same archetypal coin, revolving on endurance that demands waiting. Passivity represents obedience, but it also has individual rewards. By waiting and being obedient a young man is usually promoted by his superiors and a marriage is eventually arranged for him with someone who may not be the girl of his dreams but is at least a suitable mate. Still, in modern Japan, where hierarchy is not as strong as in the past and the "modern" idea of finding your own mate has taken hold, the persistence of passivity in male behavior cannot be attributed solely to social reinforcement. Such ingrained behavior must start in childhood.

Ezra Vogel has observed that a Japanese mother responds to the desires of her children and tries to satisfy them almost before they are aware of them themselves.[44] Consequently, after outgrowing childish tantrums, Japanese seem to mature by learning patience and waiting passively until their desires are satisfied by later mother substitutes. By Western standards, such childrearing practices would lead to the formation of a weak ego without clearly conceived desires—one that could easily be satisfied with whatever the environment has to offer. The conflict between desires and the environment is thereby toned down in Japan, where a pliant ego could adapt more easily than in the West.

Japanese mothers, like their counterparts everywhere, are simply raising their children to be good boys and girls, but in Japan that leads to an ego that readily adapts to a situation and then feels some desire or need has been satisfied. This personality type can be called Buddhist or traditional, for it posits an unchangeable social environment and an ego that can only achieve satisfaction by adapting to it. It is just the opposite in the West where the environment is often changed to satisfy some clearly conceived desire.

In Buddhism enlightenment consists of "desirelessness," for desires are attachments that are the cause of suffering. The Japanese Buddhist personality type is by no means without desires; however, they are not so strong as they would be in the West. A Japanese may be waiting for some desire to be satisfied, but he may not be completely sure just what that desire is. Therefore, adaptability coexists with passivity.

A good example of this mode of behavior is the hero in *Warm Current*. We are led to believe he really loves the rich girl, but when she turns down his marriage proposal, he accepts it philosophically. When she then suggests he propose to her girl friend, he is noncommittal. The girl friend seeks him out, however, and he then decides to marry her since it seems to be a foregone conclusion. To Japanese he appears practical; to Westerners, almost frivolous—a man who loves wisely but not too well. But then his desire for either one of them was probably not that strong to begin with, and by adapting to the situation he had at least *some* desire satisfied. Thus, while passivity often conjoins with suffering, when it combines with adaptability it actually prevents the suffering that comes from strong desires such as those expressed in Chikamatsu's plays about lovers' suicide.

The behavior of the hero in *Warm Current* was considered normal as well as respectable by Japanese standards. However, when passivity is linked with suffering, it can lead to sexual masochism, which shows that abnormal or deviant behavior can follow the same mode as normal behavior. Masochism is very evident in Japanese literature and soft-core porno films. *Daydream (Hakujitsumu)*, a story by the literary master Junichiro Tanizaki, could easily be made into a sensational but intriguing film in 1964 by director Tetsuji Takechi.

In the film a young boy accompanies his girl friend to the dentist, and while waiting for her he daydreams that the dentist is seducing her. The most arresting scene has him standing outside the window of a modern apartment and watching helplessly while the middle-aged man binds the girl and tortures her with straps and electric shocks. Gradually she begins to enjoy it and even experiences an orgasm. Before the daydream ends the young man kills the girl but the sadist eludes him.

In *Warm Current*, and generally in the love melodrama genre, there is an equivalent to the sadist in *Daydream*. He either practices premeditated seduction or coldly calculates marriage with a woman to further his career. Compared with the Weak Passive Male, he is at least mentally active. He also has a Kabuki antecedent in the rich boor or slob who either torments the lovers or obstructs their union. Neither the Kabuki slob nor the "active male" in love melodrama ever got the heroine's love or satisfied her, though. Hence, the triumph of the sadist over the Passive Male in *Daydream* can be considered counterculture in denouement, albeit similar in modes and archetypal configuration. Whereas passive behavior is often rewarded in respectable films, in porno it is punished, which is the source of masochistic pleasure.

The masochist and the sadist can be combined in one figure, and a good illustration is *The Embryo Hunts in Secret (Taiji ga Mitsuryo Suru Toki,* 1966), a typical "pink" film—the generic label for Japanese soft-core porno films (until Nikkatsu attempted to "upgrade" them with their all-color "roman" porno beginning in 1971). Still, director Koji Wakamatsu redeems this one with compelling images. A middle-aged department-store manager takes a young, pretty employee up to his apartment, drugs her, and then tortures her. But in his dreams he imagines she is tormenting him just like all the other women in his life. In one dream he is shown in a vacuumlike room naked and curled up in the fetal position. He cries out for his mommy and the young girl appears to console him with a lullaby. Here the sadist and the masochist are rolled up in one Passive Male with a mother complex who desires to return to the womb where he would have no conscious desires to torment him.

Ian Buruma has noted "the return to the womb" message of this film (whose title he translates as "When the Foetus Goes Poaching")[45] and concludes it is indicative of "the trauma at the first discovery of female sexuality."[46] Tadao Sato, on the other hand, has likened the film to a fairy tale,[47] which suggests that in Wakamatsu's own perverse way he is trying to recapture the world of childhood innocence.

Loss of innocence is a religious motif that can appear in stories of true lovers who transcend their mundane world. The Japanese film that best illustrates this motif against a background of Confucian repression and within an ambience of Buddhist evanescence is *She Was Like a Wild Chrysanthemum* (Nogiku no Gotoki Kimi Nariki, 1955), a masterpiece by Keisuke Kinoshita that resembles Bergman's *Wild Strawberries.*

The film begins in contemporary times with an old man in a river boat. He tells the boatmen that this is the first time in sixty years he has been to his native village. In an off-screen soliloquy he tells the viewer that he has returned because all he has left before he dies is childhood memories. Everything has changed—the village kids get a thrill playing in his old farmhouse because they think it is haunted—but, in soliloquy again, he tells his dead, first, and only love that she never vanished from his heart. What follows is a flashback to his youth, which the director encases in an oval white frame to evoke the mood of old photographs.

His closest childhood friend and first love was a young girl who came to his house as a live-in maid. They are often shown together in the fields picking wildflowers and edible plants and herbs, and simply enjoying each other's company. They are like brother and sister, but eventually their intimacy arouses suspicion. The other, older maid and the boy's sister-in-law tell his widowed mother that they are no longer children and would make an unsuitable match because of status and age differences. She is

The Embryo Hunts in Secret (1966), directed by Koji Wakamatsu. In Japanese porno films heroines suffer physically as well, often at the hands of sadistic middle-aged men, who are at heart masochists resembling the Weak Passive Male in respectable love stories.

seventeen and he is fifteen. The mother reluctantly agrees with them and first has the girl temporarily sent back to her home, and then has the boy sent away to high school.

Director Kinoshita had previously shown in *The Garden of Women* (*Onna no Sono*, 1954) a callous adult society keeping young lovers apart. He visualized this by photographing them as dotlike figures at the foot of a towering feudal castle, emblematic of old-fashioned authoritarianism. In *She Was Like a Wild Chrysanthemum*, however, almost all the adults are presented as sympathetic characters—the older maid eventually repents—and it seems that village custom is the culprit. The one exception is the sister-in-law, whose sole motivation is envy of a beautiful affinity she had never experienced with her own husband.

On the morning the boy is going away to school, the girl and the older maid see him off in a light rain. There is a long take of a high-angle shot of the women with paper umbrellas watching his boat gradually disappear in the mist. He will never see her again. In his absence she will be married off and will die in childbirth. The flashback ends. The old man is shown walking across a long wooden bridge over a dry riverbed.

By juxtaposing the river of youth and the old man's bridge of dreams, director Kinoshita has evoked the images of the eternal youth and the senex which are two sides of the same archetypal coin. Middle age has been left out. The old man has not changed. He reminds Westerners of Rip Van Winkle, but he is more a manifestation of Urashima Taro, who along with Momo Taro—the child-like prototype of the Chaste Warrior—is the most popular among Japanese folk heroes.

A sea turtle took Urashima Taro to the Dragon King's underwater kingdom where he had a fabulous time playing with the Maiden of the Sea. After he returned, he opened up a box like that of Pandora and became an old man immediately.[48] He skipped middle age, too, and only experienced first love and old age. Moreover, since he was merely a recipient of fate's favors and disfavors, he is the fairy tale prototype of the Weak Passive Male, who becomes more important than the All-Suffering Female in *She Was Like a Wild Chrysanthemum*.

The film ends in a graveyard with the old man appearing dwarflike under a huge tree, full-leaved but not bearing forbidden fruit. He bows in front of her grave and the titles of the poem comparing her to a wild chrysanthemum appear on the screen. The poem is written in the *tanka* style, which recalls classical poetry bemoaning the evanescence of life.

She Was LIke a Wild Chrysanthemum is unlike Western films of nostalgia in that it is not "the way we were." Death prevented the young girl from changing and his memory of her kept him pure. It is the Japanese version of the universal tragic-young-lovers motif, though. If she had not died and they had been allowed to marry, they would have simply become a mundane middle-aged couple. Village custom and the envious sister-in-law were merely pretexts. These Japanese lovers resemble the Swedish ones in Arne Mattsson's 1951 *Summer Anguish (Hon Dansade en sommar)* where the girl also died, but the Japanese never kiss nor embrace, let alone take off their drab rural clothing for a nude love scene in a sparkling river.

She Was Like a Wild Chrynsanthemum also resembles Randal Kleiser's 1980 *Blue Lagoon,* where the Adam-and-Eve-like lovers try to remain pure by eating some fruit they think is poisoned but that simply puts them asleep until they are "rescued" by civilization. But the Japanese film is Buddhist in mood. There is no Fall or One Great Loss of Innocence. Since everything is changing because of mutability, there is, however, a continual loss that is made poignant by the constancy of memory, for, as the old man said, "you never vanished from my heart."

The dominant tone of *She Was Like a Wild Chrysanthemum* was the illusory nature of existence, against which Confucian-based family and social relations seemed less important than the constancy of the young-

She Was Like a Wild Chrysanthemum **(1955), directed by Keisuke Kinoshita. Encased in the oval white frame of old photographs, this couple (Shinji Tanaka and Noriko Arita) in drab rural clothing is the Japanese version of the universal tragic-young-lovers motif.**

old man's love. This Buddhist form of transcendentalism, existing in a state of tension with Confucian norms, resulted in the creation of a truly Japanese expression of a universal theme. However, with the decline of Buddhist sentiments and the loosening of Confucian restraints in present-day Japan, Japanese love stories have come to resemble their Western counterparts more and more. In retrospect, *The Compassionate Buddha Tree* and *What Is Your Name?* represented a transitional stage, for, although Confucian repression was much in evidence in their formation, their only Buddhist quality was passivity. Moreover, despite their Weak Passive Male, they were heavily influenced by Hollywood, and by contrast make *She Was Like a Wild Chrysanthemum* seem like the last genuinely Japanese love story.

Prodigal Son, Forgiving Parent, Self-Sacrificing Sister

Introduction

MIZOGUCHI'S internationally famous *Sansho the Bailiff* was perhaps Japan's most religious film. Based on a medieval Buddhist legend, the story concerns an eleventh-century aristocratic family in which the father dies in exile and the son is reunited with the mother through the self-sacrifice of his sister. The story is well known to many Japanese as a nursery tale they learned literally at their mother's knee.[1] Mizoguchi turned it into a myth for adults with the archetypes of the Prodigal Son, Forgiving Parent, and Self-Sacrificing Sister illustrating the universal moral problem of guilt and forgiveness in the context of suffering.

Since Japan is often regarded as a "shame culture,"[2] the archetypes designated here may appear to be more Christian than Japanese. George De Vos, though, has concluded on the basis of psychological tests that there is a relation between guilt and parental suffering and that guilt feelings can be aroused in Japanese when they fail to live up to parental expectations.[3] In Mizoguchi's *Sansho the Bailiff* the son became prodigal because he did not live up to the ideals of his noble father, and in the end he seemed to be forgiven by his mother rather than by a Buddhist deity—a denouement that made her appear sacred.

Such a sacred parent can be found in the writings of Takeo Doi, a modern Japanese psychologist. Doi is a Catholic by faith, but very Japanese in his interpretation of the Biblical parable of the Prodigal Son, for he regards the forgiver as an actual parent rather than a symbol for God the Father. For Doi, the heart of this parent, or his benevolence, is so deep it is beyond the understanding of ordinary persons.[4]

Endowed with an incomprehensible love that Western Christians would attribute only to God, Doi's "Parent" takes on a sacred aspect that is not unseemly. George De Vos has stated that in place of a concern with a transcendental deity, there is among the Japanese a respectful idealization of a father image and a feeling of loving devotion to a mother who deserves eternal gratitude.[5] Conversely, among Western Christians the concept of a transcendental deity deprived their parents of the sacred ultimacy of Doi's "Parent" and the Forgiving Mother in *Sansho the Bailiff*.

The Self-Sacrificing Sister archetype may seem at first glance to be simply a miniature version of the All-Suffering Female. In contrast to the latter's multifarious forms (as mother, wife, sweetheart, and so forth), however, the former is confined within a single family for whose sake she suffers and sacrifices herself. In *Sansho the Bailiff*, though, Mizoguchi raised her above this domestic level by equating her sacrifice with adherence to her father's noble ideals of humanism, which transcended and opposed the norms of a feudal society based on privileged classes and slavery. Still, her suffering is more familial than universal or individual. Salvation is a family matter, and the sister does more penance for her prodigal brother than he does himself. She exists more in relation to him and her mother than as an individual. While this characterization is liable to modern charges of sexism, the same can be said for the other main characters in Mizoguchi's *Sansho the Bailiff*, for they too act more like members of a Holy Family than individuals.

The archetypes of this Holy Family definitely have sociopolitical implications. Some self-sacrifice is necessary for order in any society and is demanded by a nation at war. Japanese models from period film and love melodramas are simply extreme examples. The Prodigal Son exemplifies both obedience and submission when he is shown repentant and forgiven by a benevolent parent or paternalistic ruler. Mizoguchi himself was doubtless aware of these implications because he had made several films centering on suffering, self-sacrificing women exploited by their men, and on their fathers and brothers. Yet, as a devout Buddhist in his later years,[6] Mizoguchi was probably religiously moved by the myth of the Prodigal Son he saw in the medieval legend of *Sansho the Bailiff*. The archetypes that culminated in his film had existed in some form or other since antiquity. By tracing their development in Japanese family dramas, an overview of Japanese religious history also comes into focus, for in Japan religion was usually considered in a familial context. Their problematic nature will also become evident as they support, oppose, or transcend their social order.

Metamorphoses

Japan's first Prodigal Son was Susano O, an offspring of Izanami and Izanagi, the progenitor deities of the world. Susano O refused to rule the Sea, the realm entrusted to him, because he wanted to go see his mother in the Land of the Dead, and his father expelled him. Then he went to visit his sister, Amaterasu, in the Plain of Heaven, the realm entrusted to her. She was wary of his intentions and, to allay her suspicions, he suggested that they swear oaths and bear children together. Afterwards, however, he became a troublemaker whom she put up with until he caused the death of one of her heavenly maidens. Thereupon, out of fear she shut herself up in a cave.[7] As mentioned previously, the other gods coaxed her outside and exiled her brother, who nevertheless managed to lead a happy life on earth. Susano O neither suffered much for his misdeeds nor was ever forgiven by his father.

The relations between Susano O and Amaterasu suggest Hayao Kawai's view of sibling ties as an intermediate stage between the mother-child and opposite-sex relations.[8] Accordingly, the younger sister is like a pre-heterosexual love object and the older sister like a little mother. Amaterasu first acts as Susano O's lover by bearing children with him (though devout Shintoists stress that they stood on opposite shores of a river during the transaction). Then she behaves like a doting older sister or little mother making excuses for his delinquent behavior. Her ambivalence could be attributed to the fact that, although she was born before him, there is no emphasis on birth order in their relationship. Amaterasu does not really qualify as a Self-Sacrificing Sister, though, since she is merely tormented by a brother she does not save from exile.

Japan's second Prodigal Son was the mythical warrior, Yamato Takeru, who was also her first tragic hero.[9] Like Cain, he killed his older brother, and thereafter his father, Emperor Keiko, kept sending him out on dangerous expeditions to subdue enemy tribes. Aided by his aunt, he confided in her his grief over the suspicion that his father wanted him killed in battle. During one expedition a storm arose while he was on a ship, and his wife dived into the sea to calm the turbulent waters. Her death added to his sorrow and eventually he died tragically, away from his homeland.[10] Unlike Susano O, he had suffered greatly, perhaps because he was human rather than divine.

The wife of Yamato Takeru can be considered the first Self-Sacrificing Female. She dived into the sea intentionally so that he might complete his mission, unlike Izanami, who had not meant to die giving birth to fire.

The Forgiving Parent archetype, however, is not clearly formed. His aunt was like a protective mother, but she could not forgive him. There is no record of his father's reaction to his death in the Kojiki version of the myth; however, in Nihon shoki, Japan's other ancient history completed in A.D.720, the father grieved deeply and ordered that an imperial tumulus be built where his son died so that he could be entombed there according to custom. Then the corpse of Yamato Takeru was transformed into a white bird that came out of the tomb and flew toward the Land of Yamato.[11] In the Nihon shoki version, therefore, while the father could not forgive the Prodigal Son, he at least lamented his death, and the flight of the white bird suggests that Yamato Takeru was liberated from his sufferings, though he died unforgiven.

Both Susano O and Yamato Takeru were children separated from their parents. The theme of parent-child separation became important in Buddhist legends like *Sansho the Bailiff* in the medieval period from 1186 to 1600 and continues to be popular in present-day Japan. These legends were the subjects of sermons given not only in temples but also by roadsides as Buddhist priests began taking their doctrine to the masses.[12] Since mendicant monks depended on their sermons for their livelihood, they began to make them into entertaining stories.[13] Gradually these stories were told by wandering outcasts who added their own embellishments, and this oral tradition is still carried on in contemporary times by blind women minstrels called *goze*.[14]

Tadao Sato gives one version of *Sansho the Bailiff* as a sermon (*sekkyo bushi*) first recited by medieval wandering storytellers.[15] While the mother and children are journeying to visit the exiled father, they are deceived by slave traders and the children are separated from their mother and sold to Sansho, a bailiff who manages a nobleman's estate. When they try to escape, they are caught and branded on the forehead; but when they pray to the Jizo Bodhisattva image their father had given the son, their brands are miraculously transferred to the image's forehead. Eventually, the sister Anju manages to set her brother Zushio free, but later she is caught and tortured to death. Zushio finds refuge in Buddhist temples on his way to the imperial capital, where under miraculous circumstances he is made the adopted son of a nobleman. Later, after Zushio's own aristocratic origins are discovered, he is appointed governor of the same province he had been a slave in. When he returns there and finds out about his sister's cruel death, he avenges her by having Sansho beheaded with a bamboo-saw by his own son. Later he is reunited with his mother and he miraculously heals her blindness with his Buddhist image. Thereafter, he places the image in a temple built in memory of his sister.

This tale of parent-child separation is told within a Buddhist context like many tales of the medieval period—it tells of suffering and miracles and follows the doctrine of karma or the law of cause and effect. Evil doers like Sansho are punished, and the good are protected by Bodhisattvas and eventually rewarded. However, there is no forgiveness. The sister Anju is self-sacrificing, but since Zushio is not a prodigal, he does not need to be forgiven either by his suffering mother or a Buddhist deity.

The cruel aspects of this medieval legend were omitted when it was made into the famous nursery tale, *Anju and Zushio*. When Ogai Mori, one of Japan's greatest modern writers, used it as the basis for his short story published in 1915,[16] he had Anju commit suicide rather than be tortured and had Zushio forgive Sansho after he freed the slaves. According to Takeo Iwasaki, a literary critic, Ogai Mori thereby whitewashed the medieval mentality,[17] which mainly consists of the fusion of Buddhist doctrine with the resentment of the outcast storytellers.[18]

Contact between mendicant monks and wandering outcasts resulted in the incorporation of the latter's experiences of prejudice in the sermons or legends.[19] In one version of *Sansho the Bailiff* Anju and Zushio are segregated as though they were untouchables and, after they try to escape, are refused food.[20]

Probably many outcasts were regarded as untouchables because they were descendants of the slave caste of tomb guards or others who worked in such polluting occupations. Contact with death was considered one of the greatest pollutions and those associated with it were to be avoided (*imi*), since pollution was thought to be contagious (and apparently hereditary because descendants were also shunned). Although slavery had been nominally abolished during the Heian period (794–1185), children like Anju and Zushio continued to be kidnapped and bought and sold as servants through the medieval period until the seventeenth century or so, and the descendants of slaves (*hinin*) often could earn a livelihood only through begging and as itinerant entertainers.[21]

The concern with pollution in the native religion of Shinto merged with Buddhist concepts in medieval legends. The cruel punishment meted out to Sansho was not only the karmic result of his evil deeds but also the expression of the resentment outcasts felt for the suffering they experienced. Although forgiving Bodhisattvas like Kannon, the Goddess of Mercy, were characteristic of medieval Buddhism in Japan, outcast storytellers would not let mercy interfere with the just punishment their oppressors deserved. As such, the Buddhist legend of *Sansho the Bailiff* does not entirely support the political order at that time. The fact that Zushio's aristocratic origins are discovered after he lives as a beggar for a time indicates the same kind of wish fulfillment present in *The Prince and The Pauper* fairy tale, and in both cases liberation in fiction forestalls any actual revolt. However, since Zushio escaped from his master and killed a representative of authority to avenge his sister's death, familial love is placed over submission to authority in this Buddhist legend, which in many respects reflects the living conditions of the lowest classes from ancient times until the modern era.[22]

The Forgiving Parent-Prodigal Son dyad, which had been absent from the medieval legend of *Sansho the Bailiff*, became salient in the literature of the Tokugawa period (1603–1868), as Confucianism superseded Buddhism as the principal mode of thought.[23] As a consequence, tales of piety toward Buddhas and Bodhisattvas were largely replaced with those of filial piety.

Saikaku downplayed parent-child relations in his famous erotic tales, probably because guilt-inducing parents would spoil the reader's enjoyment of amorous adventures. However, he also wrote *Twenty Breaches of Filial Piety (Honcho Niju Fuko)*, in which unfilial children are punished by Heaven, an abstract Confucian equivalent of God the Father in the West.

In fact Saikaku added realism to this genre, which had been prolific since the beginning of the Tokugawa era, by omitting the miracles that had appeared as a reward for filial behavior in older stories. In this respect, however, he was also following the trend of his times toward secularism.

Saikaku also added irony and humor in a tale like *This Borrowed Good Life (Ima no Miyako mo Yo wa Karimono)*. An exceedingly unfilial son prays to the god of long life for his father's early death so that he can inherit his wealth. When the son decides to take matters into his own hands, however, he accidentally poisons himself. The father finds him dead and laments the passing of the son he did not know was out to kill him.[24]

For Saikaku's contemporary, Chikamatsu, the parent-child relation was seldom humorous and never ironical. Even in the plays about lovers' suicide for which Chikamatsu is famous, parents play an important role, and in his family dramas he continually presents benevolent parents who forgive prodigal sons. In the case of mothers this is not so unusual, for the ideal mother was supposed to be loving and protective *(jibo)*. However, Chikamatsu's fathers often outdo their wives in benevolence, and this goes against the model father, based on samurai ideology, who should be a strict disciplinarian *(genpu)*.[25]

In Tokugawa society the father was responsible for his children's behavior. Any crimes committed by them incurred punishment not only for his own family but also for his immediate neighbors. According to the *gonin-gumi* system of social control,[26] five families were mutually responsible for the actions of any of their members. Ideally a father's duty toward society or loyalty toward his master should have overriden concern for his own children. In *Battles of Coxinga* Chikamatsu presented a samurai father who reluctantly kills his own son so that the enemy will be deceived and his lord's son will escape. However, in plays about the contemporary merchant class *(sewa mono)*, Chikamatsu unfailingly has benevolent fathers forgiving prodigal sons whom they previously disowned, despite adverse effects on his own family and neighbors.

In *The Uprooted Pine* the son is placed in the father's custody after having wounded a man in a quarrel. At first the father appears strict, but when he finds his son's position is precarious because the wounded man will not accept consolation money, he makes plans for his escape. Overwhelmed by the father's love, the son refuses for fear of the repercussions. However, the father threatens suicide and after the son agrees to escape, he says, "I forgive you all your disobedience of the past. I accept this one act as the equivalent of thirty years of dutiful service as a son."[27] In respect to this Prodigal Son, the suffering father is not only forgiving but also self-sacrificing.

The distinction in Chikamatsu's plays between samurai fathers who sacrifice their children out of loyalty or social responsibility and merchant fathers who cannot do so supports the conclusions of Takeyoshi Kawashima, a modern Japanese sociologist. Kawashima claimed that, while obedience was absolute in samurai households during the Tokugawa period, among commoners it was predicated upon the benevolence of the parents.[28] Written in 1948, Kawashima's study could be considered a refutation of Ruth Benedict's conclusion that duty to a parent (ko) was unconditional since it was an expression of gratitude (on) not contingent on benevolence.[29] However, the participants in Benedict's study were usually Japanese who had been educated in a later, militaristic age when samurai values were disseminated throughout the populace. Therefore, the views of Kawashima and Benedict do not contradict each other, and the merchant fathers in Chikamatsu's plays suggest that "samuraization"[30] was not complete during the Tokugawa period. Moreover, the Forgiving Parent archetype did not necessarily support the sociopolitical order then, since he was frequently shown helping prodigal sons to escape from the authorities.

The merchant fathers in Chikamatsu's plays are so benevolent that at times they seem sacred. Sons bow in worship before a suffering father who is often hidden from their view like an omnipresent but invisible god. In *The Uprooted Pine* the son's wife reverently lifts in her hands the earth the father walked upon and asks her husband if he heard the father's words of mercy. In *The Girl From Hakata, or Love At Sea* the unseen father pokes his hand through a paper panel (shoji) and gives his son the identification pass that the smugglers want in exchange for his freedom. The son tells his sweetheart to bow in that direction, and when she swoons and cries out for something to drink, the father's hand appears again, with a cup of water. The son says, "Could a precious wine cup, an elixir, a sacred potion from the gods be more precious than this?"[31]

Modern Japanese would probably interpret the above as exaggerated displays of respect for the father rather than reverence. However, when Chikamatsu wrote his plays, the dominant philosophy was Neo-Confucianism, which had been imported from China, of course, with the metaphysical elements that had been added to the old code of social ethics. Neo-Confucian thinkers' concern with an immanent ultimate instead of a transcendental deity can be found in these words of Toju Nakae, a contemporary of Chikamatsu's.

> When we seek to investigate origins [we find that] our body is received from our parents, our parents' bodies are received from heaven and earth, heaven and earth are received from the universe (taikyo), and therefore since basically our body is a branch and transformation of the universe and the gods (shimmei), we are clearly one with the universe and the gods.[32]

Robert N. Bellah comments: "Since one's relation to the universe is mediated through the parents, one's primary religious obligation is filial piety. It is thus that one expresses one's unity with the universe."[33] Bellah also notes that for Neo-Confucianists like Nakae—and probably for Chikamatsu to some extent—parents have the first claim on reverence, and that since other objects of religious reverence like Heaven (Ten) are mediated to the individual only through the family, they have but a reflected light.[34]

The theme of filial piety continued to be popular in the nineteenth century but lost Chikamatsu's religious ambience. Consequently, Kodan heroes who were Prodigal Sons were simply used in the service of a modernizing nation. Kodan storytellers had inherited and adpated from medieval outcasts their narrative forms, but not their resentment. Since they partriotically supported nationalism, they unconsciously made forgiveness contingent on social service rather than paternal benevolence. Two of the most popular Kodan Prodigal Sons, Yasudei Nakayama and Genzo Akagaki, went on to become period film heroes—particularly Yasudei, whose *Bloody Battle at Takadanobaba (Chikemuri Taka-danobaba)* was made into classical film adaptations by some of the genre's best prewar directors, Daisuke Ito in 1928[35] and Hiroshi Inagaki and Masahiro Makino in 1937.

Yasudei Nakayama is an unemployed master swordsman who gets spending money by playing a conciliatory role in quarrels. He is usually broke, though, since he drinks up whatever he earns. The only thing he dreads is an occasional visit from his sober uncle, who invariably admonishes him to mend his prodigal ways. The uncle is killed in a duel at Takadanobaba, and, although Yasudei arrives too late to save him, he manages to avenge him by slaying all eighteen of the assailants. The 1937 film version of this tale ends with him weeping unabashedly over the dead body of his uncle.

In another tale concerning Yasudei, he marries into the Horibe family and becomes their adopted son. Now he is admonished by his father-in-law to cut down on the drinking. Since the Horibe family was attached to Lord Asano, Yasudei becomes unemployed again with his master's death, but achieves glory by taking part in the vendetta of the loyal forty-seven against Lord Kira.

When both tales are put together, it appears that the slaying of eighteen was not sufficient atonement for the death of the fatherly uncle Yasudei caused so much suffering. He had to redeem himself for not living up to his uncle's expectations through faithful service to some lord culminating in his own *seppuku*.

Genzo Akagaki is also a hard-drinking, ne'er-do-well samurai. He is reproved by his older brother, who keeps reminding him that their dead father had wanted him to become a noble samurai. Like Yasudei, Genzo also redeems himself in the vendetta of the loyal forty-seven.

Both Yasudei and Genzo had to demonstrate that they were loyal retainers in order to expiate guilt feelings over their profligate ways. This had not been the case with Chikamatsu's prodigal sons, who were forgiven when they simply obeyed their benevolent father. The development of such *Kodan* heroes shows that by the nineteenth century the virtue of filial piety had become firmly wedded to the virtue of loyalty toward a superior. This was an important ideological step in the unification of Japan through Emperor Meiji as the ultimate object of loyalty, for Yasudei and Genzo suggested that prodigal sons could redeem themselves only by becoming loyal subjects.

Yet, since Yasudei and Genzo soon committed *seppuku* after their great deed, they had not been of much service to the state. A better role model can be found in Kin-san of Toyama, a popular character in films and TV who was modeled on old Kodan heroes. In the 1938 film *The Travels of Yaji and Kita (Yaji-Kita Dochuki)* Kin-san worries his samurai father continually with his drinking and gambling. One night he comes home drunk and when his father goes to pull the bedcovers over him, he discovers a tattoo on his back which signifies underworld connections. His father breaks into tears and after he leaves, Kin-san starts weeping too.

Kin-san is not actually a Prodigal Son, however, since his tattoo and profligate ways are only a front for his undercover investigations as a police magistrate. In the 1938 film the father dies broken-hearted without discovering his son's true identity. Kin-san continued to work for law and order, in a popular film series in the 1950s,[36] and thereafter in some TV drama series with high ratings. Most Japanese nowadays only know of him as a master sleuth and do not realize that he began his career as a pseudo-Prodigal Son who continued to serve the state because he was never forgiven by his benevolent father.

In Shimpa it was also difficult for prodigal males to be forgiven. The main theme of the earliest Shimpa mother-tragedies was the ancient one of parent-child separation,[37] but a then modern twist was added by blaming it on class differences. For example, a geisha or girl from the lower classes would bear her rich lover a child, and then suffer from having the child wrested from her to be raised by his respectable legal wife.[38] *Stella Dallas*, which was first shown in Japan in 1926,[39] found a receptive audience there long before the Barbara Stanwyck version in 1937.

As "mother films" developed from their Shimpa origins to become modern melodramas, class differences became secondary to the theme of poverty pure and simple. As stated in chapter six, suffering mothers used their tears and rags to induce guilt in unfilial sons and daughters. Although she always said she forgave them everything, they knew quite well

The Fighting Magistrate (Kenka Bugyo, 1955), directed by Yasuji Sasaki. By posing as a tattooed gambler called Kin-san of Toyama, this feudal police magistrate (Chiezo Kataoka) works undercover for law and order. Ironically, he is a pseudo–Prodigal Son because his father died thinking he really was an outlaw.

that she did not mean it. Unforgiven sons could only ease their consciences through achievement that aided modernization. And one of the major goals of modernization was the elimination of the poverty that caused so many mothers so much suffering.

Culmination

Due to the influences of Kabuki and Kodan on period film and of Shimpa on contemporary film, the archetypes of the Prodigal Son, Forgiving Parent and Self-Sacrificing Sister had existed singly or in dyads in Japanese cinema since its inception. With *Sansho the Bailiff* in 1954 Mizoguchi joined them in a perfect triad. Mizoguchi began his film career in the 1920s making Shimpa-like tragedies, and female suffering and self-sacrifice remained one of his dominant, lifelong themes.[40] In the 1950s, after five years devoted to contemporary film, he tried his hand again at period film and raised the genre to a high level of historical validity and universality, thereby achieving international recognition at successive Venice film festivals. He also reintroduced the theme of forgiveness, which had lost much of its power in the ideological services of modernization, and thereby brought back the transcendental aspect of a sacred parent.

Mizoguchi's *Sansho the Bailiff* was first planned as a film adaptation of Ogai Mori's famous short story, but Mizoguchi was dissatisfied with the first draft of a faithful script. He had his main script writer, Yoshikata Yoda, rewrite it to include realistic descriptions of the slavelike conditions on some aristocratic estates.[41] As such, the final script included the resentment from the almost forgotten medieval legend, previously treated, as well as postwar democratic ideas—oppositional elements that can exist in a state of tension with traditional social norms. Moreover, through the triad Mizoguchi expressed his lifelong themes and created an idealized Japanese family that nevertheless reflected his own poverty-ridden upbringing.[42].

The first sequence of Mizoguchi's *Sansho the Bailiff* consists of beautiful dissolves between the present journey of the mother and children through a forest and flashbacks of the circumstances that led to the father's exile. The mother dominates most frames through high-angle close-ups of her serene face in three-quarter profile and reverent pans down her long black hair and flowing aristocratic robes. She is shown continually seeing to the needs of her children and husband, and doubtless Mizoguchi was paying tribute to his own beloved mother, who had died when he was seventeen.[43] Moreover, through exquisite shot compositions, and giving the mother a greater role than she had had in the medieval legend or in Ogai's story, Mizoguchi was creating his own cinematic version of the Loving Mother.[44]

The Terrible Mother is also briefly presented. In Ogai's story the family is separated and sold into slavery through the machinations of a seaman with a reassuring Buddhist rosary. In Mizoguchi's version he is replaced by an old woman disguised as a Shinto priestess, who appears out of the night at their bonfire, her rapacious eyes gleaming. In Mizoguchi's anima, respect for and fear of women created such an exaggerated contrast in their portrayal in his films.

The mother in Mizoguchi's version also suffers more. She is not only separated from her children but forced to work as a lowly prostitute. Moreover, when she tries to escape, the tendons of her feet are cruelly cut and in the end her blindness is not miraculously cured.

In the medieval legend and in Ogai's version, the reason for the father's exile is not given. Mizoguchi has him banished as a result of his compassion for the subjects under his jurisdiction. Before he leaves he gives his son a small statue of Kannon, the Goddess of Mercy, and tells him that anyone without sympathy for his fellow beings is inhuman and that he should be willing to sacrifice himself for others.

This image of the father as a humanistic leader is probably the result of postwar democratic ideas and an aging Mizoguchi's devout Buddhism. After the father goes into exile, though, he becomes the traditional father figure who is distant and idealized.[45] The mother who is close to the son aids him in the idealization process. She has him continually recite his father's words of compassion and reminds him that the father was a noble, upright man whenever the son has doubts about the circumstances of his exile. This was part of the mother's traditional role, which also extended into the modern era when sons were urged to be successful to live up to the ideals of the father.

Opposing the noble father is the cruel one, represented by the bailiff, Sansho, who wants to make his son into his own brutal image by having him brand slaves who try to escape. Sansho's son refuses, though, since he is of a gentle disposition, and befriends the enslaved brother and sister. After he hears the words of their noble father, he decides to abandon his base father and become a Buddhist monk.

Mizoguchi's own father was neither noble nor base, but a woefully inadequate provider. His family suffered such poverty that Mizoguchi's beloved sister had to be given up for adoption and wound up in a geisha house.[46] The bitter resentment Mizoguchi felt toward his own father doubtless contributed to the depictions of mean or weak men in most of his films. However, in *Sansho the Bailiff* he needed a noble father to match the suffering mother on an archetypal level, as well as a cruel villain like Sansho to inflict suffering on the enslaved brother and sister.

The sister dominates the film's middle sequences depicting the life of the grown-up brother and sister under Sansho. From a newly arrived slave

Sansho the Bailiff (1954), directed by Kenji Mizoguchi. The noble father (Masao Shimizu), an aristocrat who cares for his subjects, imbues his son with the ideal of Buddhist compassion, of which the loving mother (Kinuyo Tanaka) continually reminds him during the father's exile.

the sister learns of a song in which their names, Anju and Zushio, are called out by a blind woman on faraway Sado Island, and realizes that this woman must be their mother. In order to admonish her brother who has become brutalized from slavery, she tells him of the song and says that she is ashamed of him because he has forgotten his father's words. Later when they are gathering branches and reeds to build a shelter in a field, she asks her brother if he remembers the time they were together with their mother in the forest before they were kidnapped. Then their mother's song is heard and her hardened brother breaks down and cries, and suggests they escape.

The sister, Anju, was obviously replacing the mother, particularly in the role of reminding him of his father. Her portrayal was certainly influenced by Mizoguchi's personal circumstances, for after his mother died his sister, by becoming the mistress of a rich patron, took care of him by continually helping him find employment.[47] The nurturing attitude of

Mizoguchi's older sister (and of Anju who, though a younger sister, acts like an older one) had been prescribed role behavior in Japanese society even in the modern era.

The nature of Anju's role is further signified by the new name Sansho's son had given her: Shinobu, which means "to endure hardships." In contrast to boys, whom Japanese parents consider *wagamama* (selfish or willful), girls are expected to be *gamanzuyoi*, which means "patient and forebearing."[48] A sister would be expected to forbear for the sake of her brother or in extreme circumstances to sacrifice herself for him, which is exactly what Anju does when Zushio suggests they escape. She tells him to go on without her, since he would have a better chance and more time if she goes back, and she gives him the small statue of Kannon he had previously discarded. After he is gone she drowns herself to prevent revealing his whereabouts under torture.

Mizoguchi's treatment of Anju's suicide is probably a sublimation of his remorse over the self-sacrifice of his own sister and results in one of the

Sansho the Bailiff (1954), directed by Kenji Mizoguchi. After being separated from the mother and enslaved, the sister (Kyoko Kagawa) replaces her by reminding the Prodigal Son (Yoshiaki Hanayagi) of his father's ideals.

most memorable images in cinema. Anju walks through bamboo trees to the edge of the pond. The stationary camera creates an illusion of depth and funneling effect as it shows her gradually submerging while framed above with delicate bamboo leaves.

Anju is not a mere sacrificial lamb, since she knows exactly what she is doing; and she has determination, because she planned the whole thing. Furthermore, there is a grand purpose to her sacrifice: to return her brother to the path of their father's humanism (which eventually leads him to free the slaves) and to reunite him with their suffering mother, who had been calling her.

The virtue of self-sacrifice that Anju represents can be interpreted as a masochistic form of submission on the political level. Freda Freiberg, a feminist film researcher, calls Anju "the self-sacrificing woman who serves the patriarchal order."[49] To be sure, the emphasis on *female* self-sacrifice ideologically helps maintain the inequality of the sexes in present-day Japanese society, even though it is rationalized through family roles. However, on the religious level self-sacrifice represents the sacred aspect of overcoming selfishness, the source of all sins. In Japanese culture Anju's suicide can be particularly moving, since there is no equivalent to Christ, who sacrificed himself for everyone throughout history. This religious side to Anju's self-immersion is amplified by Mizoguchi's direction.

Before Anju enters the pond she folds her hands in prayer and bows in the direction of the song she hears, the song from her benevolent mother calling on her to save her brother from his erring ways. An old woman who had been with her becomes a witness and bows in the direction of Anju, who has become a saint. In the context of the story her sacrifice is for her family, but through such cinematic treatment Mizoguchi creates the impression that it is for all suffering humankind. Unlike Christ, who began his mission by entering a pond to be baptized and to hear His Heavenly Father's words of recognition, Anju ends hers by drowning herself in a pond. For Mizoguchi, the Divine Dyad becomes God the Mother and God the Daughter.[50] The son/brother is merely the recipient of salvation.

After the Self-Sacrificing Sister dies, the Prodigal Son dominates the film. Zushio had become a sinner after Sansho had taken a liking to him and had had him brand disobedient slaves in the place of the son who had deserted him. Under the influence of Sansho, a cruel father, Zushio had come close to hell, but his sister had shown him the way back to the path of his noble father.

Zushio is definitely a self-portrait of Mizoguchi, for Mizoguchi probably regarded himself as a sinner in his relations with women. Although he hated his father for the suffering his mother and sister had had to endure, after he himself grew up he also made women suffer, abandoning one to prostitution and contributing to the insanity of his wife.[51] Yet, like Zushio

Sansho the Bailiff (1954), directed by Kenji Mizoguchi. Bearing water as women have done for centuries all over the world, the sister (Kyoko Kagawa) represents female self-sacrifice for the sake of the family. Under Mizoguchi's direction, however, she becomes Christ-like because of her devotion to her father's humanism.

he was totally dependent on first his mother and then his sister, and he clearly exemplifies the previously mentioned, passive mode of male behavior that can alternate between sadism and masochism.

Zushio is the passive type of hero and, because of his strong sense of dependency, he needs a lot of help to achieve his objectives. After his sister sets him free, Sansho's son gives him refuge in the temple the son serves as a monk, and then helps him reach the residence of the Prince Regent (*kanpaku*). There, his beseeching appeal comes to nought, however, and he is thrown in jail. Fortunately, when he is questioned afterwards, his small statue of the Kannon is discovered, which leads to recognition of his aristocratic origins. Thereupon, he is appointed governor of the province he had been a slave in, but his joy is mixed with sadness because he learns his father died in exile. He is given the new name of Masami, which means "justice," and, backed by the authority of the government, he has Sansho arrested and exiled and all the slaves freed.

Zushio-Masami's success or failure, like Urashima Taro's happiness, depends on the winds of fortune that toss him between despair and hope. As a hero, he exemplifies the Pure-Land Buddhist principle of *tariki* or "other power" since he needed a lot of assistance. He provides a startling contrast to the solitary Musashi who manifested the Zen principle of *jiriki* or "self-power."[52] Yet, both their tales concern initiation since both undergo trials to achieve their objectives. Musashi overcame self-doubts to defeat all his opponents. Zushio-Masami tried to expiate his guilt by freeing the slaves, an act of social significance in comparison with Musashi's egoism.

Yet, Masami's victory becomes hollow when he learns that his sister killed herself for him, since freeing her had been his main objective. Unlike the hero in the medieval legend he cannot obtain satisfaction through vengeance against Sansho, for now Zushio is a Prodigal Son who had sinned against his father's ideals. Masami apologizes to a man he had once branded on the forehead, but this is not enough to expiate his guilt. Disconsolate, he hears that the former slaves are rioting in their new-found freedom, and he decides to resign from his government post and embark for Sado Island to seek his mother.

By having Masami resign, Mizoguchi not only deviated from Ogai Mori's story but also rejected the prewar ideal of success no matter what the sacrifice, which Ogai himself represented. Mizoguchi also expressed dissatisfaction with the postwar ideal of freedom. Although the rioting exslaves are not condemned, their conduct shows that freedom does not solve all problems and is not an ultimate goal. Relief from suffering is—at least for Mizoguchi in his Buddhistic twilight years—and it could only be obtained through forgiveness, not through achievement, as was the previous case during modernization. When Mizoguchi sends Zushio to Sado

Island to save his mother from further suffering, he winds up recreating the most moving Forgiving Parent archetype since Chikamatsu.

After Zushio gives his mother the Kannon statue, she recognizes him and asks about his sister, and then his father. His silence tells her they are both dead. He asks her to forgive him. She says, "There is nothing to forgive. By coming here to find me and keeping the statue your father gave you I know that you have followed his words." They embrace and the camera pans away from the emotional scene to the seashore, and the film ends.

Reunion between parent and child after long separation has always been an emotionally charged scene in Japanese drama and film, and Mizoguchi exercised proper artistic restraint with medium long shots and silent pauses in the sound track. Keiko McDonald has considered Mizoguchi's treatment of this scene to be imbued with *mujo kan*,[53] a view of the fleetingness of all things that suggests detachment. Tadao Sato, on the other hand, considering the high camera angle and the traditional musical background, has likened it to a Bunraku performance,[54] as audiences

Sansho the Bailiff (1954), directed by Kenji Mizoguchi. On an isolated island, the Prodigal Son (Yoshiaki Hanayagi) begs his blind mother (Kinuyo Tanaka) to forgive him.

could watch the emotional displays of puppets without feeling embarrassed. Still, the viewer loses detachment when shown a close-up of the blind mother touching the Kannon statue, for closed eyes are a characteristic of Buddhist images. The mother herself becomes Kannon, the Goddess of Mercy, suffering and forgiving.

When the mother says that there is nothing to forgive, the son may wonder if he has been forgiven after all, and the critical viewer may think this is merely an artistic version of "mother films," where the mother made forgiveness doubtful by "forgiving" good and bad children indiscriminately. As Ian Buruma pointed out, they were "all equally sweet."[55] The mother in *Sansho the Bailiff*, however, acknowleged that by keeping the statue Zushio at least strived toward the good, even though like all human beings he was too weak to effect it totally. For Kannon, forgiveness is simply a recognition of suffering, particularly of those who try to be good.

Conclusion

Self-Sacrifice for the ideals of a noble father is moving, but society usually supplies a noble reason when such behavior is demanded from its members. Forgiveness of unrepentant males only supports their tyranny over women, and manipulated guilt only demonstrates the power of the mother, whose sentimental portrayal in drama and film simply masks the power the state has over anyone who feels guilty about anything. Nevertheless, when guilt is firmly wedded to altruistic forgiveness, as was the case in *Sansho the Bailiff*, they become problematic. The son feels guilt for not living up to ideals that transcend his particular society—and are never fully realized in any society—and thereby can only be forgiven by a transcending agent like the sacred parent, who of course has no ulterior motives for herself or society.

Mizoguchi arrived at this juncture because he was both devoutly Buddhist and firmly against the feudalistic survivals in his culture. Very few contemporary Japanese would be capable of this, since Japanese Buddhism is mainly conservative, as is institutional religion in general, and antifeudalism usually includes the view of religion as superstition. Mizoguchi was also influenced by a Neo-Confucian tradition popularized in the plays of Chikamatsu—which, though generally used in support of the state, could still place parental love above its dictates.

8

The Archetypal Family—Extended and Rejected

Introduction

MENCIUS stated that benevolence consisted of loving one's parents and that this familial virtue should be extended to the government of the realm.[1] A good ruler had to be a filial son who became a servant of the people. In most cases in China and Japan, however, rulers preferred to think of themselves as benevolent parents to their people rather than as their servant, for obvious reasons.

Japanese rulers were compared to benevolent parents by Motoori Norinaga, an important thinker in the eighteenth century. He added a Japanese twist to Mencius' idea of extension by stating that the gods in the Shinto pantheon were the parents of the Japanese people and that utmost trust in Amaterasu, the main goddess, was the same as absolute loyalty to the Emperor as her Son.[2] Filial piety (ko) became the same as loyalty (chu), and any revolt against the state was simply considered delinquent behavior.

Norinaga's idea was rejected to a large extent on account of the defeat in World War II. Thereafter, loyalty toward leaders was regarded with some scepticism, particularly among intellectuals.[3] Furthermore, when Emperor Hirohito renounced his divinity, for most Japanese (Mizoguchi and Doi excluded, of course) parents lost whatever sacred aspect they may have had. In the postwar era several films depicted villainous leaders and fathers. Most of them were made by leftist directors who regarded the paternalism of a benevolent leader to be a camouflage for political realities that included exploitation of the ruled. The antitheses they created were purely oppositional forms without a trace of transcendentalism. Other directors, more liberal than leftist, engaged in role reversal by presenting children who were much more intelligent and mature than their parents. Finally, somewhat nihilistic directors in the 1970s showed the desolate alienation the Prodigal Son experiences because of the loss of the Forgiving Parent archetype.

Politics

The triad of the Japanese "Holy Family" had political implications even before Norinaga. In the modern era the most conspicuous political representation of the Forgiving Parent archetype took the form of the suffering military leader who grieved over the fate of the nation. The first example is General Maresuke Nogi (1849–1912), the hero of the Russo-Japanese War, who also became the first star of Japanese cinema through the newsreels of 1904 and 1905.[4] Since General Nogi committed *seppuku* on the day of Emperor Meiji's funeral,[5] he had been generally considered a paragon of the Loyal Retainer. Soon after the Manchurian Incident in 1931, he was also presented as a benevolent leader with compassion for the common people in a series of films lasting until 1937.[6]

In one entry he encounters an old couple who lost their son in the Russo-Japanese War. Unaware of his identity, they complain that General Nogi is to blame for their son's death. After his identity is revealed he reminds them that he himself lost two sons in the war and then gives them money to help them out of their economic difficulties. In another entry he helps a veteran who becomes a poor tenant farmer to escape the clutches of a wicked landowner. From these two entries it is obvious that as a film hero General Nogi provided an excellent propaganda figure for rightist militarists who claimed they were trying to save the nation from evil capitalists and greedy landowners.

Films eulogizing General Nogi were also made in the postwar era. The most recent one, *Hill Number 203 (Nihyaku-san kochi, 1980)* concerns the Russo-Japanese War itself and shows that his prewar image has not changed. An officer on horseback gives a marching soldier a cigarette. The soldier complains to him of the leadership in the present campaign, but stops short when he realizes the officer is General Nogi himself. He begins to apologize profusely, but General Nogi simply smiles sadly and rides away. The film ends with General Nogi reading the victory report to Emperor Meiji himself, and eventually convulsing into sobs when he comes to the horrendous casualty list of Hill Number 203—they were all his sons! Stoically holding back his own tears, Emperor Meiji comes down off his throne to pat General Nogi on the shoulder and console him.

Generals like Nogi were not the main benevolent father figures in Japanese war movies made from 1937 (the start of the Sino-Japanese War) to 1945. They were replaced by warm-hearted platoon and company commanders who were physically closer to their men than distant generals. An excellent example is Tomotaka Tasaka's *Five Scouts (Gonin no Sekkohei, 1938)*, which takes place on the China front. One of the scouts gets separated from his platoon in action, and when he returns from no man's land, his buddies greet him warmly, beaming smiles through their tears

Hill Number 203 (1980), directed by Toshio Masuda. Like a benevolent father, General Nogi (Tatsuya Nakadai) sobs convulsively while reading the casualty list for the Battle of Hill Number 203 during the Russo-Japanese War. Emperor Meiji (Toshiro Mifune) comes down from his throne to console him.

and tenderly helping him take off his pack and canteen belt. He reports to his squad leader, who is like their mother, and then to the fatherly platoon leader who tells him he is happy he has returned. Tears of joy come to the returnee's eyes, for he is like the Prodigal Son who has come back to the warmth of the family and has eased the heart of the platoon leader, who had worried about his absence. The suffering of the platoon leader is shown whenever he has to report a casualty or death in the daily record, since he feels fatherly responsibility for all of them.

Given such benevolent leaders, it is not so surprising that revolutionaries appear to be Prodigal Sons. In *Song of the Advancing Army* (*Shingun no Uta*, 1937) a leftist union leader is released from jail because he has been conscripted, and, touched by the warm sendoff the police give him, he fights bravely for the fatherland on the China front. In commenting on this film Tadao Sato contrasts Nazi Germany, where socialists were gotten rid of, with paternalistic Japan, where they were forgiven if they recanted.[7]

In some films like *The War at Sea from Hawaii to Malaya* (1942), the squad leaders were more like stern older brothers than kind father figures. However, as they showed their concern for their subordinates by alternating kindness with discipline, they were more like some *samurai* father types—hard on the outside and soft on the inside—and therefore not too far removed from Chikamatsu's benevolent merchant fathers.

Before 1945 Japanese emperors could not become benevolent leaders in film due to strict censorship concerning any matters relating to the royal family, past and present.[8] Even in World War II films made in the 1980s, when an appearance by the present emperor is called for, he is usually photographed from the back or at a respectable distance. Consequently, only Emperor Meiji could become a suitable film hero, beginning with the biggest box office hit in 1957, *The Emperor Meiji and the Great Russo-Japanese War (Meiji Tenno to Nichi-Ro Daisenso).*[9] During the war the emperor continually wears a military uniform and insists on eating the same kind of food his soldiers at the front have. He grieves to see wives and children seeing their men off to war and he reads the casualty list every day, like the benevolent platoon leaders in the films of the 1930s and

Five Scouts (1938), directed by Tomotaka Tasaka. This scout returning to his platoon during the Sino-Japanese War is like the Prodigal Son who has come back to the warmth of his family.

The Emperor Meiji and the Great Russo-Japanese War (1957), directed by Kunio Watanabe. Usually shown in uniform, Emperor Meiji (Kanjuro Arashi) tries to upstage General Nogi in compassionate concern for the troops at the front.

1940s. While General Nogi had played the same role for decades, it was probably particularly moving to see an emperor do so.

Beside Emperor Meiji, the most popular Japanese military leader in films after 1950 is Admiral Isoroku Yamamoto, the man who planned the attack on Pearl Harbor.[10] Toshiro Mifune played him in the American production of *Midway* in 1976, and he was the subject of a twelve-hour Japanese TV drama shown on 2 January 1983. Yamamoto strikes a responsive chord among Japanese concerning the war that caused them so much suffering, and that he had opposed from the beginning. According to the TV drama, his opposition was based on his pro-American sentiments and the cool appraisal of America's production capacity he had made while an exchange student there. Moreover, since he was killed in action in 1943, his image never suffered as a result of the war trials during the American Occupation era (1945–50).

The first film about Yamamoto, *Eagle of the Pacific* (*Taiheiyo no Washi,* 1953), begins with fascist groups out to assassinate him because he opposes an alliance with Germany and Italy. Before the outbreak of the

Pacific War he tells the prime minister he can only be a match for America for about a year and that he should continue to try to effect an early peace treaty. He refuses to rejoice over Pearl Harbor, and he cries in private over the defeat at Midway. It seems he feels he has let the emperor down, but later it becomes plain that he is grieving over the fate of the Japanese people, since, according to postwar ideology, the emperor is only their symbol.

After Midway he is often shown seeing off young pilots on dangerous missions, dressed in his white uniform and with his hand raised to his forehead in a seemingly endless salute. Although Yamamoto died before the full-scale kamikaze attacks began, missions in 1943 were already becoming suicidal because of America's overwhelming air superiority and Japan's woeful lack of fuel. Consequently, very few of these young pilots returned. During their childhood and youth they had been the recipients of the self-sacrifices of their mothers and sisters, and now it was their turn. Although the situation was already hopeless, Yamamoto would be shown sitting on a tropical porch waiting patiently late into the night for their return. He was simply playing his role: the benevolent father with no Prodigal Sons to forgive, waiting for the return of anybody. A democratic touch was added to the image when he shook hands with young pilots in a long row just before he went on his own last flight. This democratic, Suffering Father image would be continually repeated in Japanese films about the Pacific War, with other naval officers taking over Yamamoto's role and seeing off squadrons of *kamikaze* pilots.

Not all World War II military leaders qualified as benevolent commanders in Japanese film. Premier Tojo is sometimes given sympathetic treatment, particularly in *Imperial Japan* (*Dai Nippon Teikoku*, 1982), by Toshio Masuda, who also directed *Hill Number 203*; however, Tojo is still difficult to warm up to. Masuda presents him as a fine father to his own children and a devout Buddhist who usually has a rosary in his hands while he is waiting in Sugamo prison for his trial. Yet, in one scene where a civilian official expresses apprehension over the B-29 bombings that will eventually turn Tokyo into a burnt-out field, Tojo merely replies that if all the people are as loyal as he, Japan will win the war. As Loyal Retainer, Tojo suffers because he has grieved the emperor, not because so many people have died, for they are simply like grains of sand in a nirvanalike desert.

With the production of antiwar Japanese films after 1945, it was inevitable that the other side of the archetypal coin of the benevolent commander would be presented in the figure of cruel, unfeeling officers and noncoms. Two directors who excelled in this, Hideo Sekigawa and Satsuo Yamamoto, had been young leftists during the thirties[11] and seemed to be getting even for having been forced to play the Prodigal Son then.

In *Listen to the Roar of the Ocean* (*Kike! Wadatsumi no Koe*, 1950)

Eagle of the Pacific (1953), directed by Ishiro Honda. Shown here with an ace pilot (Toshiro Mifune) aboard an aircraft carrier during the Battle of Midway, Admiral Isoroku Yamamoto (Denjiro Okochi) is usually presented as a benevolent commander who democratically shook hands with his pilots before a mission.

Sekigawa begins with scenes where fat officers, who hoard food, are being massaged by starving, emaciated enlisted men. One of these enlisted men is literally treated like a dog when he is forced to crawl as a retriever for an officer hunting pheasant, who later shoots another in the back for sport. At the end of the film the spirits of the soldiers who died of starvation rise from their bodies and slowly march toward the viewer in silent protest. Since they had never revolted against their superiors, they had been like Self-Sacrificing Sisters, and now in death Sekigawa forces them to play the role of the All-Suffering Female who tries to induce guilt feelings through moral masochism. Hence, in spite of Sekigawa's leftist views, he is unable to free himself from the traditional archetypal patterns.

Although *Listen to the Roar of the Ocean* was actually based on the diaries of soldiers,[12] Sekigawa's portrayal seldom rose above caricature. In contrast, Satsuo Yamamoto in *Vacuum Zone* (*Shinku Chitai*, 1952) gave a realistic treatment of recruit harassment and showed that the "love slaps" *(ai no buchi)* administered by noncoms were simply the result of their sadistic inclinations rather than any desire to improve their charges spiritually. In one scene Yamamoto conjured up a cruel parody of the Prodigal Son motif by having one recruit crawl like a dog to beg forgiveness for a trivial oversight.

Since the benevolent commander had simply been an extension of the Forgiving Parent archetype, the debunking of the former could easily lead to the rejection of the latter. This was particularly so in the case of the Japanese father, for he not only represented the social order for his children, as is the case in any culture, but he also had been elevated to the status of "emperor" of his own family in militaristic Japan.[13] Thus, when Miyoji Ieki presented in *Stepbrothers* (*Ibo Kyodai*, 1957) a tyrannical father who was also a military officer, he was in effect killing two birds with one stone. Still, since Ieki's film was set in the wartime era, it lacked contemporary relevance. The challenge of presenting a cruel, unfeeling father who represents an exploiting, contemporary society was better met by Satsuo Yamamoto, again, particularly in *A Public Benefactor* (*Kizudarake no Sanga*, 1964).

The father in *A Public Benefactor* is an entrepreneur who uses underhanded business tactics and bribes government officials to achieve objectives he rationalizes as being in the public interest. He exploits not only workers but his own daughters, whom he marries off for financial advantage. He has a few mistresses, of course, and his neglected wife has become bedridden. His second son has had a history of mental breakdowns and relapses.

Yamamoto's film climaxes when the second son rebels and sets fire to the new school his hypocritical father had built. When the father visits him in jail, he tells him *he* is the insane one. The mother criticizes the father for his lack of paternal concern, but when she goes to visit the son now in a mental hospital, he refuses to see her.

Yamamoto's message is that such an entrepreneur is not only exploiting the Japanese people but also tormenting his own family, and that it is the nature of a capitalistic society to produce such men. Yamamoto also reversed the archetypal setup by having a good son suffer on account of a prodigal father.

Such unfeeling fathers are more thematically connected to the Japanese government itself by Nagisa Oshima in *Boy* (*Shonen*, 1969). Here the father, who is often associated visually with the national flag, has his son run close to moving cars and fake a fall in order to extort money from motorists. The fact that his son continually sustains injuries from this does not faze him in the least. As a World War II veteran who claims old wounds prevent him from working, he represents the cold, calculating political leaders who sacrificed the people then and who continue to oppress movements toward individual freedom.

A Public Benefactor (1964), directed by Satsuo Yamamoto. The sham of compassionate leaders is exposed in this portrayal of a ruthless entrepreneur (So Yamamura). Shown here chewing out a subordinate, he exploits the Japanese people and torments his own family. The Buddhist statue in his office seems ironic, but he probably purchased it as a good investment in a "priceless" art object.

The government and big business were practically linked as one in Akira Kurosawa's exposé of graft and corruption in Japan Inc. in *The Bad Sleep Well (Warui Yatsu Hodo Yoku Nemuru,* 1960), and the father became the crux of the matter. A ruthless business executive has those who could cause scandals murdered or driven to suicide. His son knows about his secrets, but when he watches his father tenderly attending his lame sister at a patio barbecue, he tells his brother-in-law that at times he cannot believe his father is an evil man. It turns out that the brother-in-law is out to expose the father to avenge the death of his own father. When the business executive learns of this, he tricks his daughter into revealing her husband's hide-out and then has him murdered. The daughter goes insane and her brother takes her away after blaming the father, who had tried to dissuade him but had been interrupted by a phone call from his superior, which had priority.

The theme of a father sacrificing his children for his superior is not new in Japan. Chikamatsu, in his plays about samurai, would place the hero in such a predicament and then have him express his internal anguish with poignant phrases and moving facial expressions. Kurosawa perhaps tried to allude to such a performance in the scene where the father is looking at himself guiltily in a mirror after he drugged his daughter to prevent her from accompanying him to her husband's hide-out. Suddenly her reflection appears behind him, just before he goes off to murder her beloved husband. However, in the last scene, where he is talking to his superior on the phone after the great sacrifice, he is as cool as ice.

Kurosawa's evil father here differs from Chikamatsu's tragic samurai fathers in that his action stemmed from his own volition, but theirs from fate. Whereas, they are truly like puppets, he is a man who by choice became a robot, mechanically bowing as he hears on the phone his masters' voices extending up the hierarchy of the business and government circles of Japan Inc. For Kurosawa, such a father could not be forgiven.

Reversal of Roles

The presentation of fathers who were the opposite of benevolent coincided with role reversal in some films where children forgive their parents. The necessary prerequisite for this, the dethronement of parents, however, had begun long before the defeat in World War II and was the result of the influx of modern or Western ideas and of increasingly better educated generations.[14]

In prewar literature writers under the influence of liberal ideas took up the theme of youthful revolt against authoritarian fathers.[15] However, *Shimpa*, the most popular drama form in the early 1920s, was more conservative. In its plays (for example, the previously treated *The Genealogy of Women*) such father figures were still presented as sympathetic, albeit behind the times, and were affectionately labeled *ganko oyaji* or "the stubborn old man." Whereas in period film father figures were modeled on Chikamatsu's benevolent merchant types or his stern-on-the-outside samurai ones, in contemporary film *ganko oyaji* dominated until the appearance of "democratic" fathers.

American films exerted a strong influence on young Japanese film makers and one notable example is Yasujiro Ozu,[16] who went on to become one of Japan's greatest directors. Ozu in 1931 with *Tokyo Chorus (Tokyo no Gassho)* presented a young office worker who as a father was no different at all from his American film counterparts, for he never displayed the slightest sign of sternness or lofty benevolence and simply played games with his kids. In 1932 with the masterpiece *I Was Born But . . .*

Tokyo Chorus (1931), directed by Yasujiro Ozu. A young office worker (Tokihiko Okada) and his wife (Emiko Yagumo) play games with their children (Hideko Takamine and Hideo Sugawara), and a new "democratic" model for Japanese fathers is formed.

(Umarete wa Mita Keredo) Ozu sets the father up as an authoritarian figure only to have him exposed as an office sycophant who has to win back his kids' favor by coming down to their level and making friends with them.

Ozu's "democratic" fathers did not actually replace or supersede the traditional types in contemporary film. Ozu himself recreated a benevolent Chikamatsu type with samurai qualities in *There Was a Father* (*Chichi Ariki*, 1942). However, with the exception of the Second World War years, the American-style father Ozu created existed side by side with the *ganko oyaji* type in films through the 1950s.

Ozu's democratic fathers were at least on the same level as their children. Some Japanese parents were not, due to the higher education their offspring received in modern schools, and this new relationship became the subject of films as early as the 1930s. In Minoru Shibuya's *Mother and Child* (*Haha to Ko*, 1938) an intelligent, steadfast daughter takes care of her superstitious, foolhardy mother until the mother dies neglected by her son and husband. Mikio Naruse recreated the same setup in his masterpiece,

Lightning (*Inazuma*, 1952), which ends with the prudent daughter sacrificing her life savings to help her ne'er-do-well mother out of financial difficulties.

From these kindhearted daughters taking care of their foolish mothers to children forgiving parents for their misdeeds and sins of omission only required one more step. Kurosawa was among the first to take it in *Scandal* (*Skyandaru*, 1950), an uneven film with a saving portrayal of a Prodigal Father.

The father in *Scandal* is a lawyer representing a young couple in their suit against a magazine that printed a false, scandalous article about them. In order to buy nice things for his bedridden daughter, though, he takes a bribe from the magazine to throw the case. That night he returns home drunk and places the presents at her bedside, begins crying, confesses that he is a bad man, and makes excuses for himself. The daughter, as though she has been through this scene many times before, pats his bowed head like a consoling mother. After she dies of tuberculosis, he atones for his sins by revealing the bribe in the courtroom.

Lightning (1952), directed by Mikio Naruse. This bright, prudent daughter (Hideko Takamine) has to help her ne'er-do-well mother (Kumeko Urabe) out of financial difficulties and hence reverses the traditional roles of parent and child.

In a scene which is a precursor to the one in *The Bad Sleep Well* where the father guiltily sees his daughter's reflection in the mirror, the father in *Scandal* looks in on a Christmas party his daughter is enjoying with his clients and her face is superimposed upon his in the window. He runs out of the house to get drunk, but the guilt felt then will lead him to take the opposite course to that of the father in *The Bad Sleep Well*. Donald Richie has appropriately commented on the maudlin treatment of this scene.[17] However, it is still moving, for, by placing a tin crown on the head of the invalid daughter, Kurosawa evoked the image of Christ the Child-King, a symbol of innocence and suffering, as well as a source of forgiveness.

In *Her Brother* (*Ototo*, 1960) director Kon Ichikawa clearly attributes a youth's delinquent activities to neglect by his parents rather than to his own perversity, which would be a traditional interpretation *(hinekureta ko)*. On his deathbed he plays the role of the Prodigal Son and asks them to forgive him; however, by nobly not holding anything against them, he induces guilt. For the first time they show him the love he needed but got only from his devoted sister. In effect he has reversed their roles by

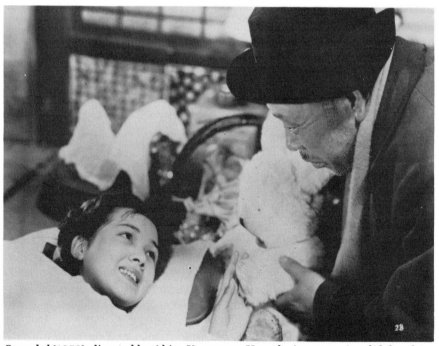

Scandal (1950), directed by Akira Kurosawa. Here the innocent, invalid daughter (Yoko Katsuragi) forgives her Prodigal Father (Takashi Shimura), a shyster lawyer who eventually atones for his sins.

forgiving them and only the role of the Self-Sacrificing Sister has remained constant.

Loss of Forgiving Parent Archetype

As parents were being dethroned through modernization, they were also losing their sacred aspect. Mizoguchi's *Sansho the Bailiff* was probably the last religious expression of the Forgiving Parent archetype in film. Four years later in the film version of Chikamatsu's *The Woman Killer and the Hell of Oil* (*Onnagoroshi Abura Jigoku*, 1958) the parents, under the direction of Hiromichi Horikawa, appeared doting rather than benevolent. (They drew chuckles from the Japanese audience I viewed the film with in 1983, and the same was probably the case in 1958.)

The demythologization of parents had different consequences for their portrayal in the cinema than on TV, which became the principal medium of family drama from the 1960s on. The TV father was usually a replica of the upper-middle-class fathers in Ozu's postwar films: understanding rather than benevolent, more accepting than forgiving.[18] In fact, he seemed to be a cross between Ozu's democratic types and Chikamatsu's feudal benevolent ones. The TV mother usually suffered only in dramas set in previous historical periods from the Occupation Days on back. In modern dramas she became increasingly cheerful and sported expensive wardrobes emblematic of Japan's economic recovery.[19]

On the other hand, in the cinema of the 1960s, dominated by young, New Wave directors,[20] poor parents often seemed ignorant and rich parents frequently appeared to be philistines. In either case, they were so easy to rebel against that they were a distant second to the main target of youthful frustration, the establishment or adult society in general. In the early 1970s, however, particularly in the films of Toshiya Fujita, the most popular director then, sentiments toward parents turned from rebellious to bitter, from sympathetic to cynical.

Parents do not play a major role in Fujita's films. His youthful characters seem to be orphans whose alienation from society makes them even more dependent on a few close friends. When parents do appear in his films, however, they never make a favorable impression. In *Virgin Blues* (*Baajin Buruusu*, 1974) two teenage girls are wanted for shoplifting. When one returns home, she finds a store detective there and tries to escape. Her own mother joins in the chase and, when they catch up with her, she spits in her mother's face. The other girl knew better and sent her middle-aged boyfriend to her home to inquire first. When he comes back and tells her the police have already contacted her mother, she realizes she has no home to go back to.

In *Did the Red Bird Escape?* (*Akai Tori Nigeta?*, 1973) a rich girl gets involved with two young hoodlums and they decide to extort money from her father by pretending to kidnap her. When the confrontation takes place, however, the father out of consideration for his reputation refuses to recognize her as his daughter, and she dies with her boy friends in a suicidal shoot-out with the police.

In these films Fujita presents the antitheses of Chikamatsu's benevolent parents, who would never begrudge ransom money for their beloved children, nor turn them in to unsympathetic authorities. Fujita's youths are prodigal sons and daughters with no parents to forgive them. Their loneliness can be partially attributed to estrangement from their parents, which is the modern form of the old theme of parent-child separation and one cause of their suicidal nihilism.

Fujita does not consider the religious significance of the loss of the Forgiving Parent or the problem of autonomy, which becomes particularly significant in the films of the later 1970s. The best treatment of these problems can be found in the analysis of postwar Japanese literature by Jun Eto, a literary critic who gives special attention to Shotaro Yasuoka's 1959 novel, *Scene by the Sea (Umibe no Kokei).*[21]

The hero of the novel has a very possessive mother and finally rebels against her. Once her existence is attacked, it disintegrates and he is freed from her and becomes an individual for the first time. However, since his mother was his second self, a deep part of him is gone, too, leaving him with a sense of emptiness.

The hero's struggle for autonomy against his mother seems perfectly natural and commonplace for Westerners. However, for Japanese living in a culture that had stressed dependency[22] and a pliant ego whose mode of behavior was passive, his action is revolutionary in the sense of a tumultuous upheaval. It took the defeat in World War II to make such an action acceptable, for afterwards Japanese intellectuals decided that one of the reasons for the rise of militarism had been the weakness of Japanese in asserting themselves as individuals and their tendency to go along with the crowd.[23] In other words, the old passive and submissive personality was to blame and now strong, self-assertive egos were advocated.

The hero in *Scene by the Sea* had simply responded to the call of his times, but the loss he felt demonstrated that it is not so easy to switch from passive to active modes overnight. Later he seeks the lost mother in his wife, but is disillusioned when she has an affair with another man, which reveals she is an ordinary woman after all.

When the hero's expectations of his wife are thus amplified, *Scene by the Sea* goes from a psychological level to a religious one: "He wanted the mother inside his wife to forgive the great sin he seemed to have committed even before the existence of his parents and was punished for even before his consciousness came into being. But when he became free he lost hope and had to face the guilt within himself. For him freedom boiled down to fear, and so it was not really freedom. . . . 'We've become free, but we're all strangers.' "[24]

For some Japanese intellectuals like Eto and Yasuoka, loss of the Forgiving Parent archetype becomes culturally equivalent to the Death of God in the West, and existentialism becomes one of the few religious recourses. Shuji Terayama, an avant-garde poet turned playwright and filmmaker, tried to resolve his mother complex in existential terms and started a vogue for films featuring matricide and patricide. In *Pastoral Hide and Seek* (*Den'en ni Shisu*, 1974) Terayama's hero ponders the problem of whether he would exist if his parents had died before he was conceived. He then takes a time-machine-like journey back into his own past with the intention of killing his mother. When he enters his house and she asks him if he is hungry, however, he realizes he cannot kill her and the film ends with her serving him soup and rice. Terayama not only concluded that matricide is out of the question but also suggested that true autonomy cannot be obtained.

In Kazuhiko Hasegawa's *Young Murderer* (*Seishun no Satsujinsha*, 1976) the young hero unintentionally kills his father in an argument about his girl friend. His mother tries to cover up the crime and even embraces him suggestively, but he rejects her. Later when she tries to kill him, he goes berserk and winds up stabbing her to death. Despite the gruesome killings and oedipal associations, the young man seems more pathetic than terrifying. On a beach he has a poignant memory of childhood and sees his father pushing an ice-candy cart and carrying him on his shoulders, with his mother trailing behind in the shade of her sun umbrella. It seems he has lost his parents rather than killed them, and the film ends with him alone and homeless in the back of a truck. He had confessed his crime to some policemen, but they had only laughed at his preposterous story. In an anonymous, modern society the Prodigal Son cannot even find recognition, let alone forgiveness, and autonomy is simply equated with loneliness.

In *Revenge is for Us* (*Fukushu Suru wa Ware ni Ari*, 1979, released in the United States as *Vengeance is Mine*) Shohei Imamura probed deeper into the problem of patricide which Hasegawa, his former protégé,[25] had raised but not resolved. After the son in Imamura's film returns home from prison he suspects that his father has had sexual intercourse with his wife and an argument ensues. Out in their yard the father picks up a sledgehammer, hands it to his son, and tells him to kill him if he does not believe him. In the Chikamatsu tradition of the Benevolent Parent he was trying to instill guilt by adopting a self-sacrificing stance. But it did not work and the son would have bashed his brains out if the daughter-in-law had not intervened. The son leaves home and thereafter commits a series of murders in which the victim is usually an old or middle-aged man, that is, a father substitute.

The last confrontation between father and son occurs during a prison visit. The son tells the father that it would have been better if he had killed *him* instead. The father spits in his face and asks if he really could have

Young Murderer (1976), directed by Kazuhiko Hasegawa. After killing the father, the son (Yutaka Mizutani) gazes at his own reflection, while his mother (Etsuko Ichihara) looks on in horror. Even though he will kill her too, he seems more like a lost boy beyond forgiveness than a murderer.

killed his own father. The son's fierce look leaves no doubt. He tells his father he does not expect to be forgiven, nor will he ever forgive him. Since childhood he had always borne his father a grudge for having recanted his Catholic faith in front of some bullying military officers during World War II. The "revenge" of the film's title was actually directed against the father, and autonomy had nothing to do with it.

Revenge is for Us ends with the father going up a lighthouse and trying to toss the son's cremated remains into the sea. By a freeze action shot of the son's bones, Imamura indicates that, just as reconciliation was unobtainable, pacification of the son's vengeful spirit could not be effected.

In the 1983 Cannes prizewinner, *The Ballad of Narayama* (*Narayama bushi-ko*) Imamura had the son commit matricide by abandoning his mother on a mountain in conformance with the custom of his marginal-existence village, where the aged are left to die so that there will be enough food for the young. Since his self-sacrificing mother had ordered him to do so, however, he could be considered filial rather than prodigal. Still, when he returned home after leaving her in the snow amid huge black crows and bleached bones and skulls, he must have felt some guilt. His wife, though, greeted him with an amiable smile and gave him some hot gruel. Imamura's camera followed his gaze from the family crest on his wife's waist-sash (obi) to his brother's pregnant wife in order to show that the women actually rule the family as they are closer to the life cycle. They warmly envelop him like the cycle they represent. He cannot escape from it, for it is as necessary as the food his wife is serving him. For Imamura, autonomy includes an acceptance of dependency, and maturity contains a belief in unspoken forgiveness.

Conclusion

Imamura's 1983 *The Ballad of Narayama* was largely a remake of an excellent 1958 film with the same title by Keisuke Kinoshita. As such,

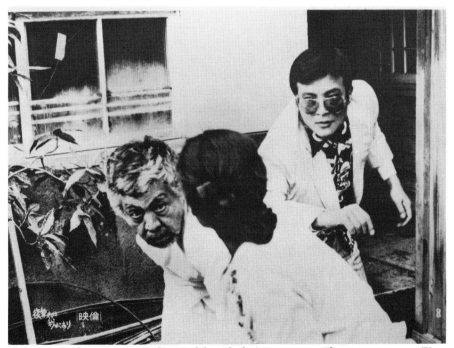

Revenge Is for Us (1979), directed by Shohei Imamura. The gangster son (Ken Ogata) here tries to kill his father (Rentaro Mikuni), but his wife (Mitsuko Baisho) restrains him. Later he will murder a number of older men resembling father substitutes, which suggests an irreconcilable breach between parent and child in contemporary Japanese society.

Imamura seemed to be expressing the sentiments of a bygone age, and the suffering mother in his film had a lot in common with the sacred one in Mizoguchi's *Sansho the Bailiff.* Although he touched upon the theme of matricide *and* patricide, since it was suggested that the son may have killed his father, his film did not express the disgust and resentment sons felt for parents who became vulgar once dethroned and demythologized. These feelings were probably the underlying motive for films featuring matricide and patricide in the late 1970s. Unlike Nietzsche's God, Japanese parents still had a secular side that remained and apparently had to be killed symbolically in films. This effect of the loss of the Forgiving Parent archetype did not continue in the films and TV dramas of the 1980s, though, probably because the present, young generation seem unaware that Japanese parents once had a sacred aspect, and consequently feel no great loss.[26]

Prodigality is no longer a viable theme in the 1980s, but delinquency still is. It is blamed either on a demanding educational system and/or on parental negligence or doting. Such parents in dramas often come to their senses and exhibit responsible concern or a stern attitude. They neither forgive, nor are forgiven, but somehow come to an understanding with children who reform. This indicates that at least some social problems can be solved within the context of a depoliticized, secular Japanese family.

The motif of self-sacrifice has declined in proportion to contemporary Japan's prosperity. It is no longer expected from modern sisters and daughters, who could also be spoiled and who actually have less pressure from parental expectations than do their brothers. Thus, prosperity and continuing secularization in Japan have created a culture in which self-sacrifice, guilt, and forgiveness, as religious sentiments, are forgotten rather than lost.

9

Modern Archetypal Antitheses

Introduction

AN important factor in the metamorphoses of Japanese archetypes has been the movement toward secularism in Japanese society. As stated previously, in the Tokugawa era medieval Buddhism was replaced as the dominant religion by Confucianism, which is this-worldly and socially oriented. While in Neo-Confucianism a "sacred parent" is a possibility, in the modern age this aspect was lost, despite Mizoguchi's notable exception. Western ideas, such as the exploitation of the ruled, helped secularize Japan even more. Yet, although such ideas undermined transcendentalism in traditional values, they also opposed authoritarianism and submission with the ideal of freedom and individual autonomy.

Such ideals were advocated by Japanese filmmakers at the urging of Occupation censors during the late 1940s, but they were hardly credible then due to the abrupt *volte face* Japanese cinema had been forced to undertake.[1] However, mainly young filmmakers from the late 1950s on began creating believable antitheses for not only the Forgiving Parent but also the Loyal Retainer and the Weak Passive Male, as well as for the All-Suffering Female and the Self-Sacrificing Sister. Their modern archetypes were solely oppositional in the beginning.

The Irresponsible Salaryman

The most popular film salaryman appeared in *The Age of Irresponsibility in Japan* (*Nippon Musekinin Jidai*, 1962). Played by the comedian Hitoshi Ueki, the hero was a shrewd opportunist who appeared to be the antithesis of the ideal of company loyalty. Revivals of this film series show that he still strikes responsive chords as an exaggerated self-reflection of actual salarymen and as a wish-fulfillment image.

Buruma has noted that this character is typical, but seems unaware of his antithetical nature.[2] Perhaps, like most Westerners, Buruma thinks of Japanese white-collar workers as modern equivalents of feudal samurai, who are as loyal to their company as the forty-seven were to their dead Lord Asano. In fact, a movie called Salaryman Chushingura (Sarariiman Chushingura) was made in 1960. This comedy set in modern times was not a parody, for the loyalty the employees felt toward the memory of their dead company president was taken seriously and the revenge they effected against his business enemy was a subject for rejoicing. Still, most real-life Japanese salarymen cringe at the word for loyalty toward a superior (chugi or chuseishin), since after the defeat in 1945 that particular value lost the most credence.[3] Their own self-image is different from the views Westerners have of them, and it was affected by their film image, which changed through history.

Films about Japanese salarymen appeared as early as the 1930s, when their numbers increased during rapid urbanization,[4] and the best ones were made by Ozu. In Tokyo Chorus in 1931 Ozu presented an upright young man who loses his job after defending a fellow worker and thereby places his own family in jeopardy. Older and wiser in I Was Born But . . . in 1932, Ozu's salaryman becomes a sycophant who loses the respect of his children and complains to his wife that, if he did not play up to the boss, they would not be able to live a better life. Ozu's view of salarymen was simply that economic conditions make them servile, and it did not change after World War II. In 1956 in Early Spring (Soshun) Ozu's young office worker was neither courageous nor obsequious, but simply resigned to the fact that he was dependent on his regular income.

Ozu's salarymen were docile rather than loyal, and not particularly industrious. They only worked hard when their supervisor was looking. Otherwise they yawned at their desks and lethargically performed their tasks. Ozu's view was shared by his contemporary, Mikio Naruse, who also portrayed lazy, spineless salarymen in Repast (Meshi, 1951) and Husband and Wife (Fufu, 1953). Ozu and Naruse had both lived through the Great Depression in the 1930s, and perhaps this experience colored their postwar presentation of servile salarymen during hard times. However, the view of the younger Kon Ichikawa is hardly different.

In Mr. Pu (Puu-san, 1953) Ichikawa satirically presented a teacher who loses his position after participating in a political demonstration. As he becomes more and more destitute he begs to be hired as an office clerk anywhere, and finally, despite his pacifistic views, consents to work for a company which clandestinely manufactures ammunition to be used in the Korean War (1950–53). Ichikawa's portrayal of the salaryman is even more dismal than that of Ozu and Naruse, and doubtless was conditioned by the acute unemployment in Japan from 1945 to 1950. Out of desperation many Japanese males were ready to accept anything, even another war, as long as they could get a job and regain their self-esteem—and they would be loyal to any company that supported them.

Ichikawa's glum view was only acceptable as satire. In contrast, a cheerful image of Japanese salarymen, which reflected postwar democratic reforms, can be found in *Third-Class Executive* (*Santo Juyaku*, 1952). Third-class executive refers to minor administrators who took over the positions of presidents who had been forced to vacate them by the Occupation authorities. As a rule, they were more democratic than their former, sometimes tyrannical superiors, and thus more acceptable objects of loyalty. The comical boss in this film is like a kind-hearted father who arranges marriages for employees, who feel they are members of one big happy family. Their loyalty is not unconditional, like that of Oishi in *Chushingura*, in that it is predicated on the proposition that their boss will take good care of them.

Sequels to *Third-Class Executive* led to the production of the extremely popular *The Boss and the Slush Fund* (*Hesokuri Shacho*, 1956), which in turn launched the famous *Company President* series (*Shacho shirizu*), whose popularity through the 1960s resulted in some thirty films. The incompetent boss in this series, played by the excellent comic actor Hisaya Morishige, was more like a big baby than a benevolent father. Still, by loyally taking care of him through prudent decision-making from the bottom up, salarymen were given initiative and the happy family remained intact. Actually, figurehead executives and middle-management decision-making is characteristic of many Japanese companies even today.[5]

Whether filled with affection for a lovable boss or servile on account of economic conditions, postwar film salarymen were ultimately loyal to their company. They sacrificed private time for it, dated only fellow employees, and felt a sense of responsibility toward their allotted position no matter how low it was. Then along came *The Age of Irresponsibility in Japan* in 1962 with its star Hitoshi Ueki singing the title song making fun of obsequious salarymen, and its hero who felt no responsibility toward his position whatsoever. Unlike obsequious salarymen who simply maintained their position, he cleverly played up to superiors after business hours to get one promotion after another.

The creation of this new salaryman hero may have been influenced by the Broadway musical *How to Succeed in Business without Really Trying*. However, unlike the young American businessman who simply used flattery to get ahead, the Japanese hero also had clandestine meetings with the heads of rival companies. When this is revealed he is suspected of being a traitor by his fellow workers and former section chief. He takes their ill feelings in stride, however, for he values individual success over loyalty. When he quits to get a better position with another company, he becomes an object of their envy, since he demonstrates a sense of freedom they had long ago exchanged for job security. While their sense of company loyalty may simply be a form of dependency, his disloyalty may actually be an independency rare in Japan. *The Age of Irresponsibility in Japan* ends with the hero coming back to his former company as a result of a merger and getting his old fellow workers and section chief better positions, and then quitting again. While he had felt no particular loyalty to any superior, he had still kept an affection for his peers and old boss, who had not been high up the hierarchial order. Hence he demonstrated a loyalty-among-equals ideal that is more appealing in postwar Japan than the old feudal sense of loyalty (chugi or chuseishin). He certainly differs from Oishi in Chushingura in this respect; however, they are similar in that they both succeeded over all obstacles in achieving their objective, and as a consequence the Irresponsible Salaryman was not yet completely antithetical to the Loyal Retainer.

A more antithetical example can be found in a sequel, Drop Dead! Long Live Irresponsibility—Crazy Maneuvers (Kutabare! Musekinin—Kureijii Sakusen, 1963), where the hero and his office gang advocate a revolt against their superiors and the Japanese business world. The Irresponsible Salaryman and his cohorts are setup in a subsidiary company to distribute a new soft drink that is not doing well on the market. By forcing their bankruptcy through insufficient funding, their parent company plans to write off a bad product as a tax loss and to get rid of some inefficient workers.

This setup reflects actual conditions in contemporary Japan's economic system, which is said to be double-structured.[6] Whereas regular employees in large enterprises are well taken care of, their counterparts in small and medium enterprises, often subsidiaries, receive no fringe benefits and lead a perilous existence because their companies might go bankrupt to protect the parent company. In short, employees in the lower half of the double structure are exploited and expendable.

The Irresponsible Salaryman's subsidiary unexpectedly succeeds, however, by making the right connections. He and his cohorts are given reward certificates at a ceremony conducted at the parent company. Aware that they had been betrayed, however, they tear up the certificates and quit in a declaration of independence. The film ends with them marching down the streets of the Marunouchi business district, Tokyo's equivalent of New York's Wall Street. They are singing a martial air urging their fellow salarymen not to be duped by appeals for loyalty, since the big companies are only using them and would sacrifice them if it was to their advantage.

The Age Of Irresponsibility series was launched by Toho studios to capitalize on the popularity of Hitoshi Ueki, the lead vocal in the Crazy Cats jazz band, which specialized in comic routines. But now the jokes were getting out of hand, for Toho itself was a large enterprise and did not relish having its interests ridiculed, let alone threatened. The series continued, but the producer made sure directors Kengo Furusawa and Takashi Tsuboshima carefully deleted the revolutionary aspects of their hero[7] and simply presented him as a humorous figure who could poke fun at the system while still conforming to it. Hence he became like actual salarymen who can complain about their companies when they are out drinking, but who still faithfully go back to work the next day. The new message of the series became: while our economic system is not perfect, still it is successful since almost everyone is working and we are getting an increasing share of the world market.[8]

As if to emphasize the theme of success above all else, Ueki the Irresponsible Salaryman was cast as Hideyoshi Toyotomi (1536–98), Japan's Napoleon, in Toho's musical-comedy extravaganza, *The Chronicle of Taiko the Braggart (Hora Fuki Taikoki,* 1964). Taiko is one of the names Hideyoshi assumed when he rose to power, and his career is Japan's greatest success story. Born and raised as a poor farmer, he joined warlord Nobunaga Oda's army as a foot soldier and worked his way up in the ranks to become Oda's most faithful retainer and his best general. After Oda's death Hideyoshi completed the unification of Japan and became the nation's real ruler in contrast to the emperor, who was a spiritual figurehead.

Ueki played Hideyoshi with all the pluck he could muster and pointed out the true significance of Hideyoshi's career: it takes more than loyalty to become a success; ambition and drive are necessary too. As such, Ueki's Hideyoshi provides a comic key to Japan's resounding economic success from the 1960s on. Ozu's servile sycophants and the loyal, contented employees in *The Company President* series provided models for status-quo salarymen, but could not account for the aggressive determination necessary to capture a large share of the world market. Young executives who possessed that were called *moretsu* salarymen in the 1960s. *Moretsu* means "ardent" or "intense" and is applied to salarymen like Hideyoshi who are not only loyal, but whose ambition will result in accomplishments that increase profits for their company. In compensation they will be promoted over mediocre employees who simply have job security.

The savage desire for success at all costs was not peculiar to the *moretsu* salarymen of the 1960s. Musashi had it and so did thousands of others in the modern era. After the Meiji Restoration in 1868 changed a feudal, stratified society—which had prevented further Hideyoshi-like success stories—into a modern mobile one, ambitious men were needed for Japan to catch up with the advanced Western nations. However, too much ambition brought about the expansionist policy in China in the 1930s, which led to Japan's first defeat as a nation. Consequently, Japanese business heads tempered drive and determination with prudent planning, especially from the 1970s on, as Japan's success got increasingly adverse reactions from Western Europe and America.

Contemporary Japanese salarymen also became prudent, and Ueki the Irresponsible Salaryman once again provided a guide for proper conduct. In *The Greatest Flatterer in Japan (Nihon Ichi no Goma-suri Otoko,* 1965), Ueki plays a young man who gets his first job. When he returns home to tell the good news, his father advises him that playing up to superiors is

The Greatest Flatterer in Japan (1965), directed by Kengo Furusawa. After buttering up the company president (Eijiro Tono), the Irresponsible Salaryman (Hitoshi Ueki) makes a point, much to the consternation of his supervisor (Eitaro Shindo). Hence, he adroitly uses flattery to get a promotion and is not merely obsequious like past salarymen in films.

the road to success. The idealistic young man disagrees, and counters that, in this age of the *moretsu* salaryman, ability is what counts. On his first day of work, however, he finds out that he had failed the company entrance examination and that he had only got the job because his father was a classmate of the vice-president. Thereafter, he soon learns that personal connections through flattery lead to promotions, and he decides to outdo all his fellow workers in that respect. Rather than cling to impractical ideals, he is prudent enough to use the method that will work in a given situation. Perhaps in another company ability really is what counts.

The above can also be said for the salarymen in the *Company President* series of the 1960s, when maneuvering for promotions ruffled the happy-family image somewhat. They were motivated neither by belief in merit based on ability nor by loyalty expressed by playing up to superiors. Rather, they were shrewd enough to know what the situation called for and then use either method accordingly. As such, they also exemplified the adaptability of the passive mode of behavior previously explained.

While the Irresponsible Salaryman expressed rebellious sentiments, eventually they were contained and prevented from disrupting the social order. Still, the oppositional nature of this modern archetype, created under the influence of antithetical Western ideas, definitely presented a challenge to traditional values resulting in a compromise that was certainly not wholly conservative, particularly in its cynical attitude toward feudalistic loyalty.

The Angry Young Man

Angry young men were popular heroes in British and American films in the 1950s, and when young Japanese filmmakers started creating their own version they refuted the traditional archetypes of youths maintained by older generations. Their young heroes actively pursued girls rather than playing a waiting game like the Weak Passive Male, and, unlike the Chaste Warrior, they did not think that sex and romance would weaken them in a fight.

Novelist Shintaro Ishihara started the fad for angry youths with his early works about "the sun tribe" (*taiyozoku*), rich teenagers who rampaged on the beaches on the outskirts of Tokyo during their summer vacation. The first film version of the "sun tribe" was *Season of the Sun* (*Taiyo no Kisetsu*, 1956), based on Ishihara's Akutagawa-Prize-winning novel of the same name. Although director Takumi Furukawa failed to capture the flair of the original, he still succeeded in changing the old love melodrama formula. After the unwed heroine becomes pregnant, she is disappointed in her lover's nonchalant attitude and decides to have an abortion performed. She then dies on the operating table in a guilt-inducing denouement meant for the Weak Passive Male. Her lover, however, feels anger instead of guilt, and at her funeral he throws a glassed candle at her memorial photograph, calls her a fool, tells the adults there that they do not understand anything, and walks away in a huff.

The best film rendition of the "sun tribe" was *Crazed Fruit* (*Kurutta Kajitsu*, 1956), for director Ko Nakahira's tongue-in-cheek treatment set the viewer up for a devastating climax. The older brother steals away his younger brother's sexy girlfriend and rationalizes that it is for the younger's own good. However, his irritation at the younger's naiveté indicates guilty feelings, which are overcome because of his passion for her. Climbing up to her second-story bedroom, he takes rather than waits. Later when the younger brother finds out, he drives his motorboat into their small launch killing both of them. In *Crazed Fruit* guilt could not inhibit desire and anger was the strongest emotion.

The best antithesis of the Weak Passive Male can be found in Kon Ichikawa's *Punishment Room* (*Shokei no Heya*, 1956), which is also based on a Shintaro Ishihara novel. For the college student hero of this film, desires are the most important thing in life. Neither vague about them nor waiting for them to be satisfied, he pursues their main object, the opposite sex, and lets nothing stand in his way. For example, even though he knows a university club brother likes a certain coed, he takes her for himself by putting sleeping tablets in her drink.

The hero in *Punishment Room* also debunks the Chaste Warrior archetype. While he is practicing rugby, he notices his girl standing on a slope watching him. Abruptly abandoning his teammates, he walks up to her; she smiles and they go off together.

Although such a scene would not be unusual in an American or European film, in a Japanese film with sports it is iconoclastic. The Chaste Warrior often took the form of a contemporary athlete whose romantic yearnings were adversely affecting his performance on the field. Ever since Japanese films of the late 1920s, he would be pressured by the team to give the girl up and in the end they would win whatever game they were playing.[9] For the hero in *Punishment Room*, however, sports and romance are not at all incompatible.

While such a hero is an obvious wish-fulfillment image, he is also an object of envy, so much so that he is bound to incur resentment from the unsatisfied, who make up the majority of any filmviewing audience. Hence the title, *Punishment Room*, and the final scene, where he is brutally beaten by a rival gang. He endures the pain stoically like the Chaste Warrior in modern *yakuza* films, but for different reasons. The *yakuza* hero becomes a masochist for the sake of a cohort or to prevent an altercation that would be disastrous for the gang. This angry young man takes a beating out of self-esteem because he refuses to apologize for satisfying his desires.

Novelist Ishihara and the directors of his "sun tribe"-based films were not the only Japanese in the late 1950s who advocated heroes with strong desires as opposed to the traditional ideal of an almost desireless youth. Yasuzo Masumura also presented an angry young hero in his debut film, *Kisses* (*Kuchizuke*, 1957), and claimed to have learned to appreciate a strong ego while living in Rome where he studied cinema at the Centro Sperimentale.[10] The youth in *Kisses* did indeed act like a Western hero and further broke with tradition by valuing the object of his desires, his girl friend, more than he did his own parents. Although he did not criticize his parents like James Dean in *Rebel Without a Cause*, he gave his girl the money he had saved to bail his father out of jail, and did not conform to the Prodigal Son archetype since he felt no guilt for having done so.

Nagisa Oshima, the leader of Japan's New Wave directors in the 1960s, had been influenced by Masumura and the "sun tribe" films.[11] However, he developed their themes much further in *Cruel Story of Youth* (*Seishun Zankoku Monogatari*, 1960) by turning the object of desire into a love

処刑の部屋

Punishment Room (1956), directed by Kon Ichikawa. Here Japan's Angry Young Man (Hiroshi Kawaguchi) takes time out from rugby practice to confront an attractive coed (Ayako Wakao). He thus refutes the traditional view that romance would interfere with athletic performance.

object and by giving anger greater social significance. A young college student rescues a coed from the unwanted attentions of a middle-aged man, but later forcibly takes her himself and thereafter uses her as sex bait to extort money from older men. When she becomes pregnant, he intimidates her into having an abortion. His cruelty toward her seems to have no bounds, until he begins to feel some sympathy for her while she is recuperating on the operating table. This sympathy goes beyond the affection the hero in *Kisses* felt for his girl and gradually deepens into love. He decides not to use her to shake down middle-aged men again, not because it is immoral but because she hates doing it and he has begun to recognize her feelings.

As the plot develops, though, the youth realizes that, in order to survive in a profit-oriented society, you have to prostitute yourself in one way or another. Although his anger has now found an appropriate target, he is still not strong enough to support her without sacrificing their self-esteem. Their tragedy is inevitable. After he refuses to turn her over to a gang of hoodlums, shots of them beating him to death are intercut with those of her in the speeding car of an older man, from which she jumps. She is shown crawling on the pavement and after dying, stretched full-length in the black frame with an open space to her right. Suddenly her lover's bloody face appears there in a double exposure and they are juxtaposed in one last close-up. Director Oshima's treatment recalls Chikamatsu's love suicides; however, his youths died more for their self-esteem than for love.

In terms of Japanese iconography, Oshima's angry young hero is certainly revolutionary. Neither the Weak Passive Male nor the Prodigal Son had much self-esteem. To be sure, the Tormented Lord and the Loyal Retainer had fierce pride, but it was based on membership in the aristocratic samurai class. *Yakuza* heroes modeled on them were often self-deprecating, since as outlaws they yearned for respectability. Pride among the common people was invested in their family honor or their affiliation with some group or area. Oshima's own sense of self-esteem may well have been based on the fact that in the 1950s he had been a student activist who led political demonstrations on his campus.[12] As such, Oshima's pride may be elitist in nature. However, by instilling it in characters who were poor and/or delinquent, such as the hero in *Cruel Story of Youth*, Oshima raised self-esteem to the level of pride as an individual human being. While not unusual in the West, this kind of humanism had been almost nonexistent in traditional Japan.

After *Cruel Story of Youth* Oshima did not create such forceful young heroes. Rather, while continuing to praise those who maintained their self-esteem, he went on to angrily impeach those who had sold out to the powerful establishment. Consequently, Oshima—along with Shohei Imamura, who developed the theme of strong desires proposed by Ishihara, and Masumura—created the most significant Japanese films in the 1960s.

Angry young heroes continued to appear through the 1960s in the modern action dramas that were the speciality of Nikkatsu studios, which had started the fad with their production of *Season of the Sun*. These Nikkatsu heroes often tried to develop a strong ego à la Oshima, but in the context of their assemblyline, commercial films, the essential element in the process—characterization—was all but impossible. Furthermore, their directors usually equated autonomy, which is almost synonymous with ego development, with solitude and loneliness. Still, the Nikkatsu heroes sometimes made up for their defects with a display of activity that put the old passive male to shame, and by cutting a dashing figure against their environment, they provided an *image* of autonomy, if not a realization of it through characterization.

Nikkatsu's first hero was Yujiro Ishihara. During his youth his best film, after *Crazed Fruit*, where he played the older brother, was *I Am Waiting* (*Ore wa Matteru ze*, 1957). Its director, Koreyoshi Kurahara, managed to transplant an American-style hero and love story, without appearing incongruous, by having Yujiro run a Western-style restaurant in the cosmopolitan port city of Yokohama. The plot is simple and consists of boy meets girl and boy avenging the death of his brother, which had ruined his dream of emigrating to Brazil. The treatment is interesting, however, for, when the hero stops waiting for a letter from his brother and is set in motion, it appears that director Kurahara is purposely dismantling the archetype of the Weak Passive Male, who was, of course, immobile.

Donald Richie has noted that part of Yujiro's appeal rests in the fact that he has unusually long legs for a Japanese,[13] and even in present-day TV dramas his walk is his trademark. In *I Am Waiting* director Kurahara took advantage of Yujiro's distinguishing feature by beginning sequences with a shot of him from the waist down and walking at a brisk pace. Yujiro always walks straight ahead to show his determination, and, through fast cutting and wipes, Kurahara emphasized this and heightened suspense in the sequence where he is tracking down his brother's murderer.

The physique of a swimmer and a boyish grin were also among the young Yujiro's assets. He often displayed his litheness by leaping over fences and jumping over stair bannisters. In *I Am Waiting* his agility as an ex-boxer is exhibited in the final slugfest where he dispatches a gang of hoodlums with ease.

In short, Yujiro provides a startling contrast to the melancholy, immobile Keiji Sada of *What Is Your Name?* fame, and it is hard to believe that they were the top male stars in 1958 and 1954 respectively.[14] *What Is Your Name?* and *I Am Waiting* also make an interesting comparison as love stories. Both films begin with chance meetings near bridges and cinematically there are alternating close-ups and bust shots to show that the boy and girl were meant for each other. However, while *What Is Your Name?* is about lovers thwarted by circumstances and obstructing third parties, *I Am Waiting* is a story of two lonely people who fall in love and later voluntarily separate because of personal problems. The latter is clearly an American-style love story where the hero is not given the heroine but wins her back after defeating the baddies.

Since action did not exist in traditional Japanese love stories like *What Is Your Name?*, a comparison between Keiji Sada and Yujiro falls short and should be supplemented with Yujiro verses the swordfighting heroes of the action-packed period film. The stars of this genre, such as Chiezo Kataoka and Utaemon Ichikawa, had been lithe and fast on their feet in their youth during the 1920s; however, even when they became older, middle-aged men in the 1950s, they continued to dominate the commercial films in the genre, in spite of the appearance of new stars like Toshiro Mifune and Kinnosuke Nakamura. With age, they became bow-legged and barrel-chested. In contrast to the long-legged Yujiro, who was often photographed from the waist down, they were usually shot from the waist up, holding their sword in front of them and glaring at their foes, and their movements were kept to a minimum. Even the young Ken Takakura in the *yakuza* films of the 1960s was best displayed in a bust shot of his muscular, tattooed chest. Consequently, these swordfighting heroes seemed like rocks of endurance who were not so active as Yujiro, who moved around with the ease of a fleet-footed boxer.

The young Yujiro in *I Am Waiting* was an American-style hero who did not belong anywhere in Japan, except for cosmopolitan places like Yokohama. And even Yokohama, with its history of Western influence and the hero's Western-style restaurant with no chopsticks, are only staging areas for his departure to his true home somewhere in the West. When his dream is destroyed, however, Yujiro becomes a tragic figure, and director Kurahara suggests that freedom cannot exist in socially restricted Japan *and* that a Japanese is not really able to escape to the liberal West.

It was difficult for Yujiro to look sad, though, for he had no acting training to speak of, had been raised in a well-to-do family, and was already a success at twenty-two. Consequently, Kurahara expressed Yujiro's alienation with a long, full-length shot of him sitting alone on a pier with the grey sea and his estranged girl friend in the background. The search for autonomy became lost in loneliness.

The western look of *I Am Waiting* was characteristic of Nikkatsu's modern action film, as well as of its counterpart at the rival Toho studios. The heroes were always dressed in the latest American fashion, guzzled expensive Scotch, and preferred Japan's version of Western food to traditional rice dishes; they cavorted in night clubs and gambling casinos where well-heeled foreign residents served as props, and a singer with a tuxedoed band cranked out a stilted rendition of the latest American popular music.

This America-in-Japan world perhaps had a connotation of freedom in

I Am Waiting (1957), directed by Koreyoshi Kurahara. This alienated young hero (Yujiro Ishihara) is estranged from his girlfriend (Mie Kitahara). Since he cannot escape across the sea to the liberal West, his search for autonomy becomes lost in loneliness.

the minds of many Japanese. Nevertheless, it was still Japan, for such places and things actually do exist in Tokyo, which has a more modern look than Paris and has been Americanized to a large extent despite crowded living conditions. Therefore, in search of "real freedom" some young Nikkatsu filmmakers created a peculiar subgenre called the No Nationality film (*Mukokuseki eiga*). By setting their story in a barren, volcanic area, or the northern island of Hokkaido with its American-style farms, they evoked the atmosphere of a place that was neither quite American nor Japanese and was actually no particular place at all. Furthermore, to go with their No Nation Land they fabricated an abstract hero played by Akira Kobayashi, Nikkatsu's second big star.

Dressed in buckskins with a guitar slung over the shoulder, Akira cut a striking figure against his barren surroundings whenever he would go riding down a mountainside on his horse. He rescued damsels in distress as well as harassed pioneers, and sang a sad song whenever he had a chance. He was not exactly a Japanese Roy Rogers, for he toted a modern

Bird of Passage in the Red Sunset (*Akai Yuhi no Wataridori*, 1960), directed by Buichi Saito. This abstract hero (Akira Kobayashi) in the No Nationality film carried a revolver and a guitar and usually rescued this damsel in distress (Ruriko Asaoka). His formation was a naïve attempt to free Japanese heroes from their restrictive social environment.

revolver and his archfoe in fast-draw contests was usually impeccably dressed in a black zoot suit.

While the No Nationality film may seem preposterous, it was taken somewhat seriously by young filmmakers trying to create new heroes who stood out against their environment rather than blended in. Donald Richie has stated that in a good Japanese film the characters regard their environment as an extension of themselves and this creates its unique atmosphere.[15] On the other hand, Yasuzo Masumura, who created his own version of Japan's Angry Young Man, hated atmosphere and felt that a particular locale restricted the freedom or ego of film characters.[16] In other words, they would merely become extensions of the environment.

Although the idea of harmony with nature is appealing, it could have freedom-denying implications when the social order is viewed as inseparable from the natural order.[17] By using Confucian ideology, the feudal powers had equated their own authoritarian rule with that of Heaven over earth, that is, the virtuous few on top should control everything.[18] In feudal towns and villages the diet and clothing of each social class were strictly regulated by the government[19] and, through group accountability, individuals were kept in line by neighbors who feared dire consequences. Accordingly, in each gestaltlike class everyone more or less dressed and thought alike, and blended in with their social as well as with their natural environment.

The revolt against Confucian social harmony by a modern Japanese like Yasuzo Masumura was probably inevitable, and he freed his subjects from their environment by making films that consisted almost solely of big close-ups of them. The young Nikkatsu directors were not on Masumura's intellectual level, but, by fabricating a No Nation Land, they could take a long shot of an abstract hero who clearly stood out in the midst of his barren environs. He became a rather naive image of autonomy.

The most popular series in the No Nationality film was the *Bird of Passage* (*Wataridori*). All but the last entry of nine from 1959 to 1962 were directed by Buichi Saito.[20] In the first one, *Leaving the Southern Country of Tosa Behind* (*Nankoku Tosa o Ato ni Shite*, 1959), Akira Kobayashi played a young ex-convict who returned to his hometown. He was like one of Shin Hasegawa's exiles who is weakened by human ties and becomes strong out of desperation only upon severing them. From the second entry on, however, director Saito turned his hero into a vagabond and freed him from the restrictions of time and particular places like Tosa. Entering the new No Nation Land like a phantom from out of nowhere and in the end vanishing, he became an invincible, abstract figure, since he had neither past memories to weaken him nor future concerns to restrict his conduct. He was now the antithesis of the Exile, and the *Bird of Passage* series provides a startling contrast to the postwar film remakes of Shin

Hasegawa's dark, cruel world of hired killers, for the slayings by Akira are unreal and even comical, and simply allow him to look cool.

In the last few entries of *Bird of Passage* the past started to creep back in, and the formerly jocular hero became sad and seemed to be repeating Hasegawa's *Muenbotoke* message that there was no human existence outside of old particularistic relations. Now as a photographed subject like Yujiro, Akira alone in his barren environment suggested that autonomy was simply solitude.

Yujiro Ishihara and Akira Kobayashi were the only significant Nikkatsu modern action heroes. In their wake came a lonely James Dean type, Keiichiro Akagi, who also died young in a sports car accident, and hard-boiled types like Jo Shido. Akagi was simply a reincarnation of the young nihilistic swordsman in *Orochi*, playing on the viewer's sympathies with his sad face. Shido merely repeated the hard-boiled message of both the Chaste Warrior and the Exile that, to win in battle or get a license to kill, you must be cut off from weakening human bonds.

Sadness tinged the early jocularity of Yujiro and Akira and added the ambience of the Tormented Lord to their image. Their youthful anger was overcome by a loneliness that equated revolt with isolation and denied the possibility of freedom based on autonomy rather than nihilism. Anger against an oppressive society was still expressed in the artistic films of the 1960s. In the 1970s and 1980s, however, the theme of youthful anger weakened in the face of a prospering society, which even seemed to allow sexual freedom. Consequently, the vague frustrations of contemporary young Japanese heroes were often relieved if not dispelled by willing, curvaceous girlfriends.

In spite of the decline of the Angry Young Man archetype, his rise presented an alternate role model to the Weak Passive Male, the Chaste Warrior, and the Prodigal Son. Although incapable of expressing autonomy in a culture emphasizing dependency and a society that still downplays individual rights, by cutting a clear figure against his environment he made traditional male virtues like passivity, restraint, and humility much less appealing.

The Girl Next Door

The All-Suffering Female archetype and her miniature, the pathetic beauty, had been maintained since the beginning of Japanese film by older generations of directors who had either felt guilty about the sufferings of their mothers and sisters or who daydreamed of rescuing a beauty in distress. These heroines, however, were not necessarily appealing to the postwar generation, and Yasuzo Masumura is a case in point. With *Kisses* in 1957 Masumura not only created a Japanese version of the Angry Young

Man but also presented a seemingly new heroine who did not want pity and who did not win the boy through suffering. In Masumura's next film, *A Cheerful Girl* (*Aozora Musume*, 1957), together with his young script writer, Yoshio Shirasaka, he changed the persevering heroine in the original novel into an outspoken, optimistic girl who rebuked everything the Self-Sacrificing Sister archetype stood for. Unlike the Angry Young Man, Masumura's new heroines did not seem like a foreign implant at all. They were simply the Girl Next Door. The actress who best embodied this image was Sayuri Yoshinaga, the most popular young female star during the 1960s.

Sayuri's best film was *A Street of Cupolas* (*Kyupora no Aru Machi*, 1962) in which she plays an intelligent, courageous teenager. The heroine's family is placed in economic jeopardy after her hard-drinking father is laid off, and she has to work part-time so as not to give up her education and a chance for a better life. Sayuri not only gave her best performance, but director Kiriro Urayama in this his first film presented a rare, realistic glimpse of the Japanese working class without Marxist polemics.

As if to refute the passivity of traditional heroines, Urayama continually shows Sayuri as an active figure. Early in the film she is playing baseball, and after she gets a hit she runs around the bases, cheered on by her kid brother and his chum. The film even ends with her giving her brother a race after they have seen their friend off on his train journey.

The All-Suffering Female never ran anywhere, but simply appeared out of the fog walking slowly toward her passive male in films like *What Is Your Name?*. When the pathetic beauty ran, she appeared to be even more pathetic, and it was best for her to meekly follow in the tracks of her hero in films about Musashi and other Chaste Warriors.

Sayuri's active image was suitable for a girl from a poor family who has to go out and work at an early age, and in other films she is often shown dressed in jeans and making some delivery on bicycle. On the other hand, the inactive existence of suffering beauties in films is often predicated on the fact that they are wrenched from a sheltered life with their parents and cannot live in the cruel world without the protection or at least support of a man. Sayuri in *A Street of Cupolas*, however, quickly learned to cope with unpleasant realities, for on her first job she came in contact with a teenage gang. After she resisted the temptation to feel sorry for herself and become delinquent, she gained self-confidence and even the pluck to criticize her self-centered father and weak-willed mother.

In Urayama's next film, *Bad Girl* (*Hiko Shojo*, 1963), the young heroine actually does become delinquent as a result of the bad influence of her immoral parents. By resolving to become independent of them, however, she reforms with the help of her boyfriend. On the other hand, Sayuri in *A Street of Cupolas* has a mind of her own from the start and even ponders social contradictions and the plight of the poor. Rather than wait for some

A Street of Cupolas (1962), directed by Kiriro Urayama. Shown with her beau (Mitsuo Hamada) on a hillside, this intelligent Girl Next Door (Sayuri Yoshinaga) does not sacrifice herself for her working-class family.

male to rescue her, she joins a labor union that provides its members with a night school. She does not play on anyone's sympathies, which was the only way suffering beauties ever got what they wanted.

The actress Sayuri Yoshinaga played many different roles, like everyone else at Nikkatsu, where she worked. Still, because of her active Girl Next Door image, she changed the All-Suffering Female role in the love melodrama, *Looking At Love and Death* (*Ai to Shi o Mitsumete*, 1964). Based on a true story, the film concerns the love between a young girl suffering from an incurable disease (Sayuri) and her boyfriend. His hospital visits recall the grand finale of *What Is Your Name?* However, while she suffers even more than that heroine, she is often shown sewing and washing clothes and even helping other patients. She keeps active and hangs in there battling against her disease, rather than passively waiting and wilting away in her hospital bed.

Unlike the Angry Young Man, there was a prewar precedent for the Girl Next Door. Kinuyo Tanaka—best known as the sacred, suffering female in Mizoguchi films like *Ugetsu*—was the most popular film actress in the 1930s. She not only starred in the hit love melodrama *The Compassionate*

Buddha Tree but also played the hard-working girl who ran the neighborhood ricecracker, or *senbei*, shop in *Kinuyo's First Love* (*Kinuyo no Hatsukoi*, 1940), also directed by Hiromasa Nomura. In Heinosuke Gosho's *Flower Basket Song* (*Hanakago no Uta*, 1937) she is the cheerful daughter of a man who runs a *tonkatsu*, or pork cutlet, restaurant, and she first appears dressed in coveralls and making a delivery, just as Sayuri would in the 1960s.

Kinuyo's dual image was best captured in Gosho's *Dancing Girl From Izu* (*Izu no Odoriko*, 1933), the first and best film adaptation of Nobel-Prize-winner Yasunari Kawabata's famous short story. Cast as the youngest member of a poor, itinerant entertaining troupe, she was put in the pathetic beauty role, for her occupation was an object of scorn in prewar Japan. Yet, through adept editing Gosho managed to present her cheerful side in one charming sequence.

The troupe had met a college student on the road and one morning she is sitting next to him under a bridge. He assures her that she can count on him if she is ever in trouble. Blushing and beside herself with joy, she goes traipsing across the large boulders toward the middle of the stream, practically hopping because of her confining kimono. He follows her and she starts splashing her feet in the water. The sun has come out and they simply sit together, enjoying the stream cascading over the boulders.

Since *Dancing Girl From Izu* was a silent film, Kinuyo Tanaka had to express the agitation of the young dancing girl through spritely movements and facial expressions. The way joy kept flashing across her face truly conveyed the meaning of the word *vivacious*.

This scene did not appear in Kawabata's story, but it may have been inspired by the passage where the student spotted the dancer coming out of an outdoor bath at some distance. Moreover, Kawabata's dancer was neither particularly pathetic nor vivacious. She was like the dream girls in the novels of Franz Kafka, enchanting phantoms who whisper intimations of another world, and hence more an image in the student's head than a lively girl beside him.

Gosho's joyful interlude on the boulders seemed to be complemented by the poignant parting scene at the end of the film, when Kinuyo's pathetic-beauty side took over. Now she runs to the end of a concrete breakwater to get one last look at his departing ship. Shots of her tear-stained face are alternated with those of the waves breaking against the rocks on shore.

Kinuyo Tanaka could also play educated women, and her role in *Mother and Child* in 1938 was the first intelligent, self-assertive heroine in Japanese film, according to Tadao Sato.[21] In this film she not only criticizes her negligent father, as Sayuri would in *A Street of Cupolas*, but also rejects her fiancé after she finds out he had been using her to aid his business career.

Previously in Japanese film, strong-willed women had appeared only as

Dancing Girl from Izu (1933), directed by Heinosuke Gosho. Sitting under a
bridge with her college student boyfriend (Den Ohinata), this vivacious dancing
girl (Kinuyo Tanaka) projects the prewar image of the Girl Next Door.

teachers of the traditional performing arts who are particularly hard on
their masochistic male disciples. But these women had simply turned the
tables. The first real criticism of the male-oriented society appeared in
1936 through the young heroines of Mizoguchi's *Osaka Elegy* (*Naniwa
Ereji*) and *Sisters of the Gion* (*Gion no Shimai*). However, their protest
could be attributed to delinquency, since as the boss's mistress and a low-
class geisha, they fell in the fallen-woman category. By contrast, the
heroine in *Mother and Child* was raised as a respectable Miss, well-
educated and cultivated in the traditional and modern arts; and thus her
discerning indictment of male society carried more weight.

Since the heroine's father in *Mother and Child* was the respected head of
a large enterprise, criticism of his lack of paternal responsibility could be
extended to society at large. Director Minoru Shibuya, however, had to
exercise restraint, for movie censorship was tightening more and more as
Japan's military and business leaders were engaged in a war of expansion
in China in 1938.[22] Postwar directors like Urayama could be more direct
in their social criticism. Nevertheless, since the heroine Sayuri plays in *A
Street of Cupolas* is only in her early teens, it appears that Urayama was

putting words of wisdom into the mouths of babes. A better example of a Girl Next Door who not only criticizes society but also raises the issue of autonomy for women can be found in *Sunshine in the Old Neighborhood* (*Shitamachi no Taiyo*, 1963), where the heroine is old enough to be engaged.

Sunshine in the Old Neighborhood was the second film directed by Yoji Yamada, who is currently the most popular Japanese director. Although Yamada is a member of the Japanese Communist Party, it is almost impossible to find anything Marxist in his Tora-san series, which expresses nostalgia for days past when Japanese were supposedly more neighborly and kind. While the character of Tora-san implies some rejection of modern society, he is simply an old vagabond rather than a future model, as stated in chapter four. Yet, in an early film like *Sunshine in the Old Neighborhood* Yamada exhibits some conformance to Marxist ideology.

Japanese Communists and progressives profess disdain for traditional heroines who merely suffer meekly, and they express their preference for cheerful, never-say-die working girls who, by having an ego, are critical of the society that exploits both them and the common people in general.[23] Yamada in *Sunshine in the Old Neighborhood* presents a heroine who not only "has an ego" but also seems to be aware of herself as a separate entity not necessarily dependent on men.

Sunshine in the Old Neighborhood was envisioned by the producer at Shochiku studios as a vehicle for the popular singer Chieko Baisho.[24] But the fact that the young, idealist Yamada subverted this intention demonstrates that rebellious sentiments could be expressed within a commercial film genre that exploits the fantasies of poor, young women.

Yamada first presents Chieko working in a factory, for, unlike Sayuri in *A Street of Cupolas*, she has already graduated from high school. She has the same cheerful, active ambience, though, which is exhibited when she plays vollyball during the lunch break.

Chieko is dating a coworker who is trying to become a white-collar worker so that he can live the good life in the suburbs far away from their air-polluted, factory area. She is seriously considering marrying him, since everyone in her neighborhood says that being a salaryman's wife is the best most women could hope for. But she begins to have doubts when she visits an old classmate who achieved that cherished status. Her friend tells her that, while it is nice to wear expensive clothes, all she seems to do is wait for her husband to come home from work, and that, although she is disappointed with her doll-like existence, she is resigned to it.

Now Chieko is irritated by the crass materialism of some of her friends and skeptical of the common saying that a woman's happiness depends on a man. Moreover, she is disturbed by her boyfriend's attitude. When she tries to console him over a lost job opportunity, he reacts angrily, saying that she cannot understand how he feels because she is a woman who

Sunshine in the Old Neighborhood (1963), directed by Yoji Yamada. By refusing to become the doll-like wife of a young businessman, this heroine (Chieko Baisho) maintains her integrity by marrying a factory hand (Homare Suguro) in her old neighborhood. She thereby provides a model for Japanese women who make their own decisions.

does not have to worry about a working career. Later when he finally becomes a salaryman, she is crestfallen upon finding out that he got the job by concealing a traffic accident a rich boy was involved in. She decides to remain in the old neighborhood and eventually marry a factory hand she had previously dated once or twice.

The star of *Sunshine in the Old Neighborhood*, Chieko Baisho, nowadays plays Tora-san's sister, Sakura, the intelligent wife of a small factory worker. She cannot always wait for him to come home because her brother's misadventures have her continually running out of her own house, and her husband is far from domineering since all family matters are decided by them jointly.

The young Yamada's attempt to grapple with the problem of autonomy for women in *Sunshine in the Old Neighborhood* may not come up to the exacting expectations of feminists in the West. Still, his portrayal of a mature Girl Next Door who makes her own decisions as she finds out about others and herself is splendid and rare in Japanese cinema. Considering the fact that Yamada's heroine is more autonomous than most young males in film, she may indeed be his alter ego.

Ultimately the Girl Next Door, when awakened in films like *Sunshine in the Old Neighborhood*, was more rebellious than the Angry Young Man, for she actually questioned traditional values rather than simply struck a belligerent pose. Traditionally, Japanese heroines simply obeyed men and were kept at home and away from society; however, if betrayed or disappointed, they could become vengeful spirits or women who criticize society more objectively than the men who were so bound up in it due to the persistence of the feudal concept of loyalty. Yet, like the Irresponsible Salaryman, who eventually limited his protest to humorous and drunken grumblings, the Girl Next Door also became contained in the system when married. Nevertheless, she paved the way for the intelligent portrayal of career women as alternate role models in some present-day Japanese TV dramas. Relevant dramas about the working class vanished on account of affluence; but the descendents of Sayuri, Kinuyo, and Chieko still flourish. This phenomenon is more attributable to the effect on Japan of the Western women's liberation movement than to Japanese Marxist theory. While *Julia* still enjoys revivals in Tokyo film theaters, most people have forgotten *Sunshine in the Old Neighborhood*.

The Earthy Woman

The biggest difference between the Girl Next Door in Japan and in the West is the virginal ambience of the Japanese girl. An American contemporary of Sayuri was Natalie Wood, who first played love scenes with James Dean in *Rebel Without a Cause* in 1955. Such scenes became much hotter with Warren Beatty in *Splendor in the Grass* in 1961, a film in which director Elia Kazan criticized the Victorian attitude of parents toward young lovers with healthy desires. In short, America's Girl Next Door through the 1960s could conceivably go to bed with the boy she loved without being degraded. This was not the case with Sayuri. If there was a kiss scene with her beau, it was always performed awkwardly for comical effect, as her fans probably could not even imagine her having any sexual desire whatsoever.

In this respect Japan's Girl Next Door is not at all different from the traditional heroines. Whether pathetic or all-suffering, they were usually virginal girls, and, if they married, they seemed to tolerate sex only because it went with their role, as was the case with the highest-class geisha and the lowest prostitute. Women who seemed to enjoy sex were degraded almost to the level of an animal.

This may come as a surprise to some Western readers who think of Japan as a sexual paradise free of the inhibitions fostered by the puritanical tradition. Fans of Shohei Imamura's films may be particularly perplexed, since his heroines are usually downright earthy. But they are a postwar phenomenon in Japanese cinema that can only be properly understood after a brief historical survey of changing Japanese attitudes toward sex.

The oldest attitude, found in *Kojiki*, is refreshingly frank, and this is still evident in some rural festivals where penis and vagina symbols are openly celebrated. The Heian courtier aristocrats had many elegant love affairs and regarded virginity as a sign of unpopularity, or even the result of possession by some troublesome spirit.[25] In the twelfth century, however, the warrior aristocrats came to power,[26] and their samurai descendants ruled into the modern era. They valued martial valor and Confucian rectitude, and virginity became a virtue that upped the bride price in marriages arranged for the mutual political and economic benefit of the families involved. In Confucianism sex is regarded as absolutely necessary for the continuance of the all-important family line, but premarital affairs and elopements could be taken as rebellion against parents.[27]

The tension between conflicting attitudes toward sex—native frankness, elegant promiscuity, and Confucian rectitude—can be found throughout the Tokugawa period (1603–1868), particularly in the development of Kabuki. In the seventeenth century the authorities prohibited the appearance of women performers in Kabuki since they had also served as prostitutes, and thereafter males called *onnagata* or *oyama* performed all female roles.[28] Kabuki did not thereby completely clean up its act, though. A critic in 1816 noted that sexual intercourse was plainly shown on stage, in contrast to the past when amorous play was suggested by exchange of glances and the *onnagata* covering his face with his sleeve to hide embarrassment.[29]

In the modern era from 1868 until 1945 Confucian rectitude governed sex attitudes. Japan's new leaders came from the old samurai class and they indoctrinated the people with their repressive values through a modern, compulsory-education system.[30] Film censorship was so strict that not only were kissing scenes prohibited, but any relations between unmarried men and women had to be handled indirectly to avoid the charge of pornography.[31]

After 1945 the American Occupation authorities encouraged kissing scenes,[32] but virginal and chaste heroines, now in modern dress, continued to dominate Japanese film. Nevertheless, some popular fiction writers and filmmakers formed their antithesis: the Earthy Woman. She was considered a product of Americanization, and so she was to some extent, but she was also a return to the native frankness toward sex found in *Kojiki*.

In 1948 Taijiro Tamura's best-selling novel about postwar prostitution, *Gate of Flesh* (*Nikutai no Mon*), was made into a movie by Masahiro Makino.[33] During the same year Mizoguchi came out with his *Women of the Night* (*Yoru no Onnatachi*), also about streetwalkers. Mizoguchi's film is considered a masterpiece and Makino's film is so forgotten there do not seem to be any extant prints. However, the latter still has some merit, since it presents a new heroine in contrast to Mizoguchi's exploited prostitutes, reminiscent to his low-class geisha in *Sisters of the Gion* back in 1936.

The streetwalkers in *Gate of Flesh* have their own code, and their first commandment is that no one in their gang should ever do it for nothing. One woman who does is cruelly tortured for her sin. In spite of bearing witness to her punishment, however, the heroine still follows her example and not only experiences sexual pleasure but also falls in love. When her turn comes, in Seijun Suzuki's 1964 remake, she even smiles condescendingly upon her sisters who torment her for her envious discovery.

The heroine in *Gate of Flesh* broke the old rule in Japanese film that a woman should not enjoy sex. Mizoguchi's prostitutes never did; however, in 1950 with *A Picture of Madame Yuki* (*Yuki Fujin Ezu*, 1950) he portrayed a woman of aristocratic origins who, while embarrassed by her crude, bourgeois husband, cannot help but experience sensual pleasure with him. Keiko McDonald has noted Mizoguchi's indirect and delicate handling of the bed scenes.[34] Yet, the heroine's self-loathing suggests that one reason for the artistic treatment lies in Mizoguchi's old-fashioned ideas about sex. When she bemoans her "sin-filled nature," she reveals the old Buddhist prejudice against women: they were considered so spiritually inferior that they had to be reborn as men to make enlightenment possible.[35] Almost every time the heroine succumbs, Mizoguchi takes a close-up of her sash ornament, which is a miniature replica of a Noh mask. Consequently, she evokes the ghosts of the aristocratic women in Noh plays who return to earth because they cannot renounce worldly passions. Only through suicide by drowning can Madame Yuki free herself from

39

A Picture of Madame Yuki (1950), directed by Kenji Mizoguchi. This ethereal beauty (Michiyo Kogure), who drowns herself because of her "carnal" desires, evokes the ghosts of passion-bound aristocratic women and also reveals the director's virgin-whore complex.

carnality, and the last image of her walking on a misty hill overlooking a lake indicates that Mizoguchi's earthy woman became an ethereal beauty. Although Mizoguchi went on to create compelling images of sacred females in such films as *Ugetsu*, he was partly so motivated by a virgin/ whore complex typical of many Japanese men.

One manifestation of the Earthy Woman at a formative stage was films about sexy high-school girls, like *Teen-Ager's Sex Manual* (*Judai no Seiten*, 1953). While no longer titillating, it is still instructive regarding sexual inhibitions among the Japanese. When one girl finds out that her roommate is going steady with a boy, she takes a knife and slashes a photograph of the two girls together during chummier days. Director Koji Shima thereby reveals the sublimated lesbianism that could obtain from sex segregation due to Confucian mores. Although coeducation became common in postwar Japan, students at even college level are still somewhat segregated by clubs that resemble the fraternities and sororities in the United States, but without much interdating.

The heroine in *Teen-Ager's Sex Manual*, like Madame Yuki, commits suicide in the end. Instead of a Buddhist-like ornament, though, her torments of the flesh are symbolized by the necklace with the Christian cross in her décolletage. Rather than succumb to her desires, she dies still a virgin in the snow at a ski resort.

As a film *Teen-Ager's Sex Manual* was simply lurid sensationalism, demonstrating that release from Confucian-engendered sexual frustration cannot be found in the symbolism of Christianity, which resembles Buddhism in its attitude toward sex. In pre-Christian, Mediterranean mythology, however, a healthy eroticism can be found, and an attempt to instill it in a Japanese setting can be found in Senkichi Taniguchi's *Sound of Waves* (*Shiosai*, 1954), based on Yukio Mishima's famous novel.

Mishima had adapted the story of Daphis[15] and Chloe in his novel, and Taniguchi best captured the lyricism of the Greek original in the scene where the two young lovers go for a swim together. They had previously taken shelter from a sudden shower in an abandoned navel fortress where the girl had resisted the boy. Now the sun is out and after wrapping her slip around her breasts she runs down the hill to the sea shore, with him behind her and dressed only in a loincloth. Their fine young bodies are photographed underwater and they seem like cavorting dolphins.

While delightful, this scene seems somehow un-Japanese. Healthy eroticism can also be found in the native mythology, and Shohei Imamura eventually went searching there for his uninhibited Earthy Woman. The Angry Young Man tradition at Nikkatsu studios where he worked aided him. Nikkatsu prided itself on its films concerned with satisfying male desires and often had the Japanese word for desire, *yokubo*, inserted in the title of its films.[36] Imamura went one step further when he started making films which frankly and humorously depicted female desires, too.

Imamura's first Earthy Woman appeared in *The Insect Woman* (*Nippon Konchuki*, 1963), the tale of an unwed mother who becomes a prostitute. The heroine in *Intentions of Murder* (*Akai Satsui*, 1964) is more significant, however, for, dressed in a dumpy sweater and skirt, she appears to be an ordinary housewife at first. Later, with her clothes off, though, a mountain of flesh is revealed, and she becomes a white beast with pale, plump thighs and aroused desires. Through flashbacks, it is suggested that her sensuality comes from her grandmother who had been the mistress of her husband's father. This sensuality leads her to fall in love with a rapist who satisfied her sexual desire.

In *Intentions of Murder* the heroine's relation with her husband seems incestuous, and incest does play an important part in the formation of Imamura's earthy women. It was implied in the relation between the heroine and her father in *The Insect Woman*.

In *The Pornographers: Introduction to Anthropology* (*Jinruigaku Nyumon*, 1966) the widow sometimes lets her son sleep with her, and her lover winds up sleeping with her daughter. Since the widow goes insane, Imamura seems to conclude that his Earthy Woman cannot survive in Japan's modern cities. In his next, feature-length drama, *The Profound Desire of the Gods—Kuragejima: Tales from a Southern Island* (*Kamigami no Fukaki Yokubo*, 1968) Imamura journeys to some primitive islands to create earthy women who exist in a native society without Confucian morality and inhibitions.

Two sisters, born of incestuous unions, are central figures there, since they are *miko*, female mediums who served in a Shinto shrine during childhood. The elder is a local shaman who is having a love affair with her brother. The younger is demented and recalls the widow in *The Pornographers*; however, her insanity is on the blissful side. Both sisters earthily enjoy sex, sometimes in natural surroundings, or at least with cross-cutting from sex to nature scenes.

Imamura's humorous treatment of these sex scenes dispels the gloom associated with incest and harkens back to Shinto myths in *Kojiki* where sister and brother deities give birth to the islands of Japan. Imamura's comical view of sex is definitely part of the native tradition and can be found in old folk tales, such as *The Demon's Laugh* (*Oni no warai*).[37]

A girl who has been kidnapped by a demon is rescued by her mother with the help of a hermit woman. As they are escaping in a boat, though, the demon begins to drink up the water in the lake. The hermit woman suggests that they all expose their privates, and when they do, the demon laughs, coughing up the water and letting them escape. This old folk tale, moreover, recalls the myth recorded in *Kojiki* about the lewd dance of the Goddess Amenouzume, which induced laughter among the Gods and brought the Sun Goddess out of the cave she had been hiding in.

In addition to a humorous aspect, Imamura's Earthy Woman has a

Intentions of Murder (1964), directed by Shohei Imamura. When sexually aroused, this ordinary housewife (Masumi Harukawa) embodies the Earthy Woman who refutes hypocritical inhibitions.

*The Profound Desire of the Gods / Kuragejima: Tales from a Southern Island
(1968),* **directed by Shohei Imamura. This Earthy Woman (Hideko Okiyama)
escapes from civilization (represented by the locomotive) to enjoy sex in a native
society free from Confucian morality.**

maternal side, as indicated by Ian Buruma.[38] For example, in *The Insect
Woman* the unwed mother-daughter also gives milk from her lactating
breast to her senile father. This motherly attitude toward sex differs
sharply from Western ideas, and its source can also be traced to the native
tradition.

In Hayao Kawai's analysis of Japanese folk tales and psychology, he
presents an ancient version of the story of Urashima Taro in which the sea
turtle who transported Taro was transformed into a sensual woman who
gave herself to him. Kawai interprets the tortoise woman to be both mother
and mate and notes the difference from Western mythology, where the
hero has to often "kill the mother" (in the form of a dragon or other
monster) to win his mate.[39]

The transformation was lost in succeeding versions of the Urashima
Taro story. Because of Buddhist and Confucian influences, the sensual
tortoise woman became Otohime, the beautiful princess whose physical
nature is negated and who ends as an eternal virgin after Taro leaves her

underwater kingdom. The sea turtle, incidently, also appears in ancient Chinese mythology;[40] and, as a probable representation of the evolution from sea to land life, she can even be said to antedate Mother Earth.

Although the sensual aspect of the sea turtle vanished from the story of Urashima Taro, she continued to coexist with ethereal heroines in Japanese culture in the form of rural statues of fertility goddesses and artistic, pornographic prints (ukiyo-e) during the Edo period from 1603 to 1868. When Imamura unearthed her in the 1960s, he was simply bringing to the screen the old native frankness about sex that had always existed in tension with inhibiting Confucian morality.

The Earthy Woman can still be found sometimes in the soft-core porno films that Nikkatsu began mass producing in 1971. With *Sayuri Ichijo—Moist Desire (Ichijo Sayuri—Nureta Yokujo*, 1972) Tatsumi Kumashiro seemed to be following in Imamura's footsteps, for in his story of two strippers, the *Miko*-sisters on Kuragejima can be envisaged and Imamura's dual attitude toward sex well expressed. One of the strippers, the professional Sayuri Ichijo of the title, is chubby and so maternal that she sympathizes with a customer masturbating during her performance. The other stripper, played by a slender young actress (Hiroko Isayama), has the comedienne role, and her misadventures provide most of the laughs.

Another Nikkatsu director, Shinya Yamamoto, synthesized the maternal and humorous sides of sex in his *The Widow's Boarding House (Mibojin Geshuku)* series from 1974 on.[41] It is about a landlady who provides solace and pleasure for sexually frustrated college students away from home.

Although Yamamoto's humor is based on the self-serving stereotype of the passionate widow, his attitude toward sex is much more positive than that found in most Japanese porno films, where women become pneumatic toys and subjects of humiliation. In this respect, Japanese porno is not different from its Western counterparts and, therefore, is not a fit vehicle for the expression of the old native frankness about sex. The representation of this frankness in the archetype of the Earthy Woman in the films of the 1960s and 1970s was a refutation of the Confucian repression of sexual desire. In *The Ballad of Narayama* in 1983, however, Imamura's earthy women came to represent family solidarity through sex, which makes men dependent on them and more likely to perform their economic, supportive role. Ultimately, on the issue of family harmony, there is no disagreement between Shintoists and Confucianists, other than the greater demands the latter would make on women, and even earthy sex can be thereby contained.

Conclusion

Although the modern archetypal antitheses started out as wholly oppositional, gradually during their metamorphoses they coalesced with traditional archetypes. The Irresponsible Salaryman demonstrated that prudence and a certain cynicism is the middle way between loyalty and opportunism. The Angry Young Man took on the airs of the Tormented Lord, while remaining active. While prototypes for the cheerful Girl Next Door had probably existed ever since feudal times, cinema, by appealing to a mass audience, placed her upstage in Japanese iconography as an alternative to the traditional suffering heroines. The Earthy Woman had doubtless existed since antiquity, but had been suppressed during modernization, which included mass indoctrination in stoic, samurai virtues. Postwar writers and filmmakers unearthed her as a protest against sexual repression. This protest eventually resulted in a changed image for the Japanese heroine in TV dramas. Joseph L. Anderson has noted that in 1982 they still suffered, but only after satisfaction,[42] and the continuing proliferation of bed scenes on TV in the late 1980s bears him out. This phenomenon suggests that nowadays heroines can experience sex without being downgraded, but that it is best to keep it in the home. In short, while the modern archetypal antitheses did not overturn or replace traditional archetypes, their challenge resulted in new, viable role models for contemporary Japanese, who are by no means replicas of their ancestors.

Conclusion

JAPANESE film began with conservative archetypes like the Loyal Retainer, Tormented Lord, Chaste Warrior, and Exile that encouraged submission and a strong sense of affiliation with Japanese society, and problematic archetypes like the Vagabond, Vengeful Spirit, tragic lovers, and parent-child types that not only supported traditional values but sometimes transcended or opposed them. Due to Western influence, modern archetypal antitheses developed that started out as oppositional but later became contained within the total iconography. Nevertheless, they changed the iconography and contemporary attitudes by presenting alternate role models which still remain alongside, or as composite formations with, traditional archetypes.

Modern Japanese heroes and heroines are not very different from their Western counterparts. The flippant, cynical attitude of the Irresponsible Salaryman can be discerned in American films critical of big business, and the Angry Young Man probably originated in the West. Every culture has its Girl Next Door type. The Earthy Woman can be found in Erskine Caldwell's *Tobacco Road*, which John Ford made into a film in 1941, and she was well embodied in perspiring Italian beauties like Sophia Loren, before Hollywood cosmeticized them. Traditional Japanese archetypes are significantly different, though, and it would be useful to reconsider why before attempting a final assessment of all the archetypes that continue to exist on TV, the principal medium of popular iconography nowadays.

Not only the Tormented Lord and the All-Suffering Female but all the traditional Japanese archetypes suffer, and this is their dominant motif. Modern antitheses like the Irresponsible Salaryman and the cheerful Girl Next Door were in fact a rejection of suffering, but this, as evidenced by the lonely youths in the films of the 1970s, was not entirely successful.

Suffering is also the dominant motif in Western drama, for Shakespeare's tragedies are much more famous than his comedies. Even in Hollywood action dramas Robert Mitchum used to be beaten bloody before he got the baddies, and Clint Eastwood often continues that tradition. Still, Japanese *yakuza* heroes are not only more masochistic but seem even to become martyrs in the end. Like Shin Hasegawa's Exile, Alan Ladd's Shane embodies loneliness, but Shane's stems from not being able to settle down rather than from being cut off from human bonds. In Hollywood religious spectaculars, Christian martyrs suffer like Zushio the

Prodigal Son, but they go to their heavenly reward with a beatific smile on their face. Poor Zushio cannot rejoice over being forgiven, since in Japan forgiveness is usually only a recognition of the suffering that continues. In short, Japanese archetypes outsuffer their Hollywood counterparts.

Even the antagonists of the Japanese archetypes suffer. In *The Yotsuya Ghost Story* Iemon is tormented by the Vengeful Spirit of his dead wife, Oiwa. As the plot develops in *What Is Your Name?*, obstructing third parties are seen in a different light: the Weak, Passive Male begins to sympathize with the husband because *he* loves her too, and the heroine consoles her formerly cruel mother-in-law who has become bedridden. The only real difference is that the archetypes suffer even more.

"Life is Suffering" is the first truth of Buddhism, and its expression in Japanese culture dims even their perception of evil. One of Japan's greatest film directors, Yasujiro Ozu, could not really portray the bad. Whenever he tried to, the results were either melodramatic, in a family drama like *Tokyo Twilight* (*Tokyo Boshoku*, 1957), or unintentionally comical, in a crime story like *Dragnet Girl* (*Hijosen no Onna*, 1933). Ozu could present the essentially tragic human condition in the form of estrangement between kin and friends in masterpieces such as *Tokyo Story* (*Tokyo Monogatari*, 1953); but the evil side of human nature was for him simply acts of delinquency against parents or parental figures.

Ozu was not alone among his countrymen, for their dim perception of evil even shows up in the period film, an action genre where confrontation between the good guys and the bad guys is absolutely necessary. Most of the villains therein, however, are usually caricatures of Lord Kira, who was base and nasty rather than evil. In those films where an "evil daimyo" is called for, there is a scene of "pagan" revels where, after he is bored with his incongruous dancing girls, he begins shooting poor peasants with his bow and arrow. He is like Nero or Caligula, and his Japanese creators were obviously influenced by Hollywood spectaculars.

With the exception of the gratuitously evil character portrayed by Tatsuya Nakadai in *Yojimbo* (*Yojimbo*, 1961), the only really evil villain in a period film is Nobunaga Oda in *A Band of Assassins, II* (*Zoku Shinobi no Mono*, 1963). Here the feudal dictator cruelly tortures prisoners and burns Buddhist temples to the ground with all their followers inside. It is significant that its director, Satsuo Yamamoto, is taken up with Marxist ideology, which posits an ideal future world in contrast to a present one of exploitation, and is a development from Christianity, with echoes of the Manichean belief that Satan, who rules this world, is battling with God in Heaven for the souls of all mankind. As an adherent of Marxism, therefore, Yamamoto could portray Oda as a diabolical monster exploiting the peasants. Even though Oda's cruelty had been documented in postwar history books, other Japanese film directors whitewashed his rise to power. Without a transcendental reference point, such as an ideal world, they could assume only that their leaders were usually good and that a few bad ones did not spoil the barrel.

But just as suffering does exist in Christianity, evil is faced in Buddhism. In Buddhism, though, it is more important to recognize suffering than to insist on an all-out battle between the forces of good and evil, and often in Buddhist mythology demons are pacified rather than conquered. A good expression of this attitude can be found in the evolution of the popular hero, Sazen Tange. As stated in chapter 1, originally Tange was simply a villain whose deformities signified a diabolical nature, but film director Daisuke Ito transformed him into a suffering, betrayed retainer. Then in *Sazen Tange and the Pot Worth a Million Ryo (Tange Sazen—Hyakuman-ryo no Tsubo,* 1935)Sadao Yamanaka changed him into a lazy, hired sword who squabbles with his plucky female keeper while doting on orphans. In *Sazen Tange (Tange Sazen,* 1952), a remake of Yamanaka's classic, director Sadatsugu Matsuda went even further. Now Tange drinks and jokes with the common people and protects them from the baddies. He is a neighborhood hero and in one scene they give him a ride on their shoulders, as they would for a Shinto god in a cart (*mikoshi*) during a festival. His female keeper is now addressed as his wife and the orphan has become his son. The demon has been domesticated as well as pacified.

Among Japan's popular heroes, the best example of the Buddhist concern with suffering over evil is Ryunosuke Tsukue, the problematic main character of Kaizan Nakazato's popular novel *The Great Bodhisattva Pass.* As stated in chapter 1, Tsukue was the prototype of the nihilistic swordsman who dominated Japanese film in the 1920s. Nakazato, however, considered his novel to be an exposition of religious thought,[1] and did not yield film rights until 1935, when Hiroshi Inagaki directed a film version that was neither nihilistic nor religious.

The first film version to take up the religious theme in Nakazato's work was that by Tomu Uchida, *The Great Bodhisattva Pass (Daibosatsu Toge,* in 3 parts from 1957 to 1959). Quoting from Uchida's autobiography, Tadao Sato points out that Uchida was intrigued by the Buddhist elements in the original and likened its dominant tone to a Buddhist hymn (*wasan*).[2] It seems the motivation behind the film lies largely in Uchida's experiences in a Manchurian internment camp after World War II,[3] which brought home the truth of the dictum, "Life is Suffering."

Uchida's film begins at the Mountain Pass of the Bodhisattva, where Ryunosuke Tsukue slays an innocent old pilgrim merely to try out a new sword stroke. That night his fencing opponent's wife visits him and begs him to spare her husband in their match. He rapes her, kills her husband the next day, and runs off with her; but after a year or so of conjugal life he kills her during an argument and abandons their child. Thereafter, he becomes a hired sword and keeps on the move since he is pursued by the brother of the fencing opponent he killed.

A Band of Assassins II (1963), directed by Satsuo Yamamoto. In this film, sixteenth-century Japanese warlords are demythologized: Mitsuhide Akechi (So Yamamura, upper left), Nobunaga Oda (Tomisaburo Wakayama, upper right), Ieyasu Tokugawa (Tomo Nagai, lower left), and Hideyoshi Toyotomi (Eijiro Tono, lower right). Unlike most Japanese film directors who benignly whitewashed Nobunaga Oda's rise to power, Satsuo Yamamoto portrays him as a diabolical monster exploiting the peasants.

In Part 1 of Uchida's version Tsukue is tormented by the ghosts of his victims and occasionally misses his native area and his abandoned son, who is fortunately being raised by his family servant. In Part 2, after he is blinded in a battle, he is reduced to the role of a mendicant who plays a *shakuhachi* (flute) to eke out a living. Thereby, he wins the sympathy of a number of women who successively attend to his needs. He accepts the death of one of them philosophically, saying that her sufferings are over now. He even rescues a young bridegroom from mercenary officials. However, just when he is on the verge of becoming a sympathetic character he starts slaying innocent people again. Cinematically, this is attributed to fits of madness by having his sword-wielding figure shot against a background of flames or an abstract red backdrop.

In Part 3, pursued by ghosts of his victims and longing for his son, Tsukue returns to his native place. In the end he goes outside during a typhoon because he imagines his son is calling him, and he is swept down a river on a bridge dislodged during the flood.

As a backdrop for the opening titles of parts 1, 2, and 3, Uchida had used scrolls of the Buddhist universe and had panned down from the heavenlike Pure Land through Earth to Hell. At the end of Part 3 he simply reversed the process and panned up to the Pure Land. This use of Buddhist scrolls may have influenced this interpretation of Uchida's film made by Tadao Sato:

> Ryunosuke Tsukue is an incarnation of suffering, not evil. . . . He has taken on the sufferings of mankind. He is wandering alone in the midst of the flames of retribution in an earthly hell. The people he kills along the way are sent to the Pure Land.[4]

Yet, to a Westerner with a Judeo-Christian background, Tsukue is evil, since his own sufferings do not justify the murder of innocent people. Macbeth is a much more appealing character, for he has a guilty conscience and his sufferings are just punishment for his sins. Conscience may be represented by the ghosts in *The Great Bodhisattva Pass*, but Tsukue himself never expresses any guilt and simply misses his son.

With Tsukue's longing for his son, though, Confucian philosophy enters the picture and makes Japanese Buddhism more palatable. Mencius' parable about saving the child about to fall in the well, previously used in the interpretation of Uchida's *Battle of Life or Death*, also applies here because it connects compassion for human suffering with love of children in general, which is in turn rooted in parental love in particular.

When Tsukue's nemesis, Utsugi, sees Tsukue's son being cared for by the family servant, he begins to pity Tsukue and has qualms about carrying out his vendetta against him. The fact that Uchida's *The Great Bodhisattva Pass* ends with a tormented Tsukue calling out for his son suggests that, by experiencing the sufferings of a parent, Tsukue can take

The Great Bodhisattva Pass II (1958), directed by Tomu Uchida. This blind swordsman (Chiezo Kataoka), who kills many during his wanderings, exemplifies the first precept of Buddhism, "Life is Suffering." Strong belief in this precept even dimmed the Japanese perception of evil.

on the sufferings of mankind. Buddhist compassion is thereby channeled through Confucian philosophy. Although the source of this kind of compassion is different from that of Western humanism, which originated in the idea that we are all children of God, the outcome is similar.

The religious significance of *The Great Bodhisattva Pass* in film versions after that of Uchida vanished almost entirely. In a 1960 version by Kenji Misumi starring Raizo Ichikawa, Dai Ei's most handsome leading man, the director continually took high-angle close-ups of Tsukue's closed eyes. This not only provided a startling contrast to Ichikawa's expressive eyes before Tsukue goes blind but also evoked Buddhist images. Because of their closed eyes, Tanizaki tells us in *A Portrait of Shunkin*, the Japanese can find a blind face aesthetically pleasing.[5] Still, by beautifying Tsukue's suffering, Misumi dilutes its religious meaning.

The 1966 version by Kihachi Okamoto—the most popular outside of Japan—simply reflects the nihilism of its director. There are so many spurts of blood, agonized screams, and dismembered arms that the slaughter in Tsukue's melees becomes ludicrous, and reminiscent of wartime horrors, which Okamoto experienced as grotesque. Okamoto's Tsukue becomes a crystalization of soldiers made insane by war and driven to monstrous acts of cruelty in which they perversely delight. Such a maniac is beyond suffering.

These post-Uchida versions seem to reflect a general tendency, for it is difficult to discern a strong Buddhist sense of suffering in Japanese film from the 1960s on. One reason for this is the accelerating rate of secularism in Japanese culture. For Uchida, born in 1898,[6] the experience of World War II stirred up religious sentiments he had probably considered feudalistic in his younger days. On the other hand, for Okamoto, born in 1924,[7] this experience simply made him nihilistic. Another reason is affluence in postwar Japan. Although the historical Buddha regarded suffering as a spiritual disease (since he rooted it in desires), most Japanese past and present have not made such a sharp distinction between the spiritual and the physical, and for them—and for many Third World people at present—suffering was usually material indeed.

Suffering is still depicted in TV dramas that trace the vicissitudes of a typical family from the 1920s to the present day. But these lengthy serials seem to reflect nostalgia for past sufferings and indulgence in self-pity, rather than any Buddhist perception of the human condition.

While Buddhist sentiments about suffering declined in Japanese film expression, the Buddhist concept of pacification continued to work on Japan's modern archetypal antitheses. In the process rebellious sentiments were contained, but not before they remolded traditional archetypes to some extent, as can be seen in the following assessment of popular iconography on Japanese TV in the 1980s.

The Loyal Retainer-Tormented Lord dyad is still intact, as evidenced by

NHK's *Chushingura* in 1982, as well as by their dramatic serialization of the story of Yoshitsune and Benkei in 1986. Still, the most conspicuous hero in period dramas on commercial TV is the feudal magistrate, modeled on Kin-san of Toyama or Lord Ooka. While on cases, he may disguise himself as a commoner or as a *yakuza* gambler, and thus exhibit a familiarity with the common people no other samurai hero can boast. His unfailing popularity can be attributed to the contemporary Japanese penchant for mysteries, as well as to their nostalgia for the days before intense modernization, when life was simpler and people were easy to understand.[8] Although he is not an advocate of loyalty toward a superior as such, he still recalls benevolent leaders like General Nogi and his feudal antecedents,[9] who protected the common people from the malevolent powers-that-be (a reflection of the dichotomy in the Japanese spirit world).

The protector-hero in TV period dramas could also be a wandering samurai, who resembles the Exile much more than the Vagabond, or a nihilistic swordsman. The latter fools around with loose women, the former, like Kin-san of Toyama, can only joke with them, and, true to the Chaste Warrior tradition, neither would conceivably lay a hand on a pathetic beauty.

The protector-hero in these fairy-tale, period dramas probably does not indicate that present-day Japanese are politically gullible. On the contrary, their political apathy suggests a rather cynical view of contemporary government leaders, which resembles the attitude of the Irresponsible Salaryman toward his superiors. The protector-hero is more likely a wish-fulfillment image for the intense dependency needs that have been fostered since child training and lead even adult Japanese to assume they can always get help in time of need, provided they remain well-behaved members of their society.

Even the Angry Young Man has become a protector-hero on TV in contemporary police serials, the most popular of which are produced by Yujiro Ishihara. These young cops are as active as Yujiro in his prime; however, the object of their anger is not their parents or adult society, but cruel criminals who torment the ordinary citizen, whose sufferings bring bitter grimaces to their handsome mugs.

Although it appears that the Angry Young Man sold out to the establishment, his continuing presence affected the behavior of the leading man in TV love stories. The Weak Passive Male still persists, perhaps as an object for the maternal affection of older housewives; however, some young male lovers, albeit shy, are more active than their immobile predecessors, and many middle-aged lovers are more understanding than weak. In either case, the heroine often comes to the hero, or circumstances bring them together. A Japanese male who actively pursues women still seems to be considered frivolous or regarded with suspicion. Nevertheless, the hero in contemporary TV love stories does satisfy the heroine; and, even if that satisfaction is only temporary, it is more that the heroine in *What Is Your Name?* ever got.

As indicated in the latter part of this study, in popular Japanese iconography rebellious sentiments are usually expressed through heroines rather than heroes, and a feudal precedent existed in the resentment of the Vengeful Spirit. Feudal female avengers continue to appear on TV. In a 1987 drama, *The Five-Petalled Camelia (Gohen no Tsubaki)*, a young girl sets about killing the men who cuckolded her bedridden father. Her resentment, however, was more an expression of filial piety than a protest against a male-dominated society.

More significant is the frequent appearance of career women in TV dramas about contemporary life, and a good example is the series *Women Friends (Onna Tomodachi)*, which had high ratings in 1986. While not exactly a protest, it indicates that times have changed for Japanese women by presenting the adventures of three friends since high school days. One of them, the cheerful Girl Next Door type, eventually opts for the traditional role of a housewife. Another winds up as a career woman after losing in love and is a melancholy version of the All-Suffering Female. The third one has an affair with a married man and wins him, but she decides to let him go because her career is more important for her. While the first two women show that traditional norms are still strong, the third demonstrates that nowadays there are alternatives, for nothing in the treatment of her character suggests that she is a bad woman for either sleeping with a married man or for deciding a career is more important than marriage. Although conservative Japanese males may still speak of career women with derision, their frequent appearance on prime-time TV indicates that a considerable number of such women are among the viewers, and that their image represents a viable role model that developed from Western influence and from the metamorphoses undergone by the Girl Next Door and the Earthy Woman.

While the contemporary drama on TV has expressed some social change, the period drama seems to have remained conservative. Still, the theme of loyalty to a superior—the cornerstone of the old commercial period film—has been considerably de-emphasized in favor of homilies about familial and neighborly ties. This indicates that, in the value system of contemporary Japanese, the family has become more important than the polity. Current TV dramas about salarymen concur by depicting husbands and fathers who are forced to pay more attention to families they had been neglecting for the sake of company loyalty. Furthermore, the frequent treatment of old age problems in TV family dramas suggests that Japanese think this is their most crucial social problem. Through the suffering of the aged in these dramas—reminiscent of that of the mother in *Sansho the Bailiff*, but not so ennobling—their sons and daughters are impeached and the old Confucian virtue of filial piety is reaffirmed.

Japanese archetypes on present-day TV are the foci of traditional and modern sentiments, and they have been modified through dialectic tension and pacification. Joseph L. Anderson has stated that the period drama is a megagenre expressed in films, plays, and books, and he has likened it to a cosmos whose narratives change with time.[10] The same can be said for popular Japanese iconography *in toto*. It is composed of constellations of old and young stars now existing in a state of harmony rather than of tension. The Loyal Retainer and the Angry Young Man both have their place in this universe, and neither has priority over the other, since both have been modified according to their times. The distinction between traditional and modern may be significant only for the Japanophile. If a Japanese were told that the young Yujiro hero was Western in origin, he would just shake his head and say Yujiro Ishihara is Japanese. Yujiro belongs just as much as Oishi or Musashi.

With secularization and the loss of an emperor-centered nationalism, Japanese cultural identity became mainly based on a strong sense of affiliation, rather than on a belief in strong principles. All the postwar books written about this cultural identity, the so-called *Nihonjin-ron*, were simply rationalizations of affiliation, produced to fill the gaps resulting from the decline of many traditional values. This strong sense of affiliation is based upon the intense dependency needs of a group-oriented people who equate autonomy with loneliness and can depend only on their own. It is the key to the modern Japanese cultural identity, as well as the guiding principle in their contemporary popular iconography.

Popular Japanese iconography, which attained full bloom in their commercial cinema and continues to be viable on TV, reflects the fact that Japanese culture has changed considerably, especially within the last hundred years. After antitraditional sentiments were expressed, they were modified and thereby contained. This containment, along with the persistence of some traditional sentiments, indicates the conservative side of a medium like commercial cinema and of modern Japanese culture in general. Submission is still encouraged, but not necessarily in a hierarchical context. The sacrifice of the modern *yakuza* hero was made more for his group than for his boss. The Angry Young Man was punished for satisfying desires that most viewers can only sublimate. Envy was just as important a motivation for his containment as the drive to control others. In short, the tyranny of many over one has to be considered, along with the lackey mentality of submission to the powers-that-be, in any evaluation of the conservative function of commercial cinema in Japan and elsewhere.

On the other hand, the fact that new heroes and heroines are an integral part of the popular iconography and provide alternate role models demonstrates the progressive side of Japan's commercial cinema. The social significance of all this can be shown through a brief reference to American film history. Movies praising romantic and conjugal love, and those glorifying youth, eventually had a part in changing the value system of the children of immigrants (whose ancestors usually prized familial ties above all else) and of rural youths with a puritanical background. When Marlon Brando and James Dean began playing the Angry Young Man in the 1950s, they doubtless provided role models for many youths who rebelled against their parents and conservative society in general. Such youthful protest, even if delinquent, had its part in the Civil Rights movement and the antiwar demonstrations, as well as in the sex revolution throughout the 1970s. By the same token, Japan's Angry Young Man also served as a model of protest for the Japanese student movement through the 1960s, and perhaps the more liberal attitude toward sex in present-day Japan is a concession to that protest.

The development of Japanese cinema demonstrates that rebellious sentiments could be expressed as long as the results were commercial. When leftist movies made money in the early 1930s and in the 1960s,[11] Japanese film studios did not hesitate to make them. Ideological control usually took the form of censorship instead of prescription. If expression went too far, it was curbed and the antithetical archetypes were contained to maintain equilibrium in the mainstream culture. Their continuing existence in the popular iconography, however, showed that the boundaries of permitted behavior had been extended. One still had to conform to the tyranny of many over one and of the powers-that-be, but only after choosing from a wider range of role models. Consequently, contemporary Japanese have more freedom than did their ancestors. Their popular iconography not only reflects this, but also, through its metamorphoses, had a part in their progressive development.

Notes

Introduction

1. Mircea Eliade, *Rites and Symbols of Initiation: The Mysteries of Birth and Rebirth*, trans. Willard R. Trask (New York: Harper and Row, 1975).
2. Joseph L. Anderson and Donald Richie, *The Japanese Film: Art and Industry* (New York: Grove Press, 1960).
3. Donald Richie, *Japanese Cinema: Film Style and National Character* (New York: Doubleday Anchor, 1971). I write "1961" in the text because this volume is based on *Japanese Movies* (Tokyo: Japan Travel Bureau, 1961) and the generalizations I make apply to both publications.
4. Joan Mellen, *The Waves at Genji's Door: Japan through Its Cinema* (New York: Pantheon Books, 1976).
5. Audie Bock, *Japanese Film Directors* (Tokyo: Kodansha International, 1978).
6. Noël Burch, *To the Distant Observer: Form and Meaning in the Japanese Cinema* (London: Scolar Press, 1979).
7. Keiko I. McDonald, *Cinema East: A Critical Study of Major Japanese Films* (Rutherford, N.J.: Fairleigh Dickinson University Press, 1983).
8. Donald Richie, *The Films of Akira Kurosawa* (Los Angeles: University of California Press, 1965). (There is a 1984 revised edition, same press.)
9. Donald Richie, *Ozu: His Life and Films* (Berkeley and Los Angeles: University of California Press, 1974).
10. Keiko I. McDonald, *Mizoguchi* (Boston: Twayne, 1984).
11. Bock, *Japanese Film Directors*, p. 9.
12. Alain Silver, *The Samurai Film*, rev. ed. (Woodstock, N.Y.: Overlook Press, 1983).
13. David Desser, *The Samurai Films of Akira Kurosawa* (Ann Arbor, Mich.: UMI Research Press, 1983).
14. Tadao Sato, *Currents in Japanese Cinema*, trans. Gregory Barrett (Tokyo: Kodansha International, 1982).
15. Richie, *Japanese Cinema*, pp. 61–62.
16. Ibid., p. 69.
17. Ibid., pp. 61–62.
18. Harumi Befu, *Japan: An Anthropological Introduction* (San Francisco: Chandler, 1971), p. 52.
19. Richie, *Japanese Cinema*, p. xxvi.
20. Richard N. Tucker, *Japan: Film Image* (London: Studio Vista, 1973).
21. Paul Schrader, *Transcendental Style in Film: Ozu, Bresson, Dreyer* (Berkeley and Los Angeles: University of California Press, 1972).
22. Burch, *To the Distant Observer*, p. 16.
23. Desser, *Samurai Films of Kurosawa*, pp. 5–8.
24. Anderson and Richie, *Japanese Film*, pp. 315–31.
25. Ibid., pp. 315–16.

26. Ian Buruma, *A Japanese Mirror: Heroes and Villains of Japanese Culture* (London: Jonathan Cape, 1984). Published in the U.S. as *Behind the Mask: On Sexual Demons, Sacred Mothers, Transvestites, Gangsters, Drifters, and Other Japanese Cultural Heroes* (New York: Pantheon Books, 1984).

27. Robert N. Bellah, *Beyond Belief: Essays on Religion in a Post-Traditional World* (New York: Harper and Row, 1976), pp. 118–24.

28. Robert N. Bellah, *Tokugawa Religion: The Values of Pre-Industrial Japan* (Glencoe, Ill.: The Free Press, 1957), p. 18.

29. C. G. Jung, *Collected Works*, vol. 9, part 1, *The Archetypes and the Collective Unconscious*, trans. R. F. C. Hull, 2nd ed. (Princeton: Princeton University Press, 1968), p. 4.

30. Ibid., p. 5.

31. Ibid., p. 153.

32. Ibid., p. 38.

33. *Man and His Symbols*, ed. with introduction Carl G. Jung (New York: Dell Laurel, 1968), p. 83.

34. Ibid., p. 68.

35. *Webster's New Collegiate Dictionary* (Springfield, Mass., 1975), p. 58.

36. Jung, *The Archetypes and the Collective Unconscious*, pp. 3–4.

37. Bellah, in a lecture at the University of California at Berkeley, 1976.

38. Bellah, *Tokugawa Religion*, p. 197.

39. Joseph Campbell, *The Mythic Image* (Princeton: Princeton University Press, 1974), p. 356.

40. Joseph Campbell, *The Hero with a Thousand Faces*, 2nd ed. (Princeton: Princeton University Press, 1968), p. 382.

41. Emile Durkheim, *On Morality and Society*, ed. with introduction R. N. Bellah (Chicago: The University of Chicago Press, 1973), p. 191.

42. James Frazer, *The Golden Bough: A Study in Magic and Religion*, abridged ed. (London: Macmillan Press, 1922), pp. 65–66.

43. Campbell, *The Mythic Image*, pp. 430–31.

Chapter 1. The Loyal Retainer and the Tormented Lord

1. Joseph L. Anderson and Donald Richie pointed out the division into two main genres in *The Japanese Film: Art and Industry* (New York: Grove Press, 1960), p. 48. I cannot say that half of the heroes were feudal because period film production was greatly reduced in the 1940s. See Tadao Sato, *Currents in Japanese Cinema*, trans. Gregory Barrett (Tokyo: Kodansha International, 1982), p. 38.

2. Ivan Morris, *The Nobility of Failure: Tragic Heroes in the History of Japan* (Tokyo: Charles E. Tuttle, 1982).

3. George Sansom, *A History of Japan to 1334* (Stanford: Stanford University Press, 1958), p. 94.

4. Donald Keene notes in the introduction to his translation of *Kanadehon Chushingura* that there were only forty-six retainers involved but that an "honorary" forty-seventh was included in most accounts. See *Chushingura* (The Treasury of Loyal Retainers), (Tokyo: Charles E. Tuttle, 1981), pp. 1–6.

5. Tadao Sato, *Chushingura: Iji no keifu* (*Chushingura: Genealogy of Honor*) (Tokyo: Asahi Sensho, 1976), p. 96.

6. Ibid., p. 30.

7. George Sansom, *A History of Japan, 1334–1615* (Stanford: Stanford University Press, 1961), p. 152–53.

8. Ibid., p. 343.

9. John W. Hall and Richard K. Beardsley, *Twelve Doors to Japan* (New York: McGraw-Hill, 1965), p. 148.

10. Tadao Sato, *Currents in Japanese Cinema*, pp. 16–17.

11. Alain Silver, *The Samurai Film*, rev. ed. (Woodstock, N.Y.: Overlook Press, 1983), p. 17.

12. Ivan Morris, *The Nobility of Failure*, p. 371n.

13. Tadao Sato, *Chushingura: Iji no keifu*, p. 11.

14. Ibid.

15. Ibid., p. 33.

16. Silver, *The Samurai Film*, p. 35.

17. Keene, *Chushingura*, pp. 3–4.

18. Tadao Sato, *Chushingura: Iji no keifu*, pp. 13–15.

19. Ibid., pp. 57–60. Sato mentions not only craftsmen but all levels of Japanese society.

20. Ibid., pp. 88–90.

21. Ibid., pp. 99–104.

22. Chie Nakane, *Japanese Society* (London: Penguin, 1973), p. 74n.

23. David Desser, *The Samurai Films of Akira Kurosawa* (Ann Arbor, Mich.: UMI Research Press, 1983), p. 24.

24. Joan Mellen, *The Waves at Genji's Door: Japan through Its Cinema* (New York: Pantheon, 1976), pp. 31–32.

25. Tadao Sato in program notes for Shozo Makino film festival, *FC* (Tokyo National Museum of Modern Art Film Center), no. 49, 1978, p. 42.

26. Tadao Sato, *Chushingura: Iji no keifu*, pp. 101, 106.

27. Ibid., p. 163.

28. Tadao Sato, in conversation.

29. Anderson and Richie, *The Japanese Film*, p. 138.

30. Rikiya Tayama, *Waga taiken teki: Nihon goraku eiga-shi—Senzen-hen* (My Experiential View of the History of Japanese Popular Movies—prewar vol.) (Tokyo: Gendai Kyoyo Bunko, 1980), p. 106.

31. Tadao Sato, *Chushingura: Iji no keifu*, pp. 117–120, 223.

32. Robert J. Smith, *Ancestor Worship in Contemporary Japan* (Stanford: Stanford University Press, 1974) pp. 21–23.

33. Film directors often showed Oishi's strong sense of affiliation by close-ups of the Asano family crest on his clothing. Even in the 1982 NHK TV version a close-up of this crest was employed during Oishi's *seppuku* scene.

34. Donald Richie, *The Films of Akira Kurosawa* (Los Angeles: University of California Press, 1965), p. 31.

35. Ian Buruma, *A Japanese Mirror: Heroes and Villains of Japanese Culture* (London: Jonathan Cape, 1984), pp. 132–35.

36. Tadao Sato, *Currents in Japanese Cinema*, p. 16.

37. Masatoshi Ohba in program notes for ToEi film festival, *FC*, no. 69, 1981, p. 24.

38. *Showa-shi jiten* (Dictionary of Showa Period History, 1925—) (Tokyo: Mainichi Shinbunsha, 1980), p. 263.

39. Siegfried Kracauer, *From Caligari to Hitler: A Psychological History of the German Film* (Princeton: Princeton University Press, 1974), p. 53.

40. Tadao Sato, *Kimi wa jidai geki eiga o mita ka* (Have you seen a Period Drama Movie?) (Tokyo: Jyacometei Shuppan, 1977), p. 186.

41. Ohba, *FC*, no. 69, 1981, p. 24.

42. Tadao Sato, *Currents in Japanese Cinema*, pp. 38–39.

43. Quoted by Tadao Sato and Chieo Yoshida in *Chambara eiga-shi* (History of Japanese Swordfighting Movies) (Tokyo: Hoga Shoten, 1972), pp. 178–80.

44. Tadao Sato, *Currents in Japanese Cinema*, p. 253.

45. Tadao Sato, "Ito Daisuke-ron" (Essay on Daisuke Ito), *FC*, no. 40, 1977, p. 6.

46. Ibid., pp. 6–7.

47. Quoted by Hayao Kawai in *Mukashi banashi to nihonjin no kokoro* (Folk Tales and the Japanese Psyche) (Tokyo: Iwanami Shoten, 1982), pp. 243–44.

48. Hayao Kawai, *Mukashi banashi to nihonjin no kokoro*, pp. 240–49.

49. Silver, *The Samurai Film*, p. 94.

50. Tadao Sato, *Currents in Japanese Cinema*, p. 259.

Chapter 2. The Chaste Warrior

1. Musashi Miyamoto, *The Book of Five Rings* (*Gorin no sho*), trans. and commentary Nihon Services Corporation (New York: Bantam, 1982), p. xvi, pp. 5–6.

2. *NHK Dorama Gaido—Miyamoto Musashi* (NHK Drama Guide: Musashi Miyamoto) (Tokyo: Nippon Hoso Shuppan Kyokai, 1984), pp. 130–33.

3. *The Tale of The Heike* (*Heike monogatari*), trans. Hiroshi Kitagawa and Bruce Tsuchida, vol. 2, (Tokyo: University of Tokyo Press, 1977), pp. 433–35.

4. *The Taiheiki: A Chronicle of Medieval Japan*, trans. with introduction and notes Helen Craig McCullough (Tokyo: Charles E. Tuttle, 1979).

5. *NHK Rekishi e no shotai* (NHK's Invitation to History), vol. 4, (Tokyo: Nippon Hoso Shuppan Kyokai, 1980), p. 57.

6. Koji Kata, "Yoshikawa Eiji izen no Musashi-zo" (The Image of Musashi Before Eiji Yoshikawa), *Rekishi yomihon* (May 1984): 120–27.

7. Ibid., p. 124.

8. Ibid., p. 125.

9. *NHK Drama Guide*, pp. 130–32.

10. Kata, "Image of Musashi Before Yoshikawa," p. 121.

11. Eiji Yoshikawa, *Musashi*, trans. Charles Terry with foreword by Edwin Reischauer (Tokyo: Kodansha, 1981), p. ix.

12. Mircea Eliade, *Rites and Symbols of Initiation: The Mysteries of Birth and Rebirth*, trans. Willard Trask (New York: Harper and Row, 1975), pp. 134–35.

13. Ibid., pp. 7–10.

14. *Kojiki*, trans. with introduction and notes Donald Philippi (Tokyo: University of Tokyo Press, 1977), pp. 79–86.

15. Eliade in *Rites and Symbols of Initiation* (pp. 81–84) gives examples of warriors who are strong because they act like wild animals; but in Musashi's case he must be tamed to become a better warrior.

16. *Kojiki*, trans. Philippi, pp. 88–92.

17. *Dokyumento Showa seso-shi—senzen-hen* (A Social History of the Showa era from 1925 to 1937), ed. Kenzo Nakashima (Tokyo: Heibonsha, 1975), p. 9.

18. Tadao Sato, "Musashi to Kojiro" in *NHK Rekishi e no shotai*, vol. 4, pp. 96–97.

19. Genzo Murakami and Tadachika Kuwata, "Ketto Ganryujima" (Duel at the Isle of Ganryu) in *NHK Rekishi e no shotai*, vol. 4, p. 67.

20. Kata, "Image of Musashi Before Yoshikawa," p. 122.

21. Musashi Miyamoto, *The Book of Five Rings*, pp. 34, 43. "Mindless consciousness" is my translation of *munen muso*.

22. Kata, "Image of Musashi Before Yoshikawa," p. 122.

23. Ibid.

24. NHK Drama Guide, pp. 132–33.

25. Ibid.

26. Alain Silver in *The Samurai Film* (Woodstock, N.Y.: Overlook Press, 1983) claims (p. 96) there is another 1954 Musashi film version, but I could not find any Japanese record of it, nor the name of its supposed director, Yasuo Kohata. There is a Yasuo Furuhata listed in Kinema Jumpo's *Nihon eiga kantoku zenshu* (Dictionary of Japanese Film Directors), but he did not begin directing films until 1966. I suspect Silver is referring to some TV drama on Musashi that was shown in the movie theater circuit in the U.S.

27. David Desser, *The Samurai Films of Akira Kurosawa* (Ann Arbor, Mich.: UMI Research Press, 1983), p. 40.

28. Ironically, in the U.S. in the 1950s the works of D. T. Suzuki were popularizing Zen among beatniks and intellectuals.

29. Donald Richie, *Japanese Cinema: Film Style and National Character* (New York: Doubleday Anchor, 1971), p. 45.

30. *Nihon eiga kantoku zenshu* (Dictionary of Japanese Film Directors) (Tokyo: Kinema Jumposha, 1976), pp. 67–68.

31. As there is hardly any Zen in Uchida's Musashi, it is curious that it was released in the U.S. as *Zen and Sword*.

32. Enlightenment consists of realizing one's own Buddha nature, which is similar to the belief of some Christian mystics that the Kingdom of God is within every individual.

33. It is strange that some U.S. businessmen regard Musashi as a model for Japan's economic success. Uchida's Musashi, for example, is closer to exemplifying America's old rugged individualism.

34. The term "worthy opponent" seems to be my own; however, Alain Silver has noted in *The Samurai Film* (p. 81) that a climactic duel with an extremely skillful opponent is characteristic of the Samurai Film genre.

35. Desser, *The Samurai Films of Kurosawa*, p. 111.

36. In regard to the slaying of the thirteen-year-old, Desser in *The Samurai Films of Kurosawa* claims that the moral rightness of Musashi's actions is never questioned (p. 41). On the contrary, in most film versions Musashi is refused sanctuary at a Buddhist temple because of his action. Still, I agree with Desser that, in general, mythical warriors are beyond morality.

37. *Mencius*, trans. with introduction D. C. Lau (London: Penguin Books, 1970), pp. 82–83.

38. Joseph Campbell, *The Mythic Image* (Princeton: Princeton University Press, 1974), p. 8.

39. Joseph Campbell, *The Hero with a Thousand Faces*, 2nd ed. (Princeton: Princeton University Press, 1968), p. 332.

40. James Frazer, *The Golden Bough: A Study in Magic and Religion*, abridged ed. (London: Macmillan Press, 1922), pp. 65–66.

41. Ibid., p. 13.

42. *Kojiki*, trans. Philippi, pp. 238–39.

43. *Nihon eiga sakuhin zenshu* (Dictionary of Japanese Films) (Tokyo: Kinema Jumposha, 1973), p. 90.

44. Ibid.

45. Ibid., p. 202.

46. Alain Silver in *The Samurai Film* also treats this interesting character (pp. 86–94) and labels him an alien hero, rather than a composite type as I do.

47. Tadao Sato, *Currents in Japanese Cinema*, trans. Gregory Barrett (Tokyo: Kodansha, 1982), p. 47.

48. Ibid., p. 46.

49. Ibid., pp. 46–49.

50. Campbell, *Mythic Image*, p. 42.

51. Somewhat similar conclusions about *Seven Samurai* are drawn by Silver in *The Samurai Film* (pp. 48–49) and by Desser in *The Samurai Films of Kurosawa* (pp. 91–92).

52. Donald Richie, *The Films of Akira Kurosawa* (Los Angeles: University of California Press, 1965), p. 108.

Chapter 3. *Yakuza* Heroes

1. Tadao Sato, *Currents in Japanese Cinema*, trans. Gregory Barrett (Tokyo: Kodansha, 1982), p. 51.

2. George A. De Vos, *Socialization for Achievement: Essays on the Cultural Psychology of the Japanese* (Berkeley and Los Angeles: University of California Press, 1975), pp. 282–83n.

3. Tadao Sato, *Currents in Japanese Cinema*, p. 259.

4. A notable exception is Zatoichi, who will be treated in chapter 4.

5. De Vos, *Socialization for Achievement*, pp. 285–86.

6. Ian Buruma, *A Japanese Mirror: Heroes and Villains of Japanese Culture* (London: Jonathan Cape, 1984), p. 167.

7. Koji Kata, *Nihon no yakuza* (Japanese Gangsters) (Tokyo: Taiwa Shobo, 1964), p. 20.

8. De Vos, *Socialization for Achievement*, pp. 286–87.

9. Ibid., pp. 288–93.

10. Sato, *Currents in Japanese Cinema*, p. 39.

11. *Nihon eiga sakuhin zenshu* (Dictionary of Japanese Films) (Tokyo: Kinema Jumposha, 1973), p. 104.

12. Donald Richie, *The Films of Akira Kurosawa* (Los Angeles: University of California Press, 1965), pp. 16–17.

13. The term "admirable ally" seems to be my own.

14. *Nihon eiga sakuhin zenshu*, pp. 132–33.

15. Masatoshi Ohba in program notes for ToEi film festival, *FC* (Tokyo National Museum of Modern Art Film Center), no. 71, 1982, p. 26.

16. Masao Maruyama, *Studies in the Intellectual History of Tokugawa Japan*, trans. Mikiso Hane (Tokyo: University of Tokyo Press, 1974), p. 195.

17. *Nihon eiga sakuhin zenshu*, pp. 193–94.

18. *Nihon eiga haiyu zenshu—Danyu-hen* (Dictionary of Japanese Film Actors) (Tokyo: Kinema Jumposha, 1979), p. 375.

19. Ohba, *FC*, no. 71, 1982, p. 36.

20. *Nihon eiga haiyu zenshu—Danyu-hen*, p. 291.

21. Ibid., pp. 648–49.

22. Shoshi Okajima in program notes for ToEi film festival, *FC*, no. 71, 1982, p. 39.

23. Buruma, *A Japanese Mirror*, p. 171.

24. Ibid., p. 175.

25. James Frazer, *The Golden Bough: A Study in Magic and Religion*, abridged ed. (London: Macmillan Press, 1922), p. 469.

26. David Desser, in *The Samurai Films of Akira Kurosawa* (Ann Arbor, Mich.: UMI Research Press, 1983) makes the same "mistake" (p. 136).

27. Frazer in *The Golden Bough* gives numerous examples of substitution in sacrifices.

28. Sato, *Currents in Japanese Cinema*, p. 52.

29. Ezra F. Vogel in *Japan's New Middle Class*, 2nd ed. (Berkeley and Los

Angeles: University of California Press, 1971) gives a good description of a salaryman's company gang (pp. 103–9).

30. In some *yakuza* films, core members of a gang have parts of a dragon tattoo on their back, which they join together, shoulder to shoulder, for the final melee.

31. De Vos, *Socialization for Achievement*, p. 277.

32. Kurt Singer, quoted by Buruma in *A Japanese Mirror*, p. 189.

33. Sato, *Currents in Japanese Cinema*, pp. 52–53.

Chapter 4. Wanderer

1. Shoko Watanabe has stated in *Japanese Buddhism* (Tokyo: Japan Cultural Society, 1968) that "the important factor which relates most Japanese to a Buddhist temple is that the graves of his ancestors are there (p. 119)."

2. *Kojiki*, trans. with introduction and notes Donald L. Philippi (Tokyo: University of Tokyo Press, 1977), pp. 85–92.

3. Ivan Morris, *The Nobility of Failure: Tragic Heroes in the History of Japan* (Tokyo: Charles E. Tuttle, 1982), pp. 41–66.

4. Tadao Sato and Chieo Yoshida in *Chambara eiga-shi* (History of Japanese Swordfighting Movies) (Tokyo: Hoga Shoten, 1972), p. 69.

5. Tadao Sato, *Hasegawa Shin-ron* (Essays on Shin Hasegawa) (Tokyo: Chuokoronsha, 1975), p. 35.

6. Ibid., p. 39.

7. Ibid., pp. 287–88.

8. Ibid., p. 287.

9. Ian Buruma treats this film under the title "Mother Behind My Eyes" in *A Japanese Mirror: Heroes and Villains of Japanese Culture* (London: Jonathan Cape, 1984), pp. 26–28.

10. Modern *yakuza* heroes are also usually orphans whose boss is a father substitute, and they often pine for a dead mother who has a greater hold on them than any pathetic beauty.

11. Sato, *Hasegawa Shin-ron*, p. 20.

12. Although there is an extant print of the 1929 version directed by Kichiro Tsuji, the 1966 version is treated here because the loneliness of the Hasegawa exile is deepened on account of the romantic interest that only a postwar period film director could develop fully.

13. While some of the film treatments in the 1960s of Hasegawa stories were technically superb, their heroes could not compete in popularity with the modern *yakuza* hero. There were considered old-fashioned, but their motif was still viable, particularly in modern dress.

14. Tadao Sato in program notes for Shozo Makino film festival, FC (Tokyo National Museum of Modern Art Film Center), no. 49, 1978, p. 54.

15. Sato, *Hasegawa Shin-ron*, p. 299.

16. Tadao Sato, *Chushingura: Iji no keifu* (Chushingura: Genealogy of Honor) (Tokyo: Asahi Sensho, 1976), pp. 128–29.

17. *Eigashi-jo besuto 200 shiriizu—Nihon eiga* (The Great Films of the World—Japan) (Tokyo: Kinema Jumposha, 1982), p. 298.

18. Alain Silver in *The Samurai Film*, rev. ed. (Woodstock, N.Y.: Overlook Press, 1983) treats Zatoichi as an "alien hero," but seems unaware that he is a *yakuza* (pp. 76–83).

19. *Nihon eiga sakuhin zenshu* (Dictionary of Japanese Films) (Tokyo: Kinema Jumposha, 1973), p. 254.

20. Jippensha Ikku, *Shank's Mare* (The Tokaido volumes of *Hizakurige*) trans. Thomas Satchell (Tokyo: Charles E. Tuttle, 1960), p. 237.

21. The thirty-seventh entry came out in January 1987.

22. George A. De Vos, *Socialization for Achievement: Essays on the Cultural Psychology of the Japanese* (Berkeley and Los Angeles: University of California Press, 1975), pp. 282–84.

23. Buruma in *A Japanese Mirror* gives a detailed treatment of Tora-san (pp. 209–18). I cannot agree with his conclusion that he is popular because he appeals to the modern Japanese sense of self-satisfaction. One Japanese told me that Tora-san behaved humanely as modern Japanese *should*, and thus is an ideal rather than an object of pity.

24. Joseph L. Anderson and Donald Richie, *The Japanese Film: Art and Industry* (New York: Grove Press, 1960), p. 99.

25. Noel Carroll, "The Gold Rush," *Wide Angle* 3, no. 2 (1979):42–49.

26. Tadao Sato, "The Comedy of Ozu and Chaplin—A Study in Contrast," *Wide Angle* 3, no. 2 (1979):51.

27. For example, Tadao Sato in *Currents in Japanese Cinema*, trans. Gregory Barrett (Tokyo: Kodansaha Intl., 1982), p. 243.

28. Keiko I. McDonald in *Mizoguchi* (Boston: Twayne, 1984) also observes that Oharu became like a forgiving Buddha (p. 115).

29. *Webster's New Collegiate Dictionary* (Springfield, Mass., 1975), p. 870.

30. Ichiro Hori, *Nihon no shaamanizumu* (Japanese Shamanism) (Tokyo: Kodansha Gendai Shinsho, 1971), pp. 197–98.

31. Joseph K. Yamagiwa, "Literature and Japanese Culture," in John W. Hall and Richard K. Beardsley, *Twelve Doors to Japan* (New York: McGraw-Hill, 1965), p. 252.

Chapter 5. Vengeful Spirit

1. Shoko Watanabe, *Japanese Buddhism* (Tokyo: Japan Cultural Society, 1968), p. 83.

2. Tadao Sato, *Chushingura: Iji no keifu* (Chushingura: Genealogy of Honor) (Tokyo: Asahi Sensho, 1976), p. 119.

3. Ivan Morris, *The Nobility of Failure: Tragic Heroes in the History of Japan* (Tokyo: Charles E. Tuttle, 1982), pp. 59–61.

4. Iwao Nikura, an expert on Japanese spiritualism, made this observation in 1982 on a popular TV show called "Anata no Shiranai Sekai" (The World You Do Not Know).

5. *Kojiki*, trans. with introduction and notes Donald L. Philippi (Tokyo: University of Tokyo Press, 1977), pp. 64–67.

6. Ian Buruma, *A Japanese Mirror: Heroes and Villains of Japanese Culture* (London: Jonathan Cape, 1984), p. 47.

7. Akiko Baba, *Oni no kenkyu* (Research on Demons) (Tokyo: San-ichi Shobo, 1971), pp. 7–8, 160–63.

8. Murasaki Shikibu, *Genji monogatari* (The Tale of Genji) trans. Edward G. Seidensticker, vol. 1 (Tokyo: Charles E. Tuttle, 1978), pp. 71–73.

9. Ibid., pp. 497–98.

10. Watanable, *Japanese Buddhism*, p. 84.

11. Masatoshi Ohba in program notes for Horror film festival, *FC* (Tokyo National Museum of Modern Art Film Center), no. 41, 1977, p. 30.

12. Seicho Matsumoto and Kiyoyuki Higuchi, *Tokyo no tabi* (Tokyo Trips) (Tokyo: Kobunsha, 1966), pp. 80–81.

13. Ibid., p. 75.

14. Donald Keene, *World Within Walls: Japanese Literature of the Pre-Modern Era 1600–1867* (New York: Holt, Rinehart and Winston, 1976), pp. 468–69.

15. Ibid., p. 457.

16. Buruma, *A Japanese Mirror,* pp. 88–89.

17. Ohba, *FC,* no. 41, p. 30.

18. C. G. Jung, *Collected Works,* vol. 9, part 1, *The Archetypes and the Collective Unconscious,* trans. R. F. C. Hull, 2nd ed. (Princeton: Princeton University Press, 1968), p. 75.

19. *Mencius,* trans. with introduction D. C. Lau (London: Penguin, 1970), p. 195.

20. Tadao Sato, *Hasegawa Shin-ron* (Essays on Shin Hasegawa) (Tokyo: Chuokoronsha, 1975), pp. 191–94.

21. The explanation of the anima in the text is adapted from that found in *Man and His Symbols,* ed. C. G. Jung (New York: Dell Laurel, 1968), pp. 186–98.

22. Jung, *The Archetypes and the Collective Unconscious,* p. 82.

23. Erich Neumann presented copious examples in *The Great Mother: An Analysis of the Archetype,* trans. Ralph Manheim (Princeton: Princeton University Press, 1972), pp. 120–208.

24. Hayao Kawai, *Mukashi banashi to nihonjin no kokoro* (Folk Tales and the Japanese Psyche) (Tokyo: Iwanami Shoten, 1982), pp. 49–51.

25. Keiko I. McDonald in *Cinema East: A Critical Study of Major Japanese Films* (Rutherford, N.J.: Fairleigh Dickinson University Press, 1983) has observed that through dissolves and fades Mizoguchi lets the natural and supernatural in *Ugetsu* interact smoothly (pp. 108–9). Her interpretation is certainly valid, but in the end the viewer realizes that not only the aristocratic lady but also the potter's wife was supernatural.

26. Keiko I. McDonald, *Mizoguchi* (Boston: Twayne, 1984), p. 124.

27. *Nihon eiga sakuhin zenshu* (Dictionary of Japanese Films) (Tokyo: Kinema Jumposha, 1973), p. 224.

28. Shoshi Okajima in program notes for ToEi film festival, *FC,* no. 71, 1982, p. 38.

29. While analyzing ancient mythology, C. G. Jung surmised that the eye could stand for female genitals, in *Collected Works,* vol. 5, *Symbols of Transformation,* trans. R. F. C. Hull, 2nd ed. (Princeton: Princeton University Press, 1967), p. 268.

30. Akiko Baba, *Oni no kenkyu,* pp. 45–46.

31. Ibid., p. 248.

32. Ibid., pp. 119–223.

33. George A. De Vos, *Socialization for Achievement: Essays on the Cultural Psychology of the Japanese* (Berkeley and Los Angeles: University of California Press, 1975), p. 269.

34. Even though many Japanese claim they are a homogeneous society, the plight of resident Koreans and other minorities attracts more and more attention in the mass media nowadays.

Chapter 6. All-Suffering Female and Weak Passive Male

1. Shiro Kido, *Nihon eiga den: Eiga seisakusha no kiroku* (The Story of the Japanese Film: A Movie Producer's Record) (Tokyo: Bungei Shunjushinsha, 1956), pp. 52–54.

2. There are examples of weak Chinese male lovers in *Stories from a Ming*

Collection—The Art of the Chinese Story-Teller, trans. Cyril Birch (New York: Grove Press, 1958).

3. John K. Fairbank, Edwin O. Reischauer and Albert M. Craig, *East Asia: Tradition and Transformation* (Tokyo: Charles E. Tuttle, 1976), p. 140. On the other hand, according to John W. Hall and Richard K. Beardsley in *Twelve Doors to Japan* (New York: McGraw-Hill, 1965), in Japan in the twelfth century the warrior aristocrat replaced the courtier aristocrat as the male ideal (pp. 141–42).

4. Stephen Neale, *Genre* (London: BFI, 1980), pp. 59–60.

5. Joseph L. Anderson and Donald Richie, *The Japanese Film: Art and Industry* (New York: Grove Press, 1960), p. 261.

6. Edward H. Schafer in *Ancient China* (New York: Time-Life Books, 1967) notes the waning of Buddhist power due to persecution because of its "exotic anti-Chinese" qualities (p. 66). In Japan, though, Buddhism was no more foreign than Confucianism.

7. *Shukan Yomiuri (The Yomiuri Weekly)* featured a spread on Japanese film love stories entitled, "merodorama" on 19 July 1975.

8. *Webster's New Collegiate Dictionary* (Springfield, Mass., 1975), p. 716.

9. Tadao Sato, *Currents in Japanese Cinema*, trans by Gregory Barrett (Tokyo: Kodansha, 1982), p. 24.

10. *Kojiki*, trans. with introduction and notes Donald L. Philippi (Tokyo: University of Tokyo Press, 1977), pp. 49–58.

11. Ibid., pp. 64–65.

12. Ivan Morris, *The World of the Shining Prince: Court Life in Ancient Japan* (New York: Alfred A. Knopf, 1964), p. 109.

13. Ibid., pp. 144–47.

14. Examples are *Heike monogatari* and *Taiheiki*, which were treated in chapter 2.

15. Yoshinobu Inoura, *A History of Japanese Theater 1: Up to Noh and Kyogen*, (Tokyo: Japan Cultural Society, 1971), pp. 51, 72, 94–95.

16. Examples can be found in *Twenty Plays of the Nō Theatre*, ed. Donald Keene (New York: Columbia University Press, 1970).

17. Hall and Beardsley, *Twelve Doors to Japan*, p. 148.

18. Ian Buruma in *A Japanese Mirror: Heroes and Villains of Japanese Culture* (London: Jonathan Cape, 1984) draws similar conclusions (pp. 85–86).

19. Keiko I. McDonald, *Cinema East: A Critical Study of Major Japanese Films* (Rutherford, N.J.: Fairleigh Dickinson University Press, 1983), p. 61. McDonald notes further that the cutting of hair was "part of initiation into nunhood or priesthood, marking their abandonment of the lay world (p. 67n.)."

20. This "pure man and woman" impression was heightened by an exchange of close-ups in Masahiro Shinoda's excellent film adaptation, *Double Suicide (Shinju Ten no Amijima, 1969)*.

21. Inoura, *A History of Japanese Theater 1*, pp. 58–59.

22. Toshio Kawatake, *A History of Japanese Theater 2: Bunraku and Kabuki* (Tokyo: Japan Cultural Society, 1971), pp. 6–10.

23. Tadao Sato, *Mizoguchi Kenji no sekai* (The World of Kenji Mizoguchi) (Tokyo: Chikuma Shobo, 1982), pp. 219–21.

24. Sato, *Currents*, pp. 17–18.

25. Ibid., p. 20.

26. Masatoshi Ohba in program notes for Kazuo Hasegawa film festival, *FC* (Tokyo National Museum of Modern Art Film Center), no. 53, 1979, p. 39.

27. Sato, *Currents*, pp. 78–79.

28. Ibid., p. 250.

29. "Ballad films" were popular in the 1920s and early 1930s, but few have survived. One interesting extant print is *Osayo in Love* (*Osayo Koi Sugata*, 1934), directed by Yasujiro Shimazu.

30. According to Motohiko Fujita in *Gendai eiga no kiten* (The Starting Point of Modern Film) (Tokyo: Kinokuniya Shoten, 1965), before soundtracks were introduced Japanese silent films were accompanied by an orchestra in the theater, as in the West; title songs would be sung by *benshi* (film narrators) or professional singers (p. 25).

31. Sato, *Currents*, p. 23.

32. Kazuko Tsurumi, *Social Change and the Individual* (Princeton: Princeton University Press, 1970), pp. 89–90n.

33. Kido, *Nihon eiga den*, p. 171.

34. Anderson and Richie, *The Japanese Film*, p. 177.

35. Ibid., p. 76.

36. Sato, *Currents*, p. 24.

37. Ibid., p. 236.

38. Ibid., p. 37.

39. Koji Kata et al., *Meiji Taisho Showa Sesoshi* (Japanese History 1868–1974) (Tokyo: Shakai Shisosha, 1977), p. 302.

40. George A. De Vos, *Socialization for Achievement: Essays on the Cultural Psychology of the Japanese* (Berkeley and Los Angeles: University of California Press, 1975), p. 149.

41. Sato, *Currents*, p. 241.

42. Buruma, *A Japanese Mirror*, p. 32.

43. Sato, *Currents*, pp. 241–42.

44. Ezra F. Vogel, *Japan's New Middle Class*, 2nd ed. (Berkeley and Los Angeles: University of California Press, 1971), pp. 245–46.

45. Buruma, *A Japanese Mirror*, p. 59.

46. Ibid., p. 63.

47. Sato, *Currents*, p. 232.

48. Hayao Kawai, *Mukashi banashi to nihonjin no kokoro* (Folk Tales and the Japanese Psyche) (Tokyo: Iwanami Shoten, 1982), p. 138.

Chapter 7. Prodigal Son, Forgiving Parent, Self-Sacrificing Sister

1. At a Kenji Mizoguchi film festival at the Pacific Film Archives in Berkeley, California in 1976, Yoshikata Yoda, Mizoguchi's chief script writer, told the audience he still remembered his mother singing a lullaby based on the legend of *Sansho the Bailiff*.

2. Ruth Benedict, *The Chrysanthemum and the Sword—Patterns of Japanese Culture* (Tokyo: Charles E. Tuttle, 1954), p. 222.

3. George A. De Vos, *Socialization for Achievement: Essays on the Cultural Psychology of the Japanese* (Berkeley and Los Angeles: University of California Press, 1975), pp. 150–53, 161–62.

4. Takeo Doi, "Oyako kankei no shinri" (Psychology of Parent-Child Relationships) in *Oya to ko* (Parent and Child) (Tokyo: University of Tokyo Press, 1973), pp. 55–57.

5. De Vos, *Socialization for Achievement*, p. 106.

6. Audie Bock, *Japanese Film Directors* (Tokyo: Kodansha, 1978), p. 52.

7. *Kojiki*, trans. with introduction and notes Donald L. Philippi (Tokyo: University of Tokyo Press, 1977), pp. 71–81.

8. Hayao Kawai, *Mukashi banashi to nihonjin no kokoro* (Folk Tales and the Japanese Psyche) (Tokyo: Iwanami Shoten, 1982), p. 118.

9. Ivan Morris, *The Nobility of Failure: Tragic Heroes in the History of Japan* (Tokyo: Charles E. Tuttle, 1982), p. 1.

10. *Kojiki*, trans. Philippi, pp. 232–49.

11. *Nihongi: Chronicles of Japan from the Earliest Times to* A.D. *697*, trans. W. G. Aston (Tokyo: Charles E. Tuttle, 1972), pp. 210–11.

12. Takeo Iwasaki, *Sanseo dayu-ko: Chusei no sekkyo katari* (The Thought in *Sansho the Bailiff*: Tales from Medieval Sermons) (Tokyo: Heibonsha, 1973), pp. 8–9, 23.

13. Ibid., p. 26.

14. Tadao Sato, *Mizoguchi Kenji no sekai* (The World of Kenji Mizoguchi) (Tokyo: Chikuma Shobo, 1982), p. 204.

15. Ibid., pp. 204–6.

16. Ibid., p. 204.

17. Iwasaki, *Sanseo dayu-ko*, pp. 31–32.

18. Ibid., pp. 27–28.

19. Ibid., p. 58.

20. Ibid., 56–59, 63–64.

21. John Price, "A History of the Outcaste: Untouchability in Japan," in George De Vos and Hiroshi Wagatsuma, *Japan's Invisible Race: Caste in Culture and Personality*, rev. ed. (Berkeley and Los Angeles: University of California Press, 1972), pp. 16–22.

22. Iwasaki, *Sanseo dayu-ko*, p. 70.

23. John W. Hall and Richard K. Beardsley, *Twelve Doors to Japan* (New York: McGraw-Hill, 1965), p. 148.

24. *Honcho niju fuko* (Twenty Breaches of Filial Piety) (Tokyo: Iwanami Bunko, 1963), pp. 237–38.

25. Hiroshi Wagatsuma, "Some Aspects of Contemporary Japanese Family— Once Confucian, Now Fatherless?," a paper prepared for the conference on "The Family" sponsored by *Daedalus*, 6–8 May 1976, pp. 3–4.

26. Masao Maruyama, *Studies in the Intellectual History of Tokugawa Japan*, trans. Mikiso Hane (Tokyo: University of Tokyo Press, 1974), p. 333.

27. *Major Plays of Chikamatsu*, trans. Donald Keene (New York and London: Columbia University Press, 1961), p. 340.

28. Michio Nagai and John Bennett, "A Summary and Analysis of the Familial Structure of Japanese Society by Takeyoshi Kawashima," in *Japanese Culture and Character*, ed. Bernard Silberman (Tuscon, Ariz.: University of Arizona Press, 1962), pp. 105–8.

29. Benedict, *The Chrysanthemum and the Sword*, pp. 115–17.

30. Harumi Befu used the term "samuraization" in *Japan: An Anthropological Introduction* (San Francisco: Chandler, 1971) to describe the adoption of samurai values by lower classes (p. 52).

31. *Major Plays of Chikamatsu*, trans. Keene, pp. 377–78.

32. Robert N. Bellah, *Beyond Belief: Essays on Religion in a Post-Traditional World* (New York: Harper and Row, 1976), p. 88.

33. Ibid.

34. Ibid., p. 87.

35. There seem to be only fragmentary extant prints of the 1928 film version.

36. Sadao Yamane, "Kanzen choaku pataan no katsugeki no tenkai" (The Development of the Promotion of Good and Chastisement of Evil Pattern in Action Films), an essay for the ToEi film festival, *FC* (Tokyo National Museum of Modern Art Film Center), no. 69, 1981, pp. 3–4.

37. *Nihon eiga-shi* (History of Japanese Film), *Sekai no eiga sakka* (Film Makers of the World series), no. 31 (Tokyo: Kinema Jumposha, 1976), pp. 12–13.

38. Tadao Sato, *Currents in Japanese Cinema*, trans. Gregory Barrett (Tokyo: Kodansha, 1982). pp. 241–42.

39. Shoshi Okajima in program notes for American Film Masters festival, *FC*, no. 86, 1986. pp. 47–48.

40. Sato, *Mizoguchi Kenji no sekai*, pp. 37–38.

41. Ibid., p. 209.

42. Bock, *Japanese Film Directors*, p. 36.

43. Ibid.

44. C. G. Jung, *Collected Works*, vol. 9, part 1, *The Archetypes and the Collective Unconscious*, trans. R. F. C. Hull, 2nd ed. (Princeton: Princeton University Press, 1968), p. 82.

45. De Vos, *Socialization for Achievement*, p. 88.

46. Bock, *Japanese Film Directors*, p. 36.

47. Ibid., pp. 36–37.

48. Ezra F. Vogel, *Japan's New Middle Class*, 2d ed. (Berkeley and Los Angeles: University of California Press, 1971), p. 240.

49. Freda Freiberg, *Women in Mizoguchi's Films* (Melbourne: Papers of the Japanese Studies Centre, 1981), p. 26.

50. Erich Neumann calls this dyad the dual Great Goddess as mother and daughter and gives Demeter and Kore as an example in *The Great Mother: An Analysis of the Archetype*, trans. Ralph Manheim (Princeton: Princeton University Presss, 1972), pp. 308–9, 325.

51. Bock, *Japanese Film Directors*, p. 40.

52. Hall and Beardsley, *Twelve Doors to Japan*, p. 325.

53. Keiko I. McDonald, *Mizoguchi* (Boston: Twayne, 1984), p. 136.

54. Sato, *Mizoguchi Kenji no sekai*, pp. 214–15.

55. Ian Buruma, *A Japanese Mirror: Heroes and Villains of Japanese Culture* (London: Jonathan Cape, 1984), p. 25.

Chapter 8. The Archetypal Family—Extended and Rejected

1. *Mencius*, trans. with introduction D. C. Lau (London: Penguin Books, 1970), p. 184.

2. Shigeru Matsumoto, *Motoori Norinaga* (Cambridge, Mass.: Harvard University Press, 1970), pp. 114–17.

3. Tadao Sato, *Currents in Japanese Cinema*, trans. Gregory Barrett (Tokyo: Kodansha, 1982), pp. 246–47.

4. *Nihon eiga-shi* (History of Japanese Film), *Sekai no eiga sakka* (Film Makers of the World series), no. 31 (Tokyo: Kinema Jumposha, 1976), pp. 7–8.

5. Ivan Morris, *The Nobility of Failure: Tragic Heroes in the History of Japan* (Tokyo: Charles E. Tuttle, 1982), p. 403n.

6. There do not seem to be extant prints of prewar General Nogi films. My plot descriptions are adapted from those in Kinema Jumposha's *Nihon eiga-shi* (History of Japanese Film), pp. 81–82.

7. Tadao Sato in program notes for festival on Prewar History As Seen In Films, *FC* (Tokyo National Museum of Modern Art Film Center), no. 42, 1977, p. 19.

8. Sato, *Currents in Japanese Cinema*, p. 252.

9. Joseph L. Anderson and Donald Richie, *The Japanese Film: Art and Industry* (New York: Grove, 1960), p. 251.

10. Morris, *The Nobility of Failure*, p. 441n.

11. *Nihon eiga kantoku zenshu* (Dictionary of Japanese Film Directors) Tokyo: Kinema Jumposha, 1976), pp. 228, 436.

12. Ibid., p. 228.

13. Sato, *Currents in Japanese Cinema*, p. 135.

14. Ibid., pp. 135–36.

15. Hiroshi Wagatsuma, "Some Aspects of Contemporary Japanese Family— Once Confucian, Now Fatherless?," a paper prepared for the conference on "The Family" sponsored by *Daedalus*, 6–8 May 1976, pp. 34–35n.

16. Sato, *Currents in Japanese Cinema*, p. 33.

17. Donald Richie, *The Films of Akira Kurosawa* (Los Angeles: University of California Press, 1965), pp. 67–68.

18. Sato, *Currents in Japanese Cinema*, p. 142.

19. Ibid., p. 242.

20. Audie Bock, *Japanese Film Directors* (Tokyo: Kodansha, 1978), pp. 265–66.

21. Jun Eto, *Seijuku to soshitsu—Haha no hokai* (Maturity and Loss: Disintegration of the Mother) (Tokyo: Kawade Shobo, 1967), pp. 11–87.

22. Takeo Doi in *Amae no kozo* (Structure of Dependency) (Tokyo: Kobundo, 1971) has expounded at length on the emphasis on dependency in Japanese culture. Doi's book has been translated by John Bester as *The Anatomy of Dependence* (Tokyo: Kodansha, 1973).

23. Sato, *Currents in Japanese Cinema*, p. 121.

24. Jun Eto, *Seijuku to soshitsu*, pp. 82, 87.

25. *Nihon eiga kantoku zenshu*, p. 314.

26. C. G. Jung, *Collected Works*, vol. 9, part 1, *The Archetypes and the Collective Unconscious*, trans. R. F. C. Hull, 2nd ed. (Princeton: Princeton University Press, 1968), claimed that if an archetype was lost it would lead to frightful discontent (p. 69); and the fad for patricide and matricide films in Japan in the late seventies would bear him out. Still, since the fad was so short-lived, one can only marvel at the resiliency of the Japanese.

Chapter 9. Modern Archetypal Antitheses

1. Tadao Sato, *Currents in Japanese Cinema*, trans. Gregory Barrett (Tokyo: Kodansha, 1982), pp. 104–5.

2. Ian Buruma, *A Japanese Mirror: Heroes and Villains of Japanese Culture* (London: Jonathan Cape, 1984), p. 203.

3. Sato, *Currents in Japanese Cinema*, pp. 246–47.

4. Ezra F. Vogel, *Japan's New Middle Class*, 2d ed. (Berkeley and Los Angeles: University of California Press, 1971), p. 5.

5. Chie Nakane, *Japanese Society* (London: Penguin, 1973), p. 72.

6. Sato, *Currents in Japanese Cinema*, pp. 167–69.

7. Rikiya Tayama, *Waga taiken teki: Nihon goraku eiga-shi—Sengo-hen* (My Experiential View of the History of Japanese Popular Movies—Postwar vol.) Tokyo: Gendai Kyoyo Bunko, 1979), p. 207.

8. The Japanese economy became so successful that eventually Irresponsible Salaryman films and socially critical ones like Kurosawa's *The Bad Sleep Well* ceased to be made.

9. An excellent example in extant print is Hiroshi Shimizu's *The Young Master in College* (*Daigaku no Wakadanna*, 1933).

10. Sato, *Currents in Japanese Cinema*, p. 212.

11. Ibid., 213.

12. Audie Bock, *Japanese Film Directors* (Tokyo: Kodansha, 1978), p. 314.

13. Donald Richie, *Japanese Cinema: Film Style and National Character* (New York: Doubleday Anchor, 1971), p. 109.

14. *Nihon eiga haiyu zenshu—Danyu-hen* (Dictionary of Japanese Film Actors) (Tokyo: Kinema Jumposha, 1979), pp. 43, 242.

15. Richie, *Japanese Cinema*, p. xx.

16. Sato, *Currents in Japanese Cinema*, p. 212.

17. Robert N. Bellah, *Beyond Belief: Essays on Religion in a Post-Traditional World* (New York: Harper and Row, 1976), pp. 101–2.

18. Masao Maruyama, *Studies in the Intellectual History of Tokugawa Japan*, trans. Mikiso Hane (Tokyo: University of Tokyo Press, 1974), pp. 195–205.

19. Charles D. Sheldon, "Feudal Japan: Politics and Society from the Eighth Century to 1868," in *Half The World: The History of China and Japan*, ed. Arnold Toynbee (New York: Holt, Rinehart and Winston, 1973), p. 224.

20. *Nihon eiga sakuhin zenshu* (Dictionary of Japanese Films) (Tokyo: Kinema Jumposha, 1973), pp. 277–78.

21. Tadao Sato in program notes for festival on Prewar History As Seen In Films, *FC* (Tokyo National Museum of Modern Art Film Center), no. 42, 1977, p. 25.

22. Sato, *Currents in Japanese Cinema*, p. 100.

23. Shin'ichi Mashita and Jun Fukuda, *Eiga no naka no josei-zo* (Cinematic Images of Women) (Tokyo: Kawade Shinsho, 1956).

24. *Nihon eiga kantoku zenshu* (Dictionary of Japanese Film Directors) (Tokyo: Kinema Jumposha, 1976), p. 424.

25. Ivan Morris, *The World of the Shining Prince: Court Life in Ancient Japan* (New York: Alfred A. Knopf, 1964), p. 213.

26. John W. Hall and Richard K. Beardsley, *Twelve Doors to Japan* (New York: McGraw-Hill, 1965), p. 141.

27. George A. De Vos, *Socialization for Achievement: Essays on the Cultural Psychology of the Japanese* (Berkeley and Los Angeles: University of California Press, 1975), p. 19.

28. Toshio Kawatake, *A History of Japanese Theater 2: Bunraku and Kabuki* (Tokyo: Japan Cultural Society, 1971), p. 89.

29. Donald Keene, *World Within Walls: Japanese Literature of the Pre-Modern Era 1600–1867* (New York: Holt, Rinehart and Winston, 1976), p. 457.

30. Sato, *Currents in Japanese Cinema*, p. 135.

31. Ibid., p. 74.

32. Ibid., 35.

33. *Nihon eiga sakuhin zenshu* (Dictionary of Japanese Films) (Tokyo: Kinema Jumposha, 1973), p. 189.

34. Keiko I. McDonald, *Mizoguchi* (Boston: Twayne, 1984), pp. 91–93.

35. Ian Buruma, *A Japanese Mirror: Heroes and Villains of Japanese Culture* (London: Jonathan Cape, 1984), p. 8.

36. Related by Shoichi Ozawa, a comic actor, at a Nikkatsu film revival in 1984.

37. Hayao Kawai, *Mukashi banashi to nihonjin no kokoro* (Folk Tales and the Japanese Psyche) (Tokyo: Iwanami Shoten, 1982), p. 75.

38. Buruma, *A Japanese Mirror*, p. 35.

39. Kawai, *Mukashi banashi to nihonjin no kokoro*, pp. 154–55.

40. Edward H. Schafer, *Ancient China* (New York: Time-Life Books, 1967), p. 102.

41. *Nihon eiga kantoku zenshu* (Dictionary of Japanese Film Directors) (Tokyo: Kinema Jumposha, 1976), p. 440.

42. Joseph L. Anderson and Donald Richie, *The Japanese Film: Art and Industry*, expanded ed. (Princeton, Princeton University Press, 1982), p. 453.

Conclusion

1. Tadao Sato, *Kimi wa jidai geki eiga o mita ka* (Have you seen a Period Drama Movie?) (Tokyo: Jyacometei Shuppan, 1977), p. 186.

2. Ibid., pp. 192–93.

3. Ibid., p. 198.

4. Ibid., pp. 196–97.

5. Junichiro Tanizaki, *Seven Japanese Tales*, trans. Howard Hibbett (New York: Berkley Medallion, 1965), p. 14.

6. *Nihon eiga kantoku zenshu* (Dictionary of Japanese Film Directors) (Tokyo: Kinema Jumposha, 1976), p. 66.

7. Ibid., p. 92.

8. Tadao Sato states in *Kimi wa jidai geki eiga o mita ka* that this nostalgia for a simpler life is a reason for the continuing popularity of the period drama (p. 100).

9. One feudal antecedent who continued to be a popular hero in TV period drama in the 1980s is Komon Mito, a daimyo closely affiliated with the Tokugawa Shogunate. Legend has it that after he retired he traveled around the countryside protecting the common people from mercenary officials and feudal gangleaders.

10. Joseph L. Anderson and Donald Richie, *The Japanese Film: Art and Industry*, expanded ed. (Princeton, Princeton University Press, 1982), pp. 444–48.

11. Tadao Sato, *Currents in Japanese Cinema*, trans. Gregory Barrett (Tokyo: Kodansha, 1982), pp. 215–17, 253.

Bibliography

Anderson, Joseph, and Donald Richie. *The Japanese Film: Art and Industry*. New York: Grove, 1960. Expanded edition. Princeton: Princeton University Press, 1982.

Aston, W.G., trans. *Nihongi: Chronicles of Japan from the Earliest Times to* A.D. 697. Tokyo: Charles E. Tuttle, 1972.

Baba, Akiko. *Oni no kenkyu* (Research on demons.) Tokyo: San-ichi Shobo, 1971.

Befu, Harumi. *Japan: An Anthropological Introduction*, San Francisco: Chandler, 1971.

Bellah, Robert N. *Beyond Belief: Essays on Religion in a Post-Traditional World*. New York: Harper and Row, 1976.

———. *Tokugawa Religion: The Values of Pre-Industrial Japan*. Glencoe, Ill.: The Free Press, 1957.

Benedict, Ruth. *The Chrysanthemum and the Sword—Patterns of Japanese Culture*. Tokyo: Charles E. Tuttle, 1954.

Birch, Cyril, trans. *Stories from a Ming Collection: The Art of the Chinese Story-Teller*. New York: Grove Press, 1958.

Bock, Audie, *Japanese Film Directors*. Tokyo: Kodansha, 1978.

Burch, Noël. *To the Distant Observer: Form and Meaning in the Japanese Cinema*. London: Scolar Press, 1979.

Buruma, Ian. *A Japanese Mirror: Heroes and Villains of Japanese Culture*. London: Jonathan Cape, 1984. Published in the U.S. as *Behind the Mask: On Sexual Demons, Sacred Mothers, Transvestites, Gangsters, Drifters and Other Japanese Cultural Heroes*. New York: Pantheon, 1984.

Campbell, Joseph. *The Hero with a Thousand Faces*. 2nd ed. Princeton: Princeton University Press, 1968.

———. *The Mythic Image*. Princeton: Princeton University Press, 1974.

Carroll, Noël. "The Gold Rush." *Wide Angle* 3, no. 2 (1979): 42–49.

De Vos, George A. *Socialization for Achievement: Essays on the Cultural Psychology of the Japanese*. Berkeley and Los Angeles: University of California Press, 1975.

Desser, David. *The Samurai Films of Akira Kurosawa*. Ann Arbor: UMI Research Press, 1983.

Doi, Takeo. *The Anatomy of Dependence (Amae no kozo)*. Translated by John Bester. Tokyo: Kodansha, 1973.

———. "*Oyako kankei no shinri*" (Psychology of Parent-Child Relationships). In *Oya to ko* (Parent and Child), pp. 52–57. Tokyo: University of Tokyo Press, 1973.

Durkheim, Emile. *On Morality and Society*. Edited by Robert N. Bellah. Chicago: The University of Chicago Press, 1973.

Eliade, Mircea. *Rites and Symbols of Initiation: The Mysteries of Birth and Rebirth*. Translated by Willard R. Trask. New York: Harper and Row, 1975.

Eto, Jun. *Seijuku to soshitsu—Haha no hokai* (Maturity and Loss: Disintegration of the Mother). Tokyo: Kawade Shobo, 1967.

Fairbank, John K., Edwin O. Reischauer, and Albert M. Craig. *East Asia: Tradition and Transformation.* Tokyo: Charles E. Tuttle, 1976.

FC (Film Center Programs). Tokyo: Tokyo National Museum of Modern Art Film Center, 1971–.

Frazer, James. *The Golden Bough: A Study in Magic and Religion.* Abridged ed. London: Macmillan, 1922.

Freiberg, Freda. *Women in Mizoguchi's Films.* Melbourne: Papers of the Japanese Studies Centre, 1981.

Fujita, Motohiko. *Gendai eiga no kiten* (The Starting Point of Modern Film). Tokyo: Kinokuniya Shoten, 1965.

Hall, John W. and Richard K. Beardsley. *Twelve Doors to Japan.* New York: McGraw-Hill, 1965.

Hori, Ichiro. *Nihon no shaamanizumu* (Japanese Shamanism). Tokyo: Kodansha Gendai Shinsho, 1971.

Ihara, Saikaku. *Honcho niju fuko* (Twenty Breaches of Filial Piety). Tokyo: Iwanami Bunko, 1963.

Ikku, Jippensha, *Shank's Mare (Hizakurige).* Translated by Thomas Satchell. Tokyo: Charles E. Tuttle, 1960.

Inoura, Yoshinobu, *A History of Japanese Theater 1: Up to Noh and Kyogen.* Tokyo: Japan Cultural Society, 1971.

Iwasaki, Takeo. *Sanseo dayu-ko: Chusei no sekkyo katari* (The Thought in *Sansho the Bailiff*: Tales from Medieval Sermons). Tokyo: Heibonsha, 1973.

Jung, C. G., *Collected Works.* Vol. 9, part 1, *The Archetypes and the Collective Unconscious.* Translated by R. F. C. Hull. 2nd ed. Princeton: Princeton University Press, 1968.

———. *Collected Works.* Vol. 5, *Symbols of Transformation.* Translated by R.F.C. Hull. 2nd ed. Princeton: Princeton University Press, 1967.

———, ed. *Man and His Symbols.* New York: Dell Laurel, 1968.

Kata, Koji. "*Yoshikawa Eiji izen no Musashi-zo*" (The Image of Musashi Before Eiji Yoshikawa). *Rekishi yomihon* (May 1984): 120–27.

———. *Nihon no yakuza* (Japanese Gangsters). Tokyo: Taiwa Shobo, 1964.

———, et al. *Meiji Taisho Showa Sesoshi* (Japanese History, 1868–1974). Tokyo: Shakai Shisosha, 1977.

Kawai, Hayao. *Mukashi banashi to nihonjin no kokoro* (Folk Tales and the Japanese Psyche). Tokyo: Iwanami Shoten, 1982.

Kawatake, Toshio. *A History of Japanese Theater 2: Bunraku and Kabuki.* Tokyo: Japan Cultural Society, 1971.

Keene, Donald. *World Within Walls: Japanese Literature of the Pre-Modern Era 1600–1867.* New York: Holt, Rinehart and Winston, 1976.

———, trans. *Chushingura (The Treasury of Loyal Retainers).* Tokyo: Charles E. Tuttle, 1981.

———, trans. *Major Plays of Chikamatsu.* New York and London: Columbia University Press, 1961.

———, ed. *Twenty Plays of the Nō Theatre.* New York: Columbia University Press, 1970.

Kido, Shiro. *Nihon eiga den: Eiga seisakusha no kiroku* (The Story of the Japanese Film: A Movie Producer's Record). Tokyo: Bungei Shunjushinsha, 1956.

Kitagawa, Hiroshi and Bruce Tsuchida, trans. *The Tale of the Heike (Heike monogatari).* Vols. 1 and 2. Tokyo: University of Tokyo Press, 1977.

Kracauer, Siegfried. *From Caligari to Hitler: A Psychological History of the German Film.* Princeton: Princeton University Press, 1974.

Maruyama, Masao. *Studies in the Intellectual History of Tokugawa Japan.* Translated by Mikiso Hane. Tokyo: University of Tokyo Press, 1974.

Mashita, Shin'ichi and Jun Fukuda. *Eiga no naka no josei-zo* (Cinematic Images of Women). Tokyo: Kawade Shinsho, 1956.

Matsumoto, Seicho and Kiyoyuki Higuchi. *Tokyo no tabi* (Tokyo Trips). Tokyo: Kobunsha, 1966.

Matsumoto, Shigeru. *Motoori Norinaga.* Cambridge, Mass.: Harvard University Press, 1970.

McCullough, Helen Craig, trans. *The Taiheiki: A Chronicle of Medieval Japan.* Tokyo: Charles E. Tuttle, 1979.

McDonald, Keiko I. *Cinema East: A Critical Study of Major Japanese Films.* Rutherford, N.J.: Fairleigh Dickinson University Press, 1983.

———. *Mizoguchi.* Boston: Twayne, 1984.

Mellen, Joan. *The Waves at Genji's Door: Japan Through Its Cinema.* New York: Pantheon, 1976.

Mencius. Translated by D. C. Lau. London: Penguin, 1970.

Miyamoto, Musashi. *The Book of Five Rings (Gorin no sho).* Translated by Nihon Services Corp. New York: Bantam, 1982.

Morris, Ivan. *The Nobility of Failure: Tragic Heroes in the History of Japan.* Tokyo: Charles E. Tuttle, 1982.

———. *The World of the Shining Prince: Court Life in Ancient Japan.* New York: Alfred A. Knopf, 1964.

Murasaki Shikibu. *The Tale of Genji (Genji monogatari).* Translated by Edward G. Seidensticker. Vols. 1 and 2. Tokyo: Charles E. Tuttle, 1978.

Nagai, Michio and John Bennett. "A Summary and Analysis of the Familial Structure of Japanese Society by Takeyoshi Kawashima." In *Japanese Culture and Character,* edited by Bernard Silberman, pp. 101–11. Tuscon, Arizona: University of Arizona Press.

Nakane, Chie. *Japanese Society.* London: Penguin, 1973.

Nakashima, Kenzo, ed. *Dokyumento Showa seso-shi—senzen-hen* (A Social History of the Showa era from 1925 to 1937). Tokyo: Heibonsha, 1975.

"Natsukashi no Merodorama" (Nostalgic Melodramas). *Shukan Yomiuri* (The Yomiuri Weekly) (19 July 1975): 40–77.

Neale, Stephen. *Genre.* London: BFI, 1980.

Neumann, Erich. *The Great Mother: An Analysis of the Archetype.* Translated by Ralph Manheim. Princeton: Princeton University Press, 1972.

NHK Dorama Gaido—Miyamoto Musashi (NHK Drama Guide: Musashi Miyamoto). Tokyo: Nippon Hoso Shuppan Kyokai, 1984.

NHK Rekishi e no shotai (NHK's Invitation to History). Vol. 4. Tokyo: Nippon Hoso Shuppan Kyokai, 1980.

Nihon eiga-shi (History of Japanese Film). *Sekai no eiga sakka* (Film Makers of the World series), no. 31. Tokyo: Kinema Jumposha, 1976.

Nihon eiga haiyu zenshu—Danyu-hen (Dictionary of Japanese Film Actors). Tokyo: Kinema Jumposha, 1979.

Nihon eiga haiyu zenshu—Joyu-hen (Dictionary of Japanese Film Actresses). Tokyo: Kinema Jumposha, 1980.

Nihon eiga kantoku zenshu (Dictionary of Japanese Film Directors). Tokyo: Kinema Jumposha, 1976.

Nihon eiga sakuhin zenshu (Dictionary of Japanese Films). Tokyo: Kinema Jumposha, 1973.

Nihon eiga 200—Eigashijo besuto 200 shiriizu (The Great Films of the World—Japan). Tokyo: Kinema Jumposha, 1982.

Philippi, Donald L., trans. *Kojiki*. Tokyo: University of Tokyo Press, 1977.

Price, John. "A History of the Outcaste: Untouchability in Japan." In *Japan's Invisible Race: Caste in Culture and Personality*, edited by George De Vos and Hiroshi Wagatsuma. Rev. ed. Berkeley and Los Angeles: University of California Press, 1972.

Richie, Donald. *The Films of Akira Kurosawa*. Los Angeles: University of California Press, 1965. Rev. ed. Berkeley and Los Angeles: University of California Press, 1984.

———. *Japanese Cinema: Film Style and National Character*. New York: Doubleday Anchor, 1971.

———. *Ozu: His Life and Films*. Berkeley and Los Angeles: University of California Press, 1974.

Sansom, George. *A History of Japan to 1334*. Stanford: Stanford University Press, 1958.

———. *A History of Japan, 1334–1615*. Stanford: Stanford University Press, 1961.

Sato, Tadao. *Chushingura: Iji no keifu* (Chushingura: Genealogy of Honor). Tokyo: Asahi Sensho, 1976.

———. "The Comedy of Ozu and Chaplin—A Study in Contrast." Translated by Gregory Barrett. *Wide Angle* 3, no. 2 (1979): 50–53.

———. *Currents in Japanese Cinema*. Translated by Gregory Barrett. Tokyo: Kodansha, 1982.

———. *Hasegawa Shin-ron* (Essays on Shin Hasegawa). Tokyo: Chuokoronsha, 1975.

———. *Kimi wa jidai geki eiga o mita ka* (Have you seen a Period Drama Movie?). Tokyo: Jyacometei Shuppan, 1977.

———. *Mizoguchi Kenji no sekai* (The World of Kenji Mizoguchi). Tokyo: Chikuma Shobo, 1982.

Sato, Tadao and Chieo Yoshida. *Chambara eiga-shi* (History of Japanese Swordfighting Movies). Tokyo: Hoga Shoten, 1972.

Schafer, Edward H. *Ancient China*. New York: Time-Life Books, 1967.

Schrader, Paul. *Transcendental Style in Film: Ozu, Bresson, Dreyer*. Berkeley and Los Angeles: University of California Press, 1972.

Sheldon, Charles D. "Feudal Japan: Politics and Society from the Eighth Century to 1868." In *Half The World: The History of China and Japan*, edited by Arnold Toynbee, pp. 213–24. New York: Holt, Rinehart and Winston, 1973.

Showa-shi jiten (Dictionary of Showa Period History, 1925–). Tokyo: Mainichi Shinbunsha, 1980.

Silver, Alain. *The Samurai Film*. Rev. ed. Woodstock, New York: Overlook Press, 1983.

Smith, Robert J. *Ancestor Worship in Contemporary Japan*. Stanford: Stanford University Press, 1974.

Tanizaki, Junichiro. *Seven Japanese Tales*. Translated by Howard Hibbett. New York: Berkley Medallion, 1965.

Tayama, Rikiya. *Waga taiken teki: Nihon goraku eiga-shi—Sengo-hen* (My Experiential View of the History of Japanese Popular Movies—Postwar vol.) Tokyo: Gendai Kyoyo Bunko, 1979.

———. *Waga taiken teki: Nihon goraku eiga-shi—Senzen-hen* (My Experiential View of the History of Japanese Popular Movies—Prewar vol.) Tokyo: Gendai Kyoyo Bunko. 1980.

Tsurumi, Kazuko. *Social Change and the Individual*. Princeton: Princeton University Press, 1970.

Tucker, Richard N. *Japan: Film Image*. London: Studio Vista, 1973.

Vogel, Ezra F. *Japan's New Middle Class*. 2d ed. Berkeley and Los Angeles: University of California Press, 1971.

Wagatsuma, Hiroshi. "Some Aspects of Contemporary Japanese Family—Once Confucian, Now Fatherless?" Paper prepared for the conference on "The Family" sponsored by Daedalus, 6–8 May 1976.

Watanabe, Shoko. *Japanese Buddhism*. Tokyo: Japan Cultural Society, 1968.

Watanabe, Takenobu. *Nikkatsu akushon no karei na sekai* (The Magnificent World of Nikkatsu Action Movies), 1954–1971. 3 vols. Tokyo: Miraisha, 1981–82.

Yamagiwa, Joseph K. "Literature and Japanese Culture." In John W. Hall and Richard K. Beardsley, *Twelve Doors to Japan*, pp. 224–62. New York: McGraw-Hill, 1965.

Yoshikawa, Eiji. *Musashi*. Translated by Charles S. Terry. Tokyo: Kodansha, 1981.

Index